THE GREATEST BLUNDERS ...EVER!

HISTORY'S DUMBEST MISTAKES

AND THE PEOPLE WHO MADE THEM

METRO BOOKS
New York

An Imprint of Sterling Publishing Co., Inc.
1166 Avenue of the Americas
New York, NY 10036

ISBN 978-1-4351-6464-2

For information about custom editions, special sales, and premium and corporate
purchases, please contact Sterling Special Sales at 800-805-5489
or specialsales@sterlingpublishing.com.

Manufactured in China

2 4 6 8 10 9 7 5 3 1

www.sterlingpublishing.com

Editorial & Design by Tall Tree

[THE GREATEST BLUNDERS ...EVER!]

HISTORY'S DUMBEST MISTAKES
AND THE PEOPLE WHO MADE THEM

IAN WHITELAW

METRO BOOKS
New York

CONTENTS

6   Introduction

8   Humans Domesticate Plants and Animals

12   Failing to Let God's People Go

16   Persia Invades Greece

20   Alexander the Great Pushes Too Far

26   Pyrrhus Achieves Costly Victories

30   The Murder of Julius Caesar

36   Choosing Caligula as Emperor

40   Emperor Julian Rejects Christianity

44   Monophysitism Is Declared Heretical

48   The Great East-West Schism

52   Harold Hurries to Meet William at Hastings

56   The French Underestimate the English at Agincourt

60   The Ming Dynasty Turns Its Back on the World

64   The Excommunication of Martin Luther

70   The Inca Atahualpa Meets Pizarro the Conquistador

74   Henry VIII Wants a Son

78   Philip II of Spain Launches the Armada

82   Charles I's Cavalier Attitude to Parliament

86   Napoleon and the Louisiana Bargain

90   Napoleon's Second Bite at the Apple

94   British Troops Massacre Workers at "Peterloo"

100   Santa Anna Attacks the Alamo

104   Britain Invades Afghanistan

108   Tragedy in the Valley of Death

112   The Assassination of Tsar Alexander II

116   Austria's Mayerling Incident

120   The German Navy Sinks the *Lusitania*

126   The Treaty of Versailles

130   Stalin's First Five-Year Plan

134   Hitler Invades the Soviet Union

140   Japan Attacks Pearl Harbor

144   Britain Partitions India

148   The Vietnam War

152   France Tries to Hold on to Algeria

158   The US Fails to Topple Cuba at the Bay of Pigs

162   Charles de Gaulle Faces Down the Students

166   Idi Amin Expels the Asian Population from Uganda

170   President Nixon and the Watergate Affair

174   Argentina Invades the Falkland Islands

180   Iraq Invades Kuwait

184   Margaret Thatcher Introduces the Poll Tax

188   The UN Fails to Prevent Genocide in Rwanda

192   Massacre at Srebrenica

198   Repealing the Glass-Steagall Act

202   Al-Qaeda Attacks the US

208   The Deepwater Horizon Blowout

214   Building Reactors in Japan's Earthquake Zone

218   Further Reading

220   Index

INTRODUCTION

Blunders, mistakes, bad decisions—we've all made them, but for most of us the consequences are slight and affect only ourselves and those close to us. Very few of us wield such power that our mistakes affect thousands of others, or are so well-known that our blunders become world news. Some people, however, are in that position. *The Greatest Blunders…Ever!* is, for the most part, about powerful and prominent individuals and the negative effects—intended or accidental—that their decisions and actions have had upon the world and/or themselves.

DEFINE NEGATIVE

The pros and cons of a historical event depend very much upon your point of view—one man's victory is another's defeat (or death)—and there are very few major events that don't have a downside from someone's perspective. Sadly, there are far too many that have no upside whatsoever: acts of greed, stupidity, selfishness, and savagery that gain nothing for anyone and cause untold suffering to many. You will find plenty of those between the covers of this book. In other instances, a decision has been labeled as negative because it achieved the opposite of what was intended. Pope Leo X, for example, tried to silence Martin Luther to prevent the Roman Catholic Church from losing its religious monopoly over Western Europe. Santa Anna attacked the Alamo to maintain Mexican control over Texas. Japan bombed Pearl Harbor to keep the US out of the war.

Causing environmental damage also counts as a negative, although, in the cases of the Deepwater Horizon blowout and the Fukushima nuclear power plant, one could argue that to find the bad decision one has to go further back than the failure to take the necessary safety precautions and look at the whole issue of risky energy sources. Bringing about one's own embarrassment or downfall is perhaps negative on a smaller scale, although Napoleon's ultimate defeat at Waterloo cost the lives of a great many soldiers, and President Nixon's behavior throughout the Watergate affair displayed an utter contempt for democracy, the legal system, and the American people.

WHAT'S THE MOTIVATION?

It's often hard to give a clear-cut answer to what drives people to issue commands or take decisions or actions that are almost bound to result in disaster in one form or another, but as a form of shorthand we have identified one or more of the seven deadly sins and the cardinal virtues as the motivating force or forces in each case. Greed and pride come up a good deal, charity less so. That having been said, if we had to choose one word to describe the cause of most of the worst outcomes in this book, it would be "ideology," ways of thinking that convince people that their belief—be it religion, politics, nationalism, or ethnic fervor—is not just right but is so utterly right that it justifies imposing it on others even if that means killing them.

BATTLE OF AGINCOURT
In 1415, the French (left) committed a
terrible blunder by underestimating the
strength of the English army.

WHO ARE THE CULPRITS?

If the measures of a blunder are the
number of people affected and the
severity of the impact, then clearly the
more power a person has, the bigger
the blunders they can commit. What is
evident from the events covered in this
book, however, is that big mistakes
require cooperation—and therefore
shared motives—on a grand scale.
Hitler could not have done that much
harm without the support of millions.
Stalin relied upon the participation of
the secret police, the army, and even
the average citizen, to shatter the lives
of millions of their compatriots. In
situations such as the widespread
conflict that accompanied the partition
of India, or the genocides that took place
in Rwanda and Bosnia, the violence
didn't even need any real leadership.
On a less dramatic level, there are plenty
of bad decisions that can't really be
pinned on any individual. No one person
deregulated the financial system in the
US, allowed dozens of oil rigs to drill
in deep water in the Gulf of Mexico,
or said it was okay to place nuclear
reactors on a tsunami-prone coast.
Interest groups, corporations,
governments, and whole societies make
these kinds of blunders possible. To
misquote a well-known phrase, for big
mistakes to happen, it only requires
sensible people to do nothing.

HUMANS DOMESTICATE PLANTS AND ANIMALS

ca. 10,000 BCE

Main Culprits: Our ancestors some twelve thousand years ago

Damage Done: Laid the foundations for all the problems of modern society

Why: It just seemed like a good idea at the time

Throughout this book we will be looking at a wide range of blunders, mistakes, and bad decisions, and the effects they have had on individuals, groups, and sometimes millions of people. It's usually people in positions of power—kings and queens, military leaders, politicians, captains of industry—who are to blame, often so they can extend their authority over people, land, or resources. However, none of their bad decisions would have been possible had there not been one mega-blunder a long, long time ago. Up until recently, it has been hailed as one of the best decisions in human history. If we go back more than fifteen thousand years and watch our ancestors, we see people feeding themselves and their families mainly by gathering wild plants, fruits, and roots, and occasionally hunting down a wild animal. This is called hunting and gathering. It's the way it had been for a very long time, and it worked just fine.

A NEW WAY OF LIFE

Over the next five thousand years, however, humankind's means of feeding itself goes through a gradual, but radical, change. We begin to catch and tend some of our food animals, such as sheep, goats, and pigs. Some are scrawny and feisty, but if you just breed the fatter and less boisterous ones then over hundreds of generations they get easier to manage and there's a lot more meat on those bones. And you don't have to go running through the hills with a spear every time you want dinner.

Something similar applies to the plants, especially cereals (various grains like wheat and corn) and pulses (edible seeds, like beans and chickpeas). Plant the seeds from the best ones and they just keep getting bigger and more productive. And it gets even better if you dig the earth over, throw some goat droppings on it, pull up the weeds, and add some water. This "domestication" of plants

Humans began to catch and tend food animals, such as sheep, goats, and pigs. The "domestication" of animals and plants seemed like a good idea.

and animals and the development of agriculture look like really good ideas.

SETTLING DOWN

This new agricultural way of life, however, has many consequences. If you're going to plant things and help them grow, then it makes sense to stick around and harvest them. So the mobile lifestyle of the hunter-gatherer gave way to a more static way of life. Shelters were built to last and settlements where people could live were created. Hunter-gatherers, who were always on the move, tended not to have (or keep) another child until the first one could walk. If you are staying in one place you

MOVING ON

The hunter-gatherers of some fifteen thousand years ago led a more mobile existence, moving from place to place in search of food and resources. If a family or group of families needed shelter they might put up a temporary structure, only to abandon it once they had used up local food sources and needed to move on.

can raise more children at the same time, so the population began to grow more quickly. That was okay because the agricultural way of life produced more food. In fact, it produced more food than they needed, a surplus, which meant that not everyone had to work. People in society could take on different roles, with

---

THE FURROW'S CURSE

This three-thousand-year-old Egyptian painting shows the land being plowed. In ancient Egypt food production was based in the fertile flood plains of the Nile.

NEOLITHIC FARMING
The inhabitants of this Neolithic stone house, the Knap of Howar in the Scottish Orkney Islands, were raising cattle, sheep, and pigs, and growing wheat and barley more than five thousand years ago. Maybe they should have stuck to fishing.

some telling other people what to do and how to organize the growing of food. Some even convinced the rest that they had all the power and that any food and harvests were theirs and were only to be shared with those who did exactly what they were told.

TOUGH GUYS
Some settlements became really big, and built up a large surplus, but then settlements that weren't doing so well or wanted to do better tried to steal it. Then the people gave their own tough guys food in return for defending the settlement, but they soon realized that an army could be used to take over other settlements and make those people grow

the food and do what they were told. There are quite a few examples of that kind of thing throughout this book.

A BETTER LIFE?
Okay, so there are some downsides to civilization, but at least it's better than being a hunter-gatherer. Just look around the world. There are very few hunter-gatherers now, and they look

as though they lead a fairly tough life. There's no doubt that we live longer, have a better diet, and have a great deal more leisure time, which is why we've been able to develop everything from art, music, and architecture to cities and science.

A LONGER LIFE?

However, we need to be careful about making comparisons between ourselves and modern hunter-gatherers. As most of the world is made up of societies that depend on agriculture, the hunter-gatherers have long since been pushed off the most fertile land. Back in the day, they had the run of the whole planet, and finding dinner wasn't that hard. If local supplies ran short, they would simply move to a more fertile area. In settled societies, a drought, a flood, or a plague could ruin the crops, so people were more likely to starve. Hunter-gatherers living in small, widely dispersed, and mobile groups are also much less prone to the infectious diseases that thrive in large communities. Recent studies of the teeth and bones of people living before and after the agricultural period indicate that hunter-gatherers were actually healthier, longer-lived, and taller than people in early agricultural societies.

MORE LEISURE TIME?

It's also not necessarily true that the hunter-gatherer had less leisure time than we do. Studies of contemporary

LOST SKILLS

There are still a few tribes around the world who have retained their hunter-gatherer skills or way of life. These include the Kalahari Bushmen of the Kalahari Desert in southern Africa, the Batak in the western Philippines, and the Pirahã, an Amazonian hunter-gatherer tribe who live on the banks of Brazil's Maici River. Some people think that by the end of this century, most, if not all, of the modern-day hunter-gatherer tribes will have vanished.

hunter-gatherers show they spend less than twenty hours a week finding all they need to survive, and that's a good deal less than the average working week in the civilized world.

The seventeenth-century philosopher Thomas Hobbes believed that the natural condition of humankind is to be at war, and that only the "civil state" can prevent this. The evidence suggests that pre-agricultural people had less to fight about, and the last two thousand years certainly show that "civilized" people find plenty of reasons to go to war. Perhaps trapping that goat and planting those grass seeds wasn't such a great decision after all.

The diet of a hunter-gatherer is much more varied and contains a wider variety of nutrients than an agriculturalist who lives on a narrow range of sugars and carbohydrates.

FAILING TO LET GOD'S PEOPLE GO

ca. 700 BCE

Main Culprit: The Egyptian Pharaoh

Damage Done: The land of Egypt and its people suffered terrible plagues and misfortunes, and many died

Why: The Pharaoh wouldn't accept that the God of the Israelites was the true God, and he wouldn't let the Israelites leave Egypt

Sometime in the first millennium BCE, the Egyptian Pharaoh at the time was given the option of doing the right thing again and again, and every time he chose not to. As a result, ever greater suffering was heaped upon him, his people, and his country, but still he persisted. According to the scriptures, God Himself was leading the Pharaoh to make these bad decisions, but is that a good enough excuse?

ISRAELITES ARE ENSLAVED

The story began when famine forced Jacob, his twelve sons, and their families to leave the land of Canaan (modern-day Israel, the Palestinian Territories, and parts of Jordan and Lebanon) and travel west to Egypt. There, they were welcomed by the Pharaoh and settled in the fertile province of Goshen. In Egypt their number grew over the generations, and the Egyptians, worried that the Israelites might take power, enslaved them and gave them a very hard time. The Israelites had taskmasters placed over them and were forced to make bricks and build cities, and work in the fields, but still their numbers increased. Eventually, the Pharaoh insisted that all male Israelite children must be thrown into the river as soon as they were born, but one woman couldn't bear to kill her baby son and so she hid him in the reeds beside the river. He was found by the Pharaoh's daughter, who named him Moses, and he was raised as her son. When he reached adulthood, he saw an Egyptian beating a Hebrew worker and, believing no one was watching, he killed the Egyptian. However, the Pharaoh heard about it, and Moses had to flee for his life. He went to live in Midian, where he married and had children.

GOD VISITS MOSES

Meanwhile, conditions for the Israelites had become even worse, and God, remembering the agreement he had made to give Abraham and his descendants the land of Canaan, visited Moses and told him to go to the Pharaoh and lead the children of Israel out of Egypt. Moses doubted whether the Israelites would believe that he had been visited by God, or that the Pharaoh would let the

THE FINDING OF MOSES
Sir Lawrence Alma-Tadema's painting depicts the Pharaoh's daughter returning from the Nile with the child that would one day lead the Jewish people out of Egypt.

Israelites go. God, however, assured him that Aaron, the elder brother of Moses, would be his spokesman and that he would be able to turn his staff into a snake, demonstrating that God was with him. Well, the Israelites did indeed believe Aaron and Moses, but when they asked the Pharaoh to let the Hebrew people go, just for a few days to sacrifice to their God in the desert, the Pharaoh not only refused but increased the amount of work that the Israelites had to do. Acting on God's instructions, Moses and Aaron returned to the Pharaoh, threw the staff on the ground, and it turned into a snake. When the Pharaoh's magicians did the same thing with their staffs, Aaron's serpent ate those of the magicians, but the Pharaoh still refused.

PLAGUES DESCEND ON EGYPT
According to the book of Exodus, God then heaped ever greater ills upon the Egyptians. To begin with, Moses waved his staff over the water in Egypt and turned it all to blood—rivers, streams, ponds, lakes, even the water in pots and barrels. The fish in the lakes and rivers died, everything stank, and there was no water to drink in the whole kingdom. This lasted for seven days, but the Pharaoh didn't give in.

Then Moses warned him that if he didn't release the Israelites then God would send a plague of frogs. The Pharaoh still refused and, sure enough, there were so many frogs and such a lot of noise that the Pharaoh gave in, saying that the Israelites could go. The following day the plague was over, but the Pharaoh's heart hardened, and he went back on his word.

Next came a plague of lice that infested all the people and all the animals. Even the Pharaoh's magicians had to admit that the hand of God was behind this, but the Pharaoh remained immovable. On God's instructions, Moses and Aaron warned the Pharaoh that a plague of flies would be next, but that it would not affect the Israelites— and that's exactly what happened. There were swarms of flies everywhere, but the province of Goshen remained free of them. The Pharaoh called for Moses and Aaron and told them to take their people into the desert and to carry out their sacrifices, but to ask their God to get rid of the flies. Again, as soon as the plague was over the Pharaoh changed his mind and forbade the Israelites to leave. God then sent a terrible illness that infected all the animals that belonged to the Egyptians—cattle, horses, camels, oxen, everything—but the animals belonging to the children of Israel were unaffected. Still the Pharaoh wouldn't give in.

Doing as God instructed, Moses then took a handful of ashes and threw it into the air, and all the people and animals in

PASSOVER

To spare the Israelites one last plague, the death of all firstborn children, God instructed that every family must sacrifice a lamb and daub its blood on the lintel and doorposts of their house. When God came to kill the firstborn he would see this sign and pass over the houses of the Israelites. This is the origin of the Passover, or Pesach.

Jacob, the grandson of Abraham, was renamed Israel by an angel, and his descendants are known as the Israelites, each of his sons founding one of the twelve tribes of Israel.

Egypt were afflicted with terrible boils. The boils were so bad that the Pharaoh's magicians couldn't even stand to face Moses, they were in such pain. Nonetheless, the Pharaoh still refused to let the children of Israel depart.

HAILSTORM WARNING

God then told Moses to warn the Pharaoh and the people of Egypt that there was going to be a hailstorm of unprecedented ferocity, and that any person or animal left outside would be killed by the hailstones. Those Egyptians who had understood that all these terrible ills were really being brought upon them by the God of the Israelites brought their animals in and hid indoors. Moses stretched his hand toward the sky and the granddaddy of all hailstorms was unleashed, killing animals and breaking the trees to pieces—except in the province of Goshen. This time, the Pharaoh was genuinely frightened, and he called Moses and Aaron to him and told them that he believed their God was the true God and he would let them go. Moses doubted whether the Pharaoh really did believe, but he raised his hands again and the storm stopped. And, sure enough, the Pharaoh's heart hardened once again and he went back on his word.

God explained to Moses that He was deliberately hardening the heart of the Pharaoh so that He could show him all these signs, and so that future generations would remember how powerful God is. Moses and Aaron asked the Pharaoh, once again, to let the children of Israel leave Egypt, and the Pharaoh asked who they intended to take with them. Moses replied that they would all go, men, women, children, and all the flocks. The Pharaoh said that only the men could leave, which wasn't good enough for Moses and Aaron, so God sent a plague of locusts. At this, the Pharaoh backed down, saying that he had sinned against God and would let the Israelites leave, so God sent a westerly wind and the locusts were blown away into the Red Sea. And yet again God hardened the Pharaoh's heart and the Israelites were not allowed to leave.

Now God told Moses to stretch out his hand and bring darkness to the land of Egypt, and for three days it was pitch black. Finally, the Pharaoh said they could go, but they had to leave their flocks behind. That was unacceptable, so God told Moses that He would send one last plague upon Egypt—He would kill all the firstborn children in the whole country.

Moses warned the Pharaoh what would happen unless he freed the Israelites, but he wouldn't listen, and on the appointed day the firstborn in every Egyptian household, from the Pharaoh's to the lowliest servant's, was killed. And now the Pharaoh did free the children of Israel from slavery and let them leave, and the Egyptians gave them silver and gold and jewels and fine clothes to take with them.

FINAL BAD DECISION

The Pharaoh's bad decisions had brought the kingdom to its knees— depleted of crops, trees, livestock, water, and even the firstborn of every family. You would think that by now he would have been convinced to let the Israelites go but, no, he had one more really bad decision to make. He decided to follow the Hebrews with his army, finally catching up with them on the shores of the Red Sea. God instructed Moses to hold up his rod and stretch out his hand over the water. The sea parted so that the Israelites could walk across on dry ground with a wall of water on either side. The Egyptian army followed but Moses raised his hand again and the waters returned, drowning every Egyptian.

DEATH OF THE FIRSTBORN

"And all the firstborn in the land of Egypt shall die, from the firstborn of the Pharaoh...even unto the firstborn of the maidservant." —Exodus 11:5

PERSIA INVADES GREECE

490–449 BCE

Main Culprits: The Persian emperor Darius I and his son Xerxes

Damage Done: Tens of thousands of Persian soldiers died and the Persian fleet was destroyed

Why: The only thing better than a large empire is a huge empire

The first Persian invasion of Greece took place in 492 BCE, but its seeds were sown ten years earlier by a rebellion known as the Ionian Revolt. The Persian Empire at the time was vast, extending from India in the east to Egypt in the west. This included Ionia, in what is now southwest Turkey, where the Greeks had established several city states that had fallen under Persian control. When, in 499 BCE, these rebelled against the harsh rule of the Persians, Eretria (a city on the island of Euboea, close to the Greek mainland) and Athens sent military aid.

By 493 BCE, the forces of the Persian Emperor Darius I had put down the Ionian Revolt and regained control. The rebellion, however, motivated him to extend his dominion further to include more Aegean islands and mainland Greece, where he intended to punish Athens and Eritrea for helping the Ionians to revolt.

OUTNUMBERED

Taking mainland Greece seemed like an easy task for the greatest empire there had even been as the Persian army and

> *"Freedom is an excellent thing."*
> —**Herodotus**

its fleet of ships could easily outnumber those of the Greeks. Under the leadership of Mardonius, the Persians quickly took the northern regions of Thrace and Macedonia. The fleet was then caught in a fierce storm and some twenty thousand soldiers lost their lives at sea. Mardonius was replaced by the generals Datis and Artaphernes, and in 490 BCE they led a naval task force across the Aegean, taking several islands on their way, to the island of Euboea and the city of Eretria, which they looted and burned.

From there it was a short crossing to the Greek mainland, and the Persians chose a bay close to the town of Marathon, some 25 miles (40 km) northeast of Athens, as their landing site. At least twenty-five thousand Persian soldiers and one thousand cavalrymen were sent ashore, and many more may have remained on the ships. The Athenian army, made up of some ten thousand hoplites (armored infantrymen carrying swords, spears, and shields) marched to the plain

BATTLE OF MARATHON
The defeat of the Persians by the much smaller Athenian army proved to be a turning point in Greek history.

of Marathon and prevented the Persians from moving inland. The two armies faced each other in a stalemate for several days.

SHOCKING DEFEAT

On the fifth day the Greek army attacked the superior Persian forces, either because they had received news that the Persian cavalry had returned to the ships to launch a direct attack on Athens or because there were signs that the Persian army was about to attack. The Battle of Marathon should have been a walkover for the Persians, who outnumbered the Athenians by at least

At the Battle of Marathon, history records that more than six thousand Persians lay dead, while the Greeks had lost less than two hundred men.

two to one, but the Greek army shocked the Persians by forming themselves into phalanxes, which were rectangular formations of men that each moved as a unit. They rushed forward and pushed steadily with their shields into the opposition. The more heavily armored Greeks overcame the sides of the Persian army and then enclosed the center, inflicting terrible damage with their swords and spears, and finally forcing the Persians to flee to their ships. The Persians then sailed south to attack Athens directly, but the Greek army was able to get there before them and prevent a landing. The Persians gave up the attempt and sailed for home.

TURNING POINT

The Athenian victory has been seen as a turning point in European history and the beginning of the rise of Classical Greece. Up until this point, Persian domination had looked inevitable, but now the Greeks had shown the Persians—and themselves—that they could fight back. Even the Spartans, to whom war was a way of life, were impressed when they arrived a few days later and inspected the battlefield at Marathon.

LEONIDAS'S LAST STAND

The bravery of Leonidas and his men at Thermopylae, where they laid down their lives to delay the advance of the Persians, has gone down in history.

GIGANTIC ARMY

Darius I began planning for another campaign against the Greeks, but he died in 486 BCE and the task passed to his son Xerxes. He led the second Persian invasion of Greece in 480 BCE with a massive force of around 250,000 troops, 1,200 triremes (warships more than 100 feet [30 m] long and with three banks of oars), and 3,000 supply ships. This time the Persians were not taking any chances.

In preparation for the inevitable return of the Persians, Athens and Sparta had been building their own fleet of triremes but could not compete when it came to manpower. They did, however, form a coalition with other city-states. Some of these city-states

had previously been at war with each other, but they were now willing to put aside their differences in the face of a much greater enemy.

SPARTAN BRAVERY

By the summer of 480 BCE, the Persian army was marching southward through the Greek mainland. The Greeks sent a force of seven thousand men under the leadership of the Spartan king Leonidas to block their path at the pass of Thermopylae, between the mountains and the sea. They were able to hold Xerxes and his army back for several days, but the Persians were then made aware of a path through the mountains and sent their infantrymen along it. Leonidas had known about the path and instructed the majority of his troops to depart, while he and fifteen hundred soldiers fought what was to become a famous last stand and one that showed the legendary bravery of the Spartans. Every last Greek in this stand-off was killed, and the Persians continued their advance, although they too had lost some twenty thousand in the fighting.

During the Battle of Thermopylae, the Greeks had also used their naval force to prevent the Persians from making their way south by sea. In the confrontation, both fleets suffered serious losses, and once news of the fall of Thermopylae reached the Greeks they sailed for the island of Salamis to the west of Athens. As the Persians approached Athens, its inhabitants were largely evacuated to the island, and the city was soon taken and burned. The Persians were now in control of the whole of mainland Greece, but still the Greeks resisted, their fleet remaining just off the coast in the hope of engaging the Persian ships. The Persians finally did attack, but their large numbers proved to be their undoing in the narrow waters between the island and the coast, where the great triremes had difficulty maneuvering. The Greeks won a decisive victory and effectively put an end to Persian naval superiority.

FINAL VICTORY

The following year, the Persian general Mardonius offered peace terms to the Athenians, hoping to break up the coalition of city-states, which was already showing signs of instability. Athens refused them, but demanded support from Sparta for a march northward to attack the Persians, only to find that the Spartans were already on their way. When Mardonius learned of this, he and

The Greeks won a decisive victory and effectively put an end to Persian naval superiority.

MARATHON RACE

During the Battle of Marathon, the Greeks' fastest runner, a man called Pheidippides, was sent on a 140-mile (225-km) trip to Sparta, southwest of Athens. He was instructed to ask the Spartans to send military aid to defend Athens, which was now undefended. The Spartans, however, replied that they would be unable to help for at least ten days as they were celebrating a festival during which peace was sacred. Pheidippides's run is said to have inspired the modern sporting race, the marathon.

his troops retreated northward. The Greek and Persian forces met near Plataea and once again the outnumbered hoplites achieved a remarkable and final victory over the Persian troops. At sea, the Athenian and allied navies attacked the Persian fleet that had now been drawn up on the beach on the island of Samos and was being guarded by some sixty thousand soldiers. The Greeks sent troops ashore, overcame the much larger Persian force, and torched the beached fleet, putting an end to the second and last Persian invasion of Greece.

Over the next few years an even stronger alliance of Greek city-states, under the leadership of Athens, succeeded in pushing the Persians back until, by 449 BCE, they had retreated from Macedonia, Thrace, and the islands of Ionia and the Aegean. It would soon be the turn of the Greek civilization to overrun the Persian Empire.

ALEXANDER THE GREAT PUSHES TOO FAR

334–323 BCE

Main Culprit: Alexander the Great

Damage Done: Pushed his army to the point of mutiny, and many thousands died on the journey home

Why: The only thing better than ruling a huge empire is ruling the whole known world

Athens emerged from the Greco–Persian Wars as top dog, but over the next hundred years, power on the Greek mainland passed from Athens to Sparta, then to Thebes, and ultimately to Macedonia in the north. The Macedonian king, Philip II, had come to the throne in 359 BCE at the age of twenty-one and had quickly unified Macedonia, taking back territory that had been lost to neighboring tribes using a highly efficient and well-organized army. Having seen the Greek army in action as a teenager, he introduced two innovations. Improving on the Greek concept of the phalanx (rectangular formations of men that each moved as a unit), he armed the soldiers with exceptionally long spears, up to 20 feet (6 m) in length, which meant they could impale their enemies long before they themselves could be reached by

ALEXANDER THE GREAT
As a young man, Alexander displayed remarkable skill and courage, and throughout his life he had a driving ambition to rule the world.

enemy weapons. He also turned the army into a full-time, well-paid, professional organization that was always training and always ready.

MACEDONIAN EMPIRE

Over the next twenty years, through a combination of military force and diplomacy, he extended Macedonian control to the east and west and then southward through Greece, culminating in the Battle of Chaeronea in 338 BCE, which put an end to Greek independence.

After the battle, thousands of Greeks fled their homes for the Ionian shores of the Mediterranean, preferring to place themselves under Persian rule rather than that of the Macedonians.

Philip now began preparations to extend his conquests into the Persian Empire. In the spring of 336 BCE, he sent an advance force of some ten thousand Macedonian soldiers into Asia Minor, but before he could join them he was assassinated while attending his daughter's wedding celebrations.

A WORTHY SUCCESSOR

Philip's son, Alexander III, was his successor and he inherited an extensive empire, a large and highly efficient army, and the preparations in place for a large-scale invasion. Alexander "the Great" soon proved himself to be more than equal to the task.

> **Alexander inherited from his father an extensive empire and a large and highly efficient army primed and ready for a large-scale invasion.**

EARLY EDUCATION

Alexander had been well prepared to be the ruler of a vast empire. As a child he had watched his father achieve military victory after victory. As a young teenager he had been tutored by the great Greek philosopher Aristotle, and educated in literature, science, and philosophy. At the age of sixteen he was considered so capable that his father left him in charge of Macedonia while he invaded Thrace. In his absence, the young Alexander assembled and led an army to put down a rebellion that threatened his country's border. Two years later, he was at the Battle of Chaeronea, where he displayed remarkable bravery and tactical wisdom.

RUTHLESS EFFICIENCY

In fact, Alexander had to put the invasion of the Persian Empire on hold for two years, as news of Philip's death had sparked revolts in many parts of his own territory. Moving his army with remarkable speed, these revolts were put down quickly and ruthlessly. In the storming of the rebellious Greek city of Thebes, for example, six thousand men, women, and children were slaughtered, and thirty thousand more were sold into slavery. The city was then demolished.

PERSIAN CAMPAIGN

In the spring of 334 BCE, Alexander crossed the Hellespont into Asia with at least fifty thousand soldiers. In the first of

Thrace

Macedon

Black Sea

Caspian Sea

Greece

Mysia

Cappadocia

Armenia

Phrygia

Lydia

Cilicia

Media

Parthia

Syria

CYPRUS

Mesopotamia

Mediterranean Sea

Babylonia

Persis

EGYPT

ARABIA

Persian Gulf

Red Sea

Extent of Alexander's empire

many battle victories, Alexander's army met the Persians at Granicus where the Persians surrendered the governorship of what is now northwest Turkey. They then headed on south down the eastern Mediterranean coast and met the army of Darius III in the Battle of Issus, which took place close to the modern Turkish city of Iskenderun (originally Alexandria ad Issum). Despite being outnumbered by more than two to one, and being taken by surprise, Alexander's army got the better of the Persians and King Darius fled, leaving both his army (which was butchered) and his family (whom

ALEXANDER THE GREAT'S EMPIRE
At its peak, the Macedonian Empire of Alexander the Great covered an area from the Balkan Peninsula, through Mesopotamia, to the Indian subcontinent.

Alexander spared). This decisive routing, the first time that the Persian army had been overwhelmed with their king at its head, was a shock to the Persians. In return for peace, Darius offered some of the Persian territory as well as a large sum of money as a ransom for his mother, wife, and two daughters. Alexander refused the offer, saying that he would

godlike, a delusion that was later to sour his relations with the army.

Having captured Egypt (where he founded the city of Alexandria), Alexander was now in control of all the coastal cities and ports in the eastern Mediterranean. His route now took him through Mesopotamia, where he triumphed over Darius's army yet again in the Battle of Gaugamela, and once again Darius fled. Alexander then took Babylon, followed by Susa, an important center in the Persian Empire, and then Persepolis, the ceremonial capital of Persia. Darius was taken captive by one of his own provincial governors, a man named Bessus, who had Darius killed and then proclaimed himself Darius's successor. Alexander pursued Bessus throughout Afghanistan and Tajikistan until Bessus was finally executed.

KING OF KINGS

The Persian Empire now belonged to Alexander. He adopted the title "King of Kings," and began to wear Persian clothing and adopt Persian customs in his court. As part of this he insisted that his subjects lie facedown before him in the manner of the Persians, but the Greeks and Macedonians refused to do this. Alexander was forced to back down, but his actions, which suggested he did indeed think he was a god, attracted some ill feeling. The situation worsened when Alexander discovered that the son of his general, Parmenion, had known about a

take the whole of the Persian Empire and would not have terms dictated to him.

Over the next nine years, Alexander did precisely that. Continuing down through Syria, he took city after city. When Tyre held out, it was besieged until it surrendered, and then the men were slain, and the women and children taken as slaves. In 332 BCE, Alexander entered Egypt, where he was welcomed as a liberator and hailed as the son of Ammon Ra, the Egyptian sun god and equivalent to the Greek god Zeus. From this point on, Alexander appears to have become increasingly convinced that he was

Despite being outnumbered by more than two to one, and being taken by surprise, Alexander's army got the better of the Persians.

plot against him and not informed him. Alexander executed both the young officer and his father, a man who had been his faithful ally and a brilliant commander throughout the campaign. Alexander also earned the contempt of many when, hurling a javelin in a fit of drunken anger, he killed a young officer who had saved his life at the Battle of Granicus but who was now criticizing him.

THE BATTLE OF HYDASPES
Alexander's army defeated the forces of King Porus at the Hydaspes, despite the Indian ruler's war elephants, but his men refused to go farther and meet even greater armies.

After further campaigns in what are now Afghanistan and Pakistan, and several bloody and brutal battles that established his control, Alexander reached the Indus River. Despite having conquered a vast empire, the son of Zeus wanted to expand the empire yet further and fulfill his aim of becoming the ruler of the world. So he led his army across the Indus and on to the Hydaspes, where, in the summer of 326 BCE, they defeated the forces of the Indian ruler Porus. Continuing eastward they reached the Beas River and here the army rose up and mutinied. They had been away from home for eight years, they had heard tales of the mighty

enemies they might meet if they were to go farther, and they had had enough.

A BAD PLAN

Unwillingly Alexander conceded to his army's demands. After building a huge fleet of ships, they sailed downstream to the Indus River and then farther south. The fleet halted some 200 miles (320 km) from the Indian Ocean and Alexander sent part of the army northwest to return overland. A hundred miles later, he and some eighty thousand soldiers disembarked, while the remaining two thousand continued their journey by river and sea. Alexander's plan was to march west through the Gedrosian desert in what is now southwestern Pakistan. It was now August, the height of summer, and there was very little water available for the army.

Women and children were among the troops, and the little transport they had was unsuitable for the harsh and rocky landscape. It was a really bad plan. By the time the army reached Susa the following spring, thousands of men, women, and children, not to mention horses and donkeys, were dead in the desert sand. A large number of women and children had also died when their camp, next to a streambed, had been washed away by a flash flood caused by rain in the distant mountains. At Susa, Alexander hosted great celebrations before continuing on to Babylon, where he began planning an invasion of the Arabian Peninsula, to the south. It was

SON OF ZEUS

During his later years, Alexander began to show signs of egomania. His incredible successes as a military commander and the adulation that he received from those around him no doubt contributed to his increasing ambitions to rule the world. He began to think of himself as a deity, the son of Zeus (the supreme Greek god), and required others to think of him in the same way. Despite this, he is still regarded as one of the greatest generals the world has ever seen, skillful, imaginative, and relentless in his pursuit of domination.

not to be because in the second week of June 323 BCE Alexander died of a severe fever. The cause of his illness is not known, but he had been unwell since drinking wine some two weeks earlier, and there was speculation that he had been poisoned by one of his generals, Antipater.

After his death, Alexander's generals divided up his empire between them, but the spread of Greek language, learning, and culture throughout the Near Eastern and Western worlds continued, and the death of Alexander ushered in the dawn of the "Hellenistic period," which lasted until the rise of the Roman Empire.

By the time Alexander had reached the Indus, he had already conquered the whole of the Persian Empire and was the ruler of more than 2 million square miles (5 million square km) of Europe and Asia.

PYRRHUS ACHIEVES COSTLY VICTORIES

280 and 279 BCE

Main Culprit: Pyrrhus of Epirus

Damage Done: He achieved his aims and beat the Romans, but lost many soldiers, commanders, and friends

Why: The Romans could recruit reinforcements, but Pyrrhus was too far from home to replenish his forces

Pyrrhus, a Greek of the fourth century BCE, was by all accounts a great military commander. Hannibal, the Carthaginian general who was no slouch when it came to battlefield tactics, rated him second only to Alexander the Great. It is therefore unfortunate that his name lives on only in the phrase "Pyrrhic victory," meaning a victory that has been achieved at too high a cost.

Born in 319 BCE, Pyrrhus was the son of Aeacides, who ruled the region of Epirus on the northwest coast of the Greek mainland. His father was deposed when the boy was just two years old and he was raised by Glaucias, the king of the Illyrians, as part of his own family.

Glaucias refused to hand Pyrrhus over to Cassander, the son of Antipater (Alexander the Great's general), even when he was offered a large sum of money.

Despite losing the Battle of Ipsus, Pyrrhus made a name for himself for his bravery and skill in battle.

When Pyrrhus was twelve years old Glaucias sent him to Epirus with an army to take back the throne. However, when he was seventeen, Pyrrhus left Epirus to attend the wedding of one of Glaucias's sons, and while he was away there was an uprising and he lost everything.

BRAVE FIGHTER

Since the death of Alexander the Great, his generals and friends, known collectively as the Diadochi, had been fighting one another for control of parts of his empire. In 301 BCE Pyrrhus fought alongside his brother-in-law Demetrius, son of Antigonus who was one of the Diadochi, in the Battle of Ipsus against a coalition that included Cassander. Pyrrhus fought courageously, but Antigonus was killed, the army was beaten, and Demetrius fled back to Greece. Pyrrhus was sent to Egypt to try to negotiate a settlement between his brother-in-law Demetrius and King Ptolemy of Egypt.

Pyrrhus clearly impressed the Egyptian court, because he was offered the hand of Ptolemy's stepdaughter,

Profiting from his own
reputation and the ill will
that the Macedonian troops
felt toward Demetrius,
Pyrrhus then entered
Macedonia as a liberator
and took over the kingdom
without even raising his
sword. He ruled from 286
until 283 BCE, when he
was ousted.

A NEW CHALLENGE

Pyrrhus's next adventure
took him to Italy, where
Tarentum, one of the
many Greek colonies in
that country, was being
threatened by Rome.

Antigone, in marriage. With her help
he raised the funds to recruit an army,
and in 297 BCE he returned to Epirus
where he negotiated an agreement to rule
jointly with a nephew of Alexander the
Great, the unpopular Neoptolemus II.
When Pyrrhus got wind of a plot to
poison him, he killed Neoptolemus and
ruled Epirus on his own.

When Demetrius, who was now king
of Macedonia, invaded Epirus in 291,
Pyrrhus defeated one of his armies and
then invaded Macedonia. Macedonian
soldiers who were fed up with
Demetrius's corrupt and pushy attitude
changed sides, and Pyrrhus almost
succeeded in taking control of the whole
kingdom before returning to Epirus.

In 280 BCE, at the invitation of the
Tarentines, Pyrrhus sailed across the
Adriatic with an army of some twenty-
five thousand soldiers, cavalrymen,
archers, and "slingers." He also brought
twenty elephants. Despite a storm that
scattered the fleet along the Italian coast,
the army was able to regroup at Tarentum
where Pyrrhus set about turning the
inhabitants into soldiers, largely against
their will. Several other Greek cities also
offered to send troops as reinforcements.

When Pyrrhus learned that a large
Roman army was on its way he decided
not to wait for the reinforcements but to
advance on the Romans before they
could approach the city. The two armies
met on the plain of Heraclea, and when

REJECTING THE PEACE OFFER
This painting by Cesare Maccari shows
Appius Claudius persuading the Roman
Senate not to accept Pyrrhus's offer of
peace unless he leaves the country.

Pyrrhus saw the size and level of
organization of the Roman camp he
reconsidered waiting for the additional
troops, but it was too late. The Romans
had no intention of waiting.

ROAD TO RUIN

The two armies were evenly matched,
but Pyrrhus's forces finally broke
through by using the elephants, which

HORNS OF A GOAT

The battle between the armies of
Greece and Rome on the plain of
Heraclea was a long one. Pyrrhus
wore distinctive armor and a
helmet adorned with the horns of a
goat. This, he realized, made him
highly recognizable and an easy
target for those who wanted to kill
him. As a result, he swapped his
helmet with a friend, which had
disastrous consequences. His friend
was soon killed (who needs friends
like Pyrrhus?), and when the
Roman victor displayed the
distinctive helmet as a trophy, the
Greek and Tarentine soldiers
believed they had lost their leader
and began to give up hope. Pyrrhus
had to ride through the battlefield
bareheaded to show them he was
still alive and rally them.

terrified the horses of the Roman cavalry.
Pyrrhus was able to take the Roman
camp and advance on Rome itself. Aware
that his army was not large enough to
take Rome, Pyrrhus suggested a peace
treaty, and the Romans agreed provided
that Pyrrhus and his men leave Italy.

Pyrrhus would not accept this, and
the following year the two armies—
Pyrrhus's army strengthened with
soldiers from other Greek colonies in
Italy—met again in battle, this time at
Asculum. Once again the battle was long,
with each side alternately advancing and

retreating, but once again the elephants carried the day and the Romans were beaten back. Nonetheless, Pyrrhus gave a witty response when he was congratulated on the victory. In both battles, the Romans had lost more men than the Greeks (approximately thirteen

Pyrrhus had won both battles against the Romans but the cost to his army and followers was too great.

thousand Romans to seven thousand Greeks), but Pyrrhus understood the reality. The army he had brought from Epirus was severely reduced, he had lost most of his faithful commanders and good friends, his Greek allies in Italy could not be relied upon as a fighting force, and there was no way he could replenish his troops. Rome on the other hand could draw on a vast resource of capable soldiers and soon replace their losses. Yes, he had won both battles, but the cost was too great. "One more victory against the Romans," he said, "and we'll be ruined."

THE MURDER OF JULIUS CAESAR

44 BCE

Main Culprits: The Liberatores, a group of Roman senators

Damage Done: Removed a harmless dictator from power and opened the door to the tyrannical rule of the Roman emperors

Why: In order to retain or regain their personal privileges and influence over matters of state in the Roman Republic

Murdering someone is always bad, but did the assassination of Julius Caesar achieve what its conspirators, the people behind his murder, wanted? Although he ultimately paid the price for enormous personal power, Julius Caesar was certainly an extremely talented man, and his life story is quite remarkable.

Gaius Julius Caesar was born in about 100 BCE into a noble, though not particularly wealthy or influential, family. His family had ties with the Populares, aristocratic leaders whose political power was founded on the people's assemblies and drew support from the plebs (land-owning citizens). The more conservative Optimates derived their power from the Senate and the nobility.

At the age of sixteen, on the death of his father, Caesar became head of the

> As a young man, Caesar spent several years in the army, where he soon excelled in battle and diplomacy.

family, and at eighteen he married the daughter of a leading member of the Populares, who bore him a daughter called Julia. He became a high priest of Jupiter, but was forced into hiding by the Optimate dictator Sulla, who was trying to get rid of his political enemies. Without his priestly position, wealth, and inheritance, Caesar then spent several years in the army, where he soon excelled in battle and diplomacy.

SOLDIER AND POLITICIAN

When Sulla died in 78 BCE, Caesar returned to Rome. He set himself up as a lawyer and became an eloquent orator with a talent for self-promotion. At the age of twenty-eight, he took his first step on the political ladder when he was elected as a tribune (an official of the republic), followed by positions as quaestor (an elected treasury official), as the high priest of the Roman religion, and then as a member of the Senate (the governing council of the Roman Republic). At great personal cost, he also organized the Roman games in 65 BCE, which proved increasingly popular.

"… The noble Brutus Hath told you Caesar was ambitious…"
—Antony in *Julius Caesar*, Act 3, Scene II

As consul, in 59 BCE he introduced laws that granted land to retired soldiers, and this brought him the support of the army.

Caesar was then appointed governor of Spain, but he was still deeply in debt and therefore turned to the wealthy politician Crassus for financial help. Crassus agreed to do so in return for Caesar's political support against his rival

JULIUS CAESAR

He distinguished himself in battle and as a governor and politician, but his success caused resentment among the nobility.

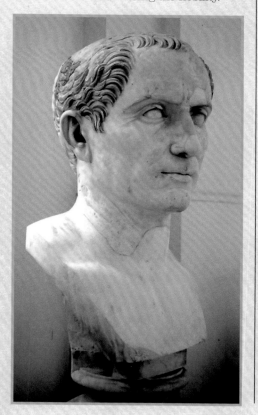

Pompey. On his return from Spain and as newly elected consul, Caesar formed an informal alliance with Crassus and Pompey, who were both Populares. With the help of Caesar's armed followers, they aggressively pushed through legislation in the Roman Senate.

CONQUEST OF GAUL

With the support of powerful allies, Caesar then became governor of northern Italy, southern Europe, and southern France. This meant he was now in control of four legions of the army. He went on to extend Roman control northward as far as the Rhine river, conquering tribe after tribe. As his armies sacked and looted towns, he also acquired considerable personal wealth. In 55 BCE he crossed the English Channel and brought the Roman army into Britain for the first time, although he was unable to establish a permanent presence there. Over the next five years he brought Gaul under complete Roman control with a number of outstanding military victories that were widely reported back home.

ALARM BELLS

By 50 BCE, Caesar's growing popularity and power were ringing alarm bells at the Senate in Rome. Pompey, who had been appointed sole consul, ordered Caesar to return to Rome without his army. Caesar refused to comply and crossed into Italy with a legion of his army, an act that was the equivalent of declaring war. As a result, Pompey and his legions fled the country along with the majority of the

Senate who had expressed opposition. Over the next few years Caesar defeated Pompey's forces and then followed Pompey to Egypt. Here the Pharaoh, King Ptolemy XIII, presented Caesar with Pompey's decapitated head, hoping that the murder of his rival would please him. The plan backfired, however.

Caesar, enraged at the murder of a noble Roman, took control of Egypt, sided with the twenty-one-year-old Cleopatra in a civil war against the Pharaoh (who was her brother, husband, and co-ruler), and installed her as queen. She bore Caesar's only son, Caesarion, in the summer of 47 BCE.

ROMAN SENATE
In the last years of his life, Caesar appointed many of his own allies as senators and effectively robbed the Senate of its power and its independence.

Some members of the Senate were unhappy with the nature of Caesar's rule, preferring the ideals of the Roman Republic before Caesar. He had reduced the power of the public assemblies and the Senate, giving them no choice but to agree to his wishes. Although Caesar had expanded the Senate, he had filled it with his own followers. This was very different from the principles of a republic, which did give at least some of the people a voice in the running of the affairs of state. Added to this, the heads of the noble families of Rome — who had once made up the Senate — had seen their power, wealth, and privileges dramatically reduced. They were desperately seeking a return to their

STRONG EMPIRE

After military triumphs in the Middle East and Africa, Caesar was made sole consul of Rome as well as the position of dictator for the next ten years. He then introduced a new constitution that not only consolidated his power but also sought to bring peace and unity to the Roman Empire.

NEW TIMES

As sole consul and dictator of the Roman Empire, Caesar introduced a host of reforms affecting everything from the legal system and taxation to land allocation and personal debt. He also replaced the lunar calendar (which was based on the cycles of the moon) with the solar year (based on the revolution of the earth around the sun). He also had great plans for major constructions, such as temples, ports, and canals, but they were never to happen.

ET TU, BRUTE?

According to one historian, Caesar's last words, directed at his friend Marcus Brutus at the moment of his assassination, were "You too, child?" spoken in Greek. However, another historian recorded that he said nothing. The Latin phrase "Et tu, Brute?" ("You too, Brutus?") was Shakespeare's invention and is now a well-known quotation representing betrayal.

former status and positions of influence. In either case, removing Caesar appeared to be the solution to the problem.

IDES OF MARCH

In February 44 BCE Caesar was appointed dictator for life. This step toward tyranny (rule by one person with absolute power) was the final straw for a large group of disgruntled senators who called themselves Liberatores, or liberators. The conspirators set the date for his assassination for March 15, the Ides of March, when Caesar would be present at a meeting of the Senate and the conspirators could smuggle in daggers beneath their togas.

On March 14, Marcus Antonius (Mark Antony), Caesar's faithful friend and second in command, got wind of the plot and attempted to warn Caesar but was prevented by a group of senators.

Casca called out for help, and the group of conspirators then drew their daggers and stabbed Caesar.

Caesar's wife, too, had fears for his safety and begged him not to attend the Senate, but Decimus Brutus (the brother of Marcus Brutus, one of the leading conspirators) successfully persuaded Caesar not to disappoint the senators. The details of what then occurred were subsequently recorded by several Roman historians, and Shakespeare's play *Julius Caesar* is a fair reflection of these accounts.

When he entered, Caesar was approached by Tillius Cimber who pretended he was presenting him with a petition for the return of his brother from exile. As the conspirators closed in around him, Caesar waved Cimber away who then grabbed Caesar by the shoulders and pulled down his toga. A senator named Casca then struck at Caesar's neck with a dagger, but Caesar grasped his arm. Casca called out for help, and the group of conspirators then drew their daggers and stabbed Caesar. Realizing what was happening and understanding that resistance was pointless, Caesar wrapped his toga around his head. With a total of twenty-three wounds to his body, Caesar then fell lifeless to the floor at the feet of a statue of his great rival Pompey. (He was to lie there for several hours until three slaves took the body to his home.)

TREACHEROUS MURDER

While the rest of the senators fled the building, the conspirators made their way to the capital, shouting to the citizens of Rome that they were once again free. However, most of the people in the city hid in their homes, fearing what might follow.

If the Liberatores thought their deed would either restore their power or save

Antony may have hoped to become ruler, but Caesar had made his grandnephew Octavian his heir and adopted son. There followed many years of civil wars, initially involving Octavian and Mark Antony against the leading conspirators and their armies, but finally pitting Octavian against Mark Antony and his former master's lover, Cleopatra. Octavian's troops triumphed over the Egyptians in 31 BCE (both Mark Antony and Cleopatra committing suicide as a result), and Rome claimed Egypt. In 27 BCE he became not only the first emperor of the Roman Empire (Imperator Gaius Julius Caesar Augustus) but also supreme spiritual leader of the Roman people.

the Roman Republic, they were truly mistaken. Mark Antony's eulogy at Caesar's funeral highlighted all the good that the late leader had done for his people and painted the conspirators' act as treacherous murder, turning the Roman people against them and causing them to flee the country for their lives. With the people on his side, Mark

Although some elements of the people's representation remained, the head of the Roman Empire was in effect an autocratic (all-powerful) tyrant. The assassination of Caesar had put an end to any personal ambitions the conspirators may have had, and ended any hopes of a return to the ideals of the Roman Republic.

CHOOSING CALIGULA AS EMPEROR

37–41 CE

Main Culprit: When Emperor Tiberius chose Caligula as his successor, he had no reason to suspect that his adopted grandson would prove to be completely off his rocker

Damage Done: Bankrupted the state and led to the deaths of many innocent Romans

Why: Caligula was a megalomaniac with delusions of godliness

With the transformation of the Roman Republic into an empire, the emperor became leader for life and was able to choose who should succeed him. The first emperor, Augustus, passed the throne to his stepson and adopted son Tiberius, who proved capable but fairly brutal in dealing with any opposition. He in turn nominated as his joint heir Gaius Julius Caesar Germanicus (better known by his nickname Caligula), the son of his nephew and adopted son Germanicus, together with Tiberius's grandson Tiberius Gemellus. When Tiberius died in around 37 CE (possibly with a little help from Caligula), Rome celebrated the arrival of the young new emperor. Caligula benefited from the popularity of his father, the highly successful and much-loved general Germanicus, which also guaranteed him the backing of the army.

Apart from having the young Tiberius Gemellus put to death, Caligula began his reign well, repealing some unpopular laws, putting an end to the bloody treason trials started by Tiberius, and spending a small fortune on gladiatorial games. But the honeymoon was to be short-lived. After a few months, Caligula was taken ill, and when he returned to public life he was a different person — self-important, power mad, cruel, irrational, deluded, and twisted.

PARTY ANIMAL

Believing himself to be godlike, and insisting on being treated as such, he demanded that his sisters be honored by the people and the army. It is also said that he had an unhealthy relationship with all three of them and may have prostituted them to other men. He treated the Senate with utter disrespect

> *"I am nursing a viper in Rome's bosom. I am educating a Phaethon who will mishandle the fiery sun-chariot and scorch the whole world."*
>
> **—Tiberius about his heir Caligula**

and even tried to have his favorite horse, Incitatus (which lived in the palace and had dinner parties held in its name), elevated to the position of consul.

Although accounts of his behavior may have been exaggerated, Caligula certainly liked to indulge in all the pleasures of the senses, openly sleeping with other men's wives, hosting numerous parties, practicing a range of sexual perversions, and enjoying killing for its own sake.

MAKING ENEMIES

Within two years of his rule, Caligula's luxurious lifestyle and out-of-control spending had exhausted the government's money reserves. To solve the problem,

EMPEROR CALIGULA

As a child, the emperor went on campaign with his father to Germania, where his father's soldiers gave him the nickname "Caligula," meaning "Little Boots."

Caligula reinstated the treason trials favored by his predecessor Tiberius so he could get his hands on the fortunes and possessions of wealthy citizens. To do this, he banished many of them from Rome, even killing some of his chosen victims. As the rumblings from an increasingly hostile Senate grew louder, Caligula turned his attention on them, opening investigations into the loyalty of some senators and having some of them executed.

SPLASHING OUT

Emperor Caligula liked to spend money and lots of it. He went through money like water, building public entertainment and construction projects that benefited the people, such as harbor improvements, aqueducts, and canals. He also delighted in erecting buildings and monuments that were dedicated to him and in his glory. In one particularly wasteful stunt he oversaw the construction of a 2.5-mile (4-km) floating bridge across the Bay of Baiae, to the west of Naples, so that he could ride his horse from one side to the other. This act was intended to pour scorn on a fortune-teller's earlier prediction that Caligula had as much chance of becoming emperor as he had of riding a horse across the bay. He also commissioned a luxurious floating palace in which to entertain his guests on Lake Nemi, a volcanic crater dedicated to the Roman goddess Diana.

Plots were undoubtedly being hatched against him, and in 39 CE one was uncovered involving Lepidus (the husband of Caligula's favorite sister, who had died the previous year) and Caligula's other two sisters. Lepidus was executed and the sisters were sent into exile (banished from Rome).

EGOMANIAC

By 40 CE Caligula seems to have been fully convinced that he was a god, turning his palace into a temple, presenting himself to the people dressed as various gods, and demanding that he be treated as one. He even commanded that a statue of himself be erected in the Temple of Jerusalem, which would probably have led to civil war had the order been carried out.

Despite his outrageous behavior, which included having a section of the

FLOATING PALACE

Caligula's floating palace on Lake Nemi, south of Rome. It included marble floors and plumbing.

crowd thrown to wild animals when the games ran out of gladiators, the people remained largely in favor of Caligula.

TIME TO GO

Increasing hostility toward him among the senators, the nobility, and the army finally resulted in a successful plot against Caligula. In January 41 CE, officers of the Praetorian Guard (personal guards of the emperor) attacked Caligula in a corridor beneath the Imperial Palace. They stabbed him repeatedly, just as Julius Caesar had been murdered a hundred years before.

> **Caligula seems to have been fully convinced that he was a god, turning his palace into a temple, presenting himself to the people dressed as various gods, and demanding that he be treated as one.**

Caligula's wife and daughter were murdered soon afterward as the Senate hoped to eliminate the imperial family and reinstate the republic. However, support for the position of emperor was greater than they realized. Another section of the Praetorian Guard found and protected the last male member of the family—Caligula's uncle, Claudius—and he was soon hailed as Caligula's successor. Caligula's reign of murder and debauchery had lasted for less than four years, but during that time he had virtually bankrupted the state. It fell upon Claudius to bring order and decency back to the empire, a task that he was thankfully able to achieve.

ON TO BRITAIN

Possibly feeling the need to follow in the legendary footsteps of his father, Germanicus, and his predecessor, Tiberius, Caligula embarked on a military campaign northward through Gaul. His intention was to add Britain to the empire, but it is reported that when he reached the English Channel, he instructed his soldiers to collect seashells from the shore, and the campaign ended there.

EMPEROR JULIAN REJECTS CHRISTIANITY

362 CE

Main Culprit: Roman emperor Flavius Claudius Julianus (Julian)

Damage Done: Persecuted Christians and harmed the development of the early Christian Church

Why: Believed in the earlier Roman gods and wished to make paganism the principle of the empire

By all accounts (and his life is well documented), Emperor Julian, who only ruled from 361 to 363 CE, was a remarkable man. Unfortunately for him, and for many throughout the Roman Empire, he decided to swim against the already-flowing current of religious change.

Flavius Claudius Julianus was born into the imperial family in 331 CE. He was the son of Julius Constantinus and half-brother of Constantine I (Constantine the Great), and it is with that emperor that this story begins. It was Constantine who made the great city of Byzantium, or Constantinople as it was renamed, the capital of the Roman Empire, and it was here that Julian was born. Constantine was also the first Christian emperor, committing himself to the religion after experiencing a vision before a great battle in 312 CE. In 313 he legalized Christian worship, and during his reign Christianity became the dominant religion throughout the empire. Although he was not baptized until shortly before his death, Constantine the Great became deeply involved in matters

of the Christian Church. This involved bringing together councils of the bishops, attempting to heal some deep religious rifts, as well as entrusting certain government functions to the clergy. He also took steps to suppress pagan (non-Christian) worship of the old gods by ordering temples to be closed or confiscated, removing temple treasures, and banning animal sacrifice.

THREE BROTHERS

Constantine the Great died when Julian was six years old and was succeeded by his three sons—the confusingly named Constans, Constantius II, and Constantine II. The three emperors immediately eliminated possible rivals with a bloody purge of the families of their father's half-brothers. Julian and his younger half-brother, Gallus, were the only male members to survive, probably because they were considered too young to pose a threat. Julian was sent to Nicomedia, the former capital of the eastern Roman Empire, where he was given a strict Christian education. When Julian was thirteen, he and Gallus

BEARDED THINKER
With his old-fashioned philosopher's beard, Emperor Julian was considered by many to be inappropriately scruffy for his position as ruler.

were sent to Cappadocia, where their Christian education continued. Julian became very knowledgeable about the Bible and Christianity, but he also began to study classical Greek teachings.

In 351, after the death of his two brothers, Constantius II made Gallus a consul and Julian returned to Nicomedia, where he became deeply interested in the Greek religious philosophy of Neoplatonism, pagan beliefs based on the work of Plato. He studied under some of the greatest Neoplatonist philosophers and was introduced to the Eleusinian Mysteries, an ancient system of beliefs and ceremonies dating back more than a thousand years.

GREEK SCHOLAR

In 354 Gallus was executed for treason and Julian was briefly brought back to Italy, although he returned to Greece the following year to continue his studies. Not long after, Constantius II, needing a representative to help him govern the vast Roman Empire, brought Julian back, appointed him as Caesar (or sub-emperor), and sent him to Gaul. The bearded scholar soon proved himself to be an able administrator and a skilled military tactician. Over the next five years he conquered and negotiated peace with many of the tribes of the region, and won over the people through just rule and fair taxation. He also secured the approval and admiration of his troops, many of whom were natives of the area. By 360 CE his popularity and success had aroused the jealousy of the emperor. Constantius II began by depriving Julian of some of his legions. However, when Petulantes, an infantry unit composed largely of Germanic men, were ordered to march east, they rebelled against the orders of Constantius II. Instead they hailed Julian as emperor.

POPULAR TOUCH

Despite his refusal to accept the honor, the troops insisted, carrying him on a shield and placing a chain about his head to symbolize a royal crown. Julian remained reluctant and later said that he only accepted after receiving guidance from the god Zeus. He also claimed that

> After the death of his two brothers, Julian became deeply interested in ancient systems of beliefs dating back more than a thousand years.

JULIAN THE APOSTATE

Julian's rejection of Christianity led to history labeling him "Julian the Apostate," apostasy meaning standing away from or abandoning a religion. Blaming the weakness of the Roman Empire on its adoption of Christianity, he reduced the power of the clergy, forbade Christians to teach the Greek classics (referring, as they did, to gods whose existence the Christians denied), and removed many of their privileges. He allowed rebellious bishops to return from exile, possibly in an attempt to generate divisions within the Christian Church.

the troops commanded him to return to the ancient rituals, leading them in sacrifices to the gods.

Julian wrote to Constantius II, explaining that receiving the title of emperor was not his wish but that of the soldiers. The situation remained unresolved for a year, but then Julian decided to settle the matter and headed east with his army to meet Constantius II in battle. Julian probably felt little loyalty to the emperor, having seen his family murdered on the orders of Constantius and his brothers. Civil war

was looming, but as the armies drew closer the danger was averted by the sudden death, from natural causes, of the emperor. He is said to have named Julian as his successor with his dying words. Entering Constantinople on December 11, 361, Julian gave his former rival a full Christian burial and then set about fulfilling his aim of returning the Roman Empire to its former glory. He installed his own advisers in government positions and stamped out the corruption that had become rife. He now openly declared his rejection of Christianity and his conversion to the ancient Greco-Roman religion.

ROMAN GODS RETURN

If Rome was to be great again, Julian needed the help of the gods. He took steps to resurrect the ancient Roman religion by reopening the temples, encouraging and even demanding the performance of animal sacrifices to the Roman gods, and setting up a structured pagan church organized in a similar way to the Christian churches. While he attacked Christian beliefs, he showed greater tolerance for Judaism, possibly in the hope of striking a blow against Christianity.

He even instigated the reconstruction of the Temple of Jerusalem, which was destroyed by the Romans in 70 CE. The project, however, was abandoned, supposedly because balls of fire kept

Although Julian largely succeeded in bringing down a powerful Christian elite, with some Christians suffering real persecution, his attempt to return Rome to its former religion failed.

erupting from beneath the foundations, preventing the workers from carrying out their task.

CHRISTIANITY SURVIVES
Although Julian largely succeeded in bringing down a powerful Christian elite, with some Christians suffering real persecution in parts of the empire, his attempt to return Rome to its former religion failed. This was because, in the main, the people did not follow his lead. His own particular mix of paganism and philosophy was highly intellectual and had little popular appeal. By its very nature paganism was, unlike Christianity, a private rather than public religion. It was made up of a wide range of

DIVIDE AND CONQUER
Julian the Apostate encouraged the many different groups within Christianity, with the intention of creating splits within the Christian Church.

different beliefs and failed to provide a clear, organizing principle for the empire. In any case, the experiment was a short-lived one. Julian ruled for less than two years, dying in June 363 from an arrow wound while leading a military campaign against the Persians. Although his reign had succeeded in doing enormous harm to the organized Christian Church, Christianity was there to stay, and it was paganism that soon came to be outlawed by the emperors of Rome.

MONOPHYSITISM IS DECLARED HERETICAL

451 CE

Main Culprits: Stubborn theologians and an authoritarian church

Damage Done: Led to a major split in the Christian community

Why: The Catholic Church (with state backing) assumed the right to determine what was acceptable doctrine and tolerated no deviation from orthodoxy ("straight belief")

Conflict between religions has been at the root of some of the world's worst and longest wars, but don't let that lead you to thinking that all is sweetness and light within religions. In its first few centuries, Christianity was riven with deep divisions, and one that tore the community apart permanently arose from disagreements about something that many would consider unknowable—the relation between the divine and human natures of Christ.

The doctrine of the Trinity—that God exists in three persons: the Father, the Son, and the Holy Spirit—has been central to Christianity since its beginning. But according to the scriptures Jesus Christ is both God and man, so what, then, is the relation of Jesus Christ to God the Father, and how can He be both divine and human? This difficult problem led to many different attempts at understanding, and they proved to be extremely divisive.

> "According to the apostolic teaching and the doctrine of the Gospel, let us believe in the one deity of the Father, the Son and the Holy Spirit, in equal majesty and in a holy Trinity. We authorize the followers of this law to assume the title of Catholic Christians; but as for the others, since, in our judgment they are foolish madmen, we decree that they shall be branded with the ignominious name of heretics, and shall not presume to give to their conventicles the name of churches."
>
> —From the Edict of Thessalonica, delivered by the Roman emperors Theodosius I, Gratian, and Valentinian II in 380 CE

HUMAN AND DIVINE?

The orthodox line was, and is, that the three elements of the Trinity are co-equal, co-existent, and co-eternal. None is greater than the others, and they exist at the same time and forever. The first attempt at upsetting the apple cart came during the reign of Constantine the Great, when the very learned Alexandrian scholar Arius declared that Christ was neither co-equal nor co-eternal with God the Father. Citing a range of Bible verses, Arius taught that whereas God the Father had always existed, Christ was created by God the Father as the means of bringing salvation to the world. Christ was not only subordinate to God the Father but was not of the same substance and was in fact human, and not divine. This went directly against the mainstream Trinitarian doctrine.

The Church immediately pronounced his views to be heretical (contrary to Church teaching) and Arius was excommunicated (banished from the church), but not before his teachings had gained significant influence throughout the eastern Mediterranean. In order to put an end to this flourishing heresy, which was threatening to divide the Church, in 325 CE, Emperor Constantine convened the first Council of Bishops, in Nicaea (now the Turkish town of Iznik). Here an assembly of bishops from throughout Christendom debated the issue for several weeks. Their discussions centered around definitions, in many languages, of such terms as "existence," "substance," "essence," "begotten," and "created," and arguments such as, if God the Father is eternal and has always been regarded as the Father, then the Son must also be eternal.

CO-EQUAL, CO-ETERNAL

The nature of Christ, and his relation to the two other elements of the Trinity, proved to be highly divisive issues in the early Christian Church.

DECLARATION

The outcome of the debate was a declaration by the First Council of Nicaea that God the Father and God the Son are of one substance and are co-eternal, and this element of doctrine was then incorporated into the Nicene Creed, a statement of faith that is still proclaimed (in an amended form) today. The bishops at Nicaea also determined that Christ is one substance but is both fully human and fully divine, one person in whom two natures—one divine and one human—are united. This is known as the hypostatic union—one person, two natures.

MONOPHYSITISM

The Syrian bishop Apollinaris held an opposite view to Arius. He maintained that, although Christ had a human body, he had only one nature—divine. This, too, was rejected by the Church, as it denied that Christ was fully human, and was declared heretical by the next Council of Bishops, held in Constantinople in 381. The belief that Christ has only one nature became known as monophysitism (one-nature-ism), and it was later to lead to a fundamental split in the Church and ultimately to the weakening of its influence.

HERETICAL BELIEFS

Nestorius, appointed Bishop of Constantinople in 427, went to the opposite extreme of Arius. Unwilling to accept that the Son of God could have a solely human form, he taught that Christ had two natures but that he was also two persons, one divine and one human. He maintained that Mary the Virgin should be called not the Mother of God (since God had always existed), but the Mother of Christ, since she gave birth only to the human person of Christ who was later imbued with a divine nature. Nestorius was a great speaker, and his teachings quickly became popular, but there were also many who thought his views were heretical.

His strongest opponent was Cyril, the Bishop of Alexandria, and the argument between them became so heated that Emperor Theodosius II convened another council, this time at Ephesus, in 431.

Here Cyril, who had already ensured that the majority of the bishops would be on his side, charged Nestorius with heresy and the council condemned him. He was sent into exile in the Libyan desert, but his followers remained true to his teachings, leading to the formation of the Nestorian Church, or the Church of the East, mainly in Persia and later throughout parts of Asia. This church still exists, and it rejects the declarations of the First Council of Ephesus.

Present at the First Council of Ephesus, and vehemently opposed to Nestorius, was an elder of the Church in Constantinople called Eutyches. He later asserted the belief that in their union in Christ, human nature and divine nature were combined into a single nature, as though the first were dissolved in the second. Although he was careful to say that this did not diminish Christ's humanity, he put his views forward with such force that they were regarded as monophysite heresy, and he was excommunicated in 448. The following year, the Second Council of Ephesus reversed this decision, but this in turn was overruled by the Council of Chalcedon in 451, which declared that although the divine nature and the human nature were united in Christ, they each remained distinct and unaltered, and that Christ is "in two natures." Eutyches was sent into exile, but the patriarch of Alexandria, in Egypt, and

> Modern-day Christian groups who hold similar non-Trinitarian beliefs include the Unitarian Church and the Jehovah's Witnesses.

CYRIL
The Bishop of Alexandria crushed the "Nestorian heresy" and created the first major split. The Nestorian Church still exists today.

his bishops refused to accept the declarations of the Council of Chalcedon, believing that the formulation "in two natures" smacked of Nestorian heresy.

SCHISM
In the late fifth century this led to a permanent schism between the "non-Chalcedonian" Oriental Orthodox Church, as it became known, and the rest of the Church, which declared the Alexandrian position to be monophysite and therefore heretical.

The Oriental Orthodox Church flourished in northeast Africa and the Levant, and its rejection by the rest of Eastern Christianity was to have major historical consequences. In the seventh century, when the armies of Islam set out from Arabia to the north and the west, the Oriental Orthodox Christians of Egypt, Syria, and Palestine, already alienated from the rest of Christendom and oppressed by Byzantium, offered little resistance. This was in part because they practiced greater tolerance than the rest of the Christian Church. As a result these areas soon fell under Arab rule, being taken from the Byzantine Empire and becoming part of the growing Islamic Empire—a high price for Christendom to pay for a disagreement over the unprovable.

Fourteen hundred years later, the Oriental Orthodox Church today comprises several churches, including the Coptic Orthodox, the Armenian Apostolic, the Ethiopian Orthodox, and the Malankara (Indian) Orthodox Churches. They reject the accusation of being monophysite, since their position is not the same as that of Eutyches, and describe their position as miaphysite ("joined-nature"), that Christ has one nature in which the divine and the human are combined but with the character of each fully preserved.

THE GREAT EAST– WEST SCHISM

1054 CE

Main Culprit: The oppressive leadership of the Roman Catholic Church

Damage Done: Led to a major split between the Western and Eastern Churches

Why: Rome claimed the right to rule the Christian Church, and introduced changes in doctrine and practice

Growing disagreement between the Western Church based in Rome and the Eastern Church based in Constantinople finally led to breaking point in the middle of the eleventh century. Although the dispute stemmed from many things, the clincher was the interpretation of the Holy Trinity (one god in three persons: the Father, Son, and Holy Spirit). A thousand years later, this rift has still not yet been healed. After Constantine moved the capital of the Roman Empire from Rome to Constantinople in the early fourth century, the Church was divided into five "patriarchates," each administered by a separate patriarch, or archbishop. These patriarchates were Rome, Antioch, Constantinople, Jerusalem, and Alexandria. While they acknowledged that the pope in Rome was the "first among equals," when it came to religious doctrine and theology, the patriarchates considered themselves to be equal. But when Rome fell in the fifth century, the head of the Church in Rome began to assume both secular (non-religious) and religious authority, to the growing annoyance of the other patriarchates.

GREEK VERSUS LATIN

Other factors, too, distanced the patriarchates from Rome. The language of the Church in Rome was Latin, while the rest of the Church used Greek. The Western Church imposed its teachings on a largely illiterate people: in the east, more people could read and write, and were given access to a Bible translated into a language they could understand,

The dispute between the Eastern and Western Church stemmed from many things. The clincher, however, was the interpretation of the Holy Trinity (the Father, Son, and Holy Spirit).

> *"… the Giver of Life, who proceeds from the Father and the Son…"*
> —The Nicene Creed

which led to discussion about Christian doctrine. This resulted in philosophical differences between the two, although the first major bone of contention was born out of the increasing power of the pope and a matter of doctrine.

HOLY TRINITY

In Spain in the first half of the sixth century, the Nicene Creed, a formal statement of Christian beliefs, was altered. At the end of the sentence, "And I believe in the Holy Ghost, the Lord and Giver of Life; who proceeds from the Father," the words "and the Son," or, in Latin, *filioque*, were added. Some had claimed that the original wording implied that the Holy Spirit proceeded from just the Father, meaning that the Son cannot fully be God. To them, the revision made the persons of the Trinity equal and enabled God to be experienced in the Father, Son, and Holy Spirit.

Although it had been agreed in the fourth century that no changes could be made to the Nicene Creed without the agreement of the Council of Bishops, this change was accepted throughout the Western Church. But it was not accepted by the other four patriarchates. They maintained that to say that the Holy Spirit proceeds from the Son suggests that the Son is also some kind of god. This undermines the fundamental belief of the Christian Church: that there is one god (known as monotheism). They also questioned the right of the pope to make such a change to the creed without consulting them.

DEEPENING DIVISION

The dispute notched up a gear in the ninth century when the papacy disputed the appointment of Photius as the patriarch of Constantinople, and also insisted that the filioque be included in the creed in Bulgaria, a region that Constantinople regarded as its own. Photius responded by denying the authority of Pope Nicholas I to interfere with matters of Constantinople. He also excommunicated him (officially excluded from the Church) on the basis of a list of

COUNCIL OF NICAEA

The original wording of the Nicene Creed dates from the First Council of Nicaea, held in 325 CE under the emperor Constantine.

PERMANENT RIFT

The rift between the Eastern and Western Church has proved to be permanent and certain events that have taken place since the eleventh century have deepened the division. In 1204, the soldiers of the Fourth Crusade, sent by Pope Innocent II to take Egypt from the Muslims, instead sacked Constantinople. There, they carried out horrendous atrocities, looting hundreds of churches and cathedrals in the majestic city, and stealing priceless treasures and relics belonging to the Greek Orthodox Church. These were taken back to the cities of Western Europe, and most notably to the official residence of the pope, the Vatican in Rome. In 1870, the pope's claim to supremacy was further backed by the declaration by the Vatican Council that the pope cannot be wrong on matters of faith or morals. This did not help to bring the two Churches closer together.

successor of St. Peter and so is the vicar of Christ. As a result, the pope has spiritual supremacy over the whole Church and all the bishops. This doctrine, which had been expressly rejected by earlier Church Councils, was perceived by the Eastern Church as an excessive use of power. In 1054 the patriarch of Constantinople, Michael Cerularius, wrote a letter to Bishop John of Trani in Italy. In it he outlined the many changes that had been introduced by the Roman Church, condemning some of them as sinful. He asked the bishop to make known the contents of the letter as widely as possible.

EXCOMMUNICATION

In response, Pope Leo IX sent a delegation to Constantinople to remove the patriarch and to demand that Constantinople recognize the Church of Rome as the head of the Church. The patriarch refused to see the legates

ONE TRUE POPE
Leo IX attempted to force the church in Constantinople to admit Rome's authority.

"errors." These included insisting upon celibacy for priests and adding the filioque to the creed. This "Photian Schism" drove the wedge deeper between Rome and the rest of the Church.

PAPAL AUTHORITY

In the early eleventh century, in what became known as the Petrine Doctrine, the Roman Church claimed that the apostle St. Peter was given special authority over the Church by Jesus Christ, that the bishop of the Church in Rome is the

The Western Church claimed that the pope had spiritual supremacy over the whole Church, East and West, and all the bishops.

EAST VS WEST
In 2000, Pope John Paul II apologized for the siege of Constantinople by forces of the Western Church in 1204.

and finally they departed, but not before placing on the altar of the great Hagia Sophia church a papal bull excommunicating Patriarch Michael Cerularius. He in turn excommunicated them. The Great Schism between the Roman Catholic Church and the Greek (or Eastern) Orthodox Church was complete, with each claiming to be the true church.

Over the years, attempts have been made to heal the breach: the mutual excommunications were overruled in 1965 and the Roman Catholic and Greek Orthodox Churches are now at least talking. Despite this, there are still disputes over elements of doctrine and practice—the list of which is a long one.

HAROLD HURRIES TO MEET WILLIAM AT HASTINGS

1066 CE

Main Culprit: King Harold II of England

Damage Done: The throne of England passed to Duke William of Normandy, who shared the country out among his friends

Why: Harold's army was weary and depleted, but he was too impatient to wait for reinforcements

The Battle of Hastings, which took place in the south of England in 1066, is one of history's most famous battles, seen as marking the point at which Anglo-Saxon Britain became Norman Britain. The causes of William of Normandy's invasion had its roots in a long-standing connection between the English monarchy and the Norman nobility. King Harold's failure to defeat the Normans certainly led to a sea change in British history, but the fault lay not with his army or his strategy. He may just have been in too much of a hurry to engage the enemy.

LAND OF THE NORTHMEN

The story behind the conflict between Harold and William begins 150 years earlier, in 911, when the king of France gave Rollo the Viking land in the northwest of France in return for an end to Viking aggression. The area became known as Normandy, the land of the

Northmen, and the Normans adopted the French language and customs. In 1002, the English king Ethelred II married Emma, the sister of Richard II, Duke of Normandy, and she introduced many

NORMAN LANDINGS
William of Normandy's forces land on the south coast of England.

A long-standing connection between the English monarchy and the Norman nobility ultimately led to the invasion of William of Normandy.

of her Norman friends to the English court. When the Danish king Sweyn Forkbeard invaded England in 1013 Ethelred and Emma fled to Normandy. Sweyn's son Canute became king of England, and when Ethelred died, Emma married Canute, possibly to save the lives of her sons Alfred and Edward, who had a claim to the throne. This created yet another bond between Normandy and England.

When Canute died in 1035, Alfred and Edward returned to England, but Edward had to flee again to Normandy when Alfred was taken captive by Godwin, Earl of Wessex, one of England's most powerful lords. Handed over to Canute's son Harold (known as King Harold Harefoot), Alfred was intentionally blinded and he died of his wounds shortly after. In 1041 Harold's half-brother King Harthacnut invited Edward back and made him his heir, and Edward "the Confessor" came to the throne the following year.

RIGHTFUL KING

During his rule, King Edward (who had no children) had invited his uncle William, Duke of Normandy, to England and named him as heir to the English throne. Although Edward was married to Godwin's daughter Edith, Godwin and his family remained fiercely opposed to the increasing influence of the Normans. When Godwin died in 1053, his son, Harold Godwinson, became the rallying

point for anti-Norman feeling in England. At the end of 1065, Edward became gravely ill and he died on January 5, 1066, but not before entrusting his wife (Harold Godwinson's sister) and his kingdom to Harold's care. At a meeting of the Witenagamot (the king's assembly of noblemen) it was decided that Edward's words made Harold the rightful king and he was crowned the following day. This did not suit William, who immediately set about preparing a fleet of ships and an army. Harold's reign was to be a short one.

As William prepared to invade, the English armies suffered considerable

HARALD HARDRADA

William of Normandy wasn't the only one with his eye on the English throne. In September 1066, the armies of Harold's brother Tostig and Viking king Harald Hardrada of Norway arrived off the east coast of England. Harold hoped the armies of the Earls of Mercia and Northumberland would repel them, but the Vikings beat them hands down at the Battle of Fulford. When Harold heard what had happened, he force-marched his army 200 miles (320 km) north in just five days and took the Vikings by surprise. Having left their armor on the ships, the Norsemen suffered huge losses as Harold's army overran them. Both Tostig and Harald Hardrada (who received an arrow through the throat) were killed, and the invaders finally surrendered.

losses fighting off another invasion attempt on the east coast by Harold's brother Tostig and Viking king Harald Hardrada of Norway. Just after this hard-won defeat came the news that William's fleet had landed on the south coast of England. Battle weary, Harold's soldiers headed south with as much speed as they could muster.

William had been ready to set sail from Normandy with a fleet of more than five hundred long ships and possibly as many as twenty thousand men since the middle of August, but bad weather had prevented him. He was finally able to put to sea on September 27. After a night crossing, William made a first muddy landing at Pevensey Bay, but soon decided to move the fleet and the army to a better location at Hastings. For the next two weeks the soldiers pillaged the surrounding countryside, killing villagers and taking what they wished. As well as providing the army with meat and grain, this was a deliberate ploy to goad Harold into an early battle—and it worked.

BATTLE WEARY

Harold's tired army marched south, pausing for a few days in London, where opinion began to favor delaying before going into battle. The army was extremely tired and unprepared, and it was felt that Harold should wait a while to rest the soldiers and drum up more reinforcements before going into battle. For the moment, William's men were well rested, well provisioned, and ready for battle, but if they were to remain at Hastings throughout the winter they would soon run short of food and morale. Harold's brother also suggested that he, Earl Gyrth, should lead the army against William. Harold had once sworn an oath

KING HAROLD IS KILLED
The Bayeux Tapestry depicted events leading up to the Norman conquest of England, ending with the Battle of Hastings. Here King Harold is fatally injured in the battle, his eye pierced by an arrow.

promising to support William's accession to the throne, whereas Earl Gyrth owed him no such loyalty. What was more, if the Normans won, Harold would be able to raise a second army against William or destroy everything ahead of the advancing Normans and starve them into abandoning their attempt on the throne.

THE ATTACK

When the battle began at about nine o'clock the following morning, Harold had the tactical advantage because his army was stationed on a high ridge. The Norman archers began the attack, but the English front ranks used their shields to form a wall. William then sent in the cavalry, but they struggled on the uphill slope and had to pull back. At this stage, the English front lines followed them and almost broke through the Norman lines. Some of the Normans fled and William had to remove his helmet and show his face to put down a rumor that he had been killed. The English had come close to routing the Normans, but it was as close as they were to come.

William once again sent in the archers and this time, by aiming higher and overshooting the wall of shields, they did considerably more damage. It may have been at this point that Harold received an arrow in the eye. William's troops kept up a relentless assault, and the weariness of the English troops began to show. The Normans finally broke through the English defensive lines, and, despite a brave rearguard action by the fleeing soldiers, the Normans, as we all know, won the day.

A NEW CHAPTER

The impatient Harold, fielding a weary and under-strength army, had lost the battle and his life. October 14, 1066, marked the start of a new chapter in English history.

Harold, who had a reputation for being headstrong, ignored the advice of his brother and decided to go into battle as soon as possible. After a few days, Harold and his army continued their journey south. They reached Caldbec Hill, a few miles north of Hastings, on the evening of October 13 and here they set up camp. Norman scouts, however, had seen them arriving and Harold's armies had lost the element of surprise.

Harold, who had a reputation for being headstrong, ignored the advice of his brother and decided to go into battle as soon as possible.

THE FRENCH UNDERESTIMATE THE ENGLISH AT AGINCOURT

1415

Main Culprit: The weak leadership of the French army

Damage Done: Brought about the wholesale destruction of a large part of the army and most of the French nobility

Why: Too much misplaced confidence and not enough planning and organization

In 1415, almost 350 years after the Battle of Hastings, which won for William, Duke of Normandy, the crown of England, an English army led by King Henry V was on French soil. The Plantagenet kings, of which Henry was one, laid claim to the throne of France and had been engaged in a series of wars (known jointly as the Hundred Years' War) against the French House of Valois since 1337. The Plantagenet claim was based on their descent from Edward III, the son of Isabella of France, wife of Edward II. The Valois kings only recognized the male line and denied the legitimacy of a claim based on descent through a female.

TOWARD BATTLE

Since his accession to the throne in 1413, Henry had been in negotiations with the French, but his demands had proved unacceptable. Henry had declared himself willing to give up his claim to the throne of France in return for various concessions. These included payment of an outstanding ransom of 1.6 million crowns owed to the English crown, the hand of French king Charles VI's daughter Princess Catherine in marriage, with a dowry of two million crowns, and acknowledgment of the English claim to Aquitaine and certain other French lands. In response, the French offered marriage to Princess Catherine, a dowry of six hundred thousand crowns, and Aquitaine, which Henry refused. Meanwhile, the preparation of an army of English and Welsh soldiers had been underway, and Henry had decided to press his claim in battle.

The English fleet, carrying a force of some eight thousand men (six thousand archers and two thousand mounted men-at-arms), landed on the French coast in the mouth of the River Seine on

The French had great confidence in their nobles and knights, who made up a large proportion of their army and wore armor of thick steel plate.

August 13. The plan was to take the French seaport of Harfleur, and then to march to Paris, some 125 miles (200 km) away. But two things went wrong. First of all, Harfleur was not the pushover that Henry expected. The French reinforced the small garrison of one hundred soldiers with three hundred more, and the siege lasted for just over a month.

Second, his soldiers were struck by an outbreak of dysentery that killed some and weakened many. By the time the army was ready to set off, on October 8, with around five thousand men, the weather was worsening and it was too late in the year to contemplate attacking Paris. Henry decided instead to head for Calais, farther up the coast, and to make a show of strength as his army marched through the countryside. His advisers counseled against this risky plan, as a powerful French force was on its way, but he persisted. His advisers were right.

KNIGHTS IN ARMOR

When the army reached the River Somme, the presence of French troops forced Henry to take a wide detour. When they were within 30 miles (50 km) of Calais one of the army scouts reported that the valley along which they were marching was blocked by the French army. Unless Henry was willing to renounce his claim to the throne, he and his army would have to do battle. Estimates of the French numbers vary, but they outnumbered the English by at least two to one, and possibly by as many as six to one. The English and Welsh soldiers made camp and spent a somber night contemplating their imminent defeat.

The French, on the other hand, were brimming with confidence and spent the night partying. Not only

HENRY V

After Agincourt, Henry returned to France on two more campaigns, but he died (probably of dysentery) before he could be crowned king of France.

BAND OF BROTHERS

In Shakespeare's *Henry V*, the English king gives an impassioned speech to his men to spur them on to victory.

> "This story shall the good man teach his son;
> And Crispin Crispian shall ne'er go by,
> From this day to the ending of the world,
> But we in it shall be remember'd;
> We few, we happy few, we band of brothers;
> For he to-day that sheds his blood with me
> Shall be my brother; be he ne'er so vile,
> This day shall gentle his condition."

—*Henry V*, Act IV, Scene 3

were there more of them, but they had great confidence in their knights, who made up a large proportion of the army and who wore armor of thick steel plate. The rest of the army was made up of peasants enlisted for the occasion. Henry's army, by contrast, was a professional outfit of permanent soldiers, well paid and disciplined, a large proportion of whom were archers armed with the very latest in lethal weaponry— powerful longbows and armor-piercing arrows. The match was less uneven than it looked. The French had chosen a very poor field on which to do battle, and the weather was not helping.

On the morning of October 25, the two armies faced each other in a rain-sodden valley that had been plowed, with dense woodland on either side. The valley was less than three-quarters of a mile (1.2 km) wide at the French end and narrowed toward the English. Henry arranged his army with the mounted armed soldiers in the center and the bowmen forming a wing on each side. The French formed three tightly packed lines, one in front of the other.

HAIL OF ARROWS

Tired of waiting for the French to attack, Henry ordered his men to advance, stopping some 300 yards (275 m) from the French front line. Here the archers placed a row of sharpened staves in the ground, sloping forward to block any cavalry advance, and then fired a volley of arrows. The French charged, the front rows of heavily armored knights running forward over the thick, wet earth that turned to mud as thousands of feet churned it up. Under a hail of arrows (each archer was capable of firing an arrow every ten seconds), pressed shoulder to shoulder by the narrowing valley and unable to even swing their two-handed swords, the French knights fell and were trampled by the rows behind them. Unaware of what was happening ahead of them, the French cavalry then swept forward and added to the pandemonium. Horses, pierced by arrows, threw their riders and bolted away from the danger.

NOBILITY MASSACRED

The lightly clad English and Welsh archers now threw down their longbows and ran into the battle wielding their swords. The carnage was terrible, and some seventeen hundred knights and nobles (for whom the English could demand a ransom) were captured.

A major part of Henry's army was made up of archers, armed with the very latest in lethal weaponry—powerful longbows and armor-piercing arrows.

At this point word reached Henry that a further wave of French forces was attacking from the rear. At this he ordered his men to kill all their prisoners so that they could not escape and rejoin the battle. Henry's men, however, had to be threatened by a group of his archers before they would put their charges to death. Hundreds were killed before it was learned that the "attack from the rear" was in fact local villagers looting the English camp. Virtually an entire generation of the French nobility had been massacred.

CONQUERING HERO

By now the rest of the French army was in flight, and the valley was littered with the dead. It is thought that while Henry's army lost less than two hundred men, the French losses may have topped ten thousand. The English, laden with booty from the battlefield, continued their march to Calais and King Henry V returned to England victorious. There were those, especially among the French side, who felt that Henry had acted dishonorably in having the prisoners put to death. Nonetheless, he was received as the conquering hero, although he himself gave credit for the success of his army to God.

In fact, by underestimating the threat posed by the English longbows, and by choosing to do battle in a location that prevented them from using their cavalry, weapons, and skills to the full, it was the French who had snatched defeat from the jaws of victory.

HENRY V LEADS THE VICTORY
English archers ran into the battle, wielding their swords. A huge swathe of the French nobility were wiped out.

THE MING DYNASTY TURNS ITS BACK ON THE WORLD

1435

Main Culprits: The emperors of the Ming dynasty

Damage Done: China's lead in so many aspects of culture and technology was lost

Why: Chinese civilization became focused inward, believing that the country could function better on its own

In the early fifteenth century, after dominating the world in areas of technology, culture, agriculture, and science for more than a thousand years, China went through a period of exceptional exploration and self-promotion. It was on the verge of becoming a dominant power when the ruling Ming dynasty suddenly and deliberately closed the door on the wider world. It was a decision that plunged China into centuries of isolation from commercial and intellectual exchange, making it a minor player on the international stage.

FOUR GREAT INVENTIONS

The Middle Ages in Europe, which lasted from around the decline of the Roman Empire to the Italian Renaissance (the fifth to the fourteenth centuries), have been described as the Dark Ages. This suggested a period during which there was little fine literature, great architecture, or intellectual and scientific progress. The characterization is an unfair one or at least can only refer to what was happening in Europe at the time. Throughout that same thousand years, China became the world's most advanced civilization, due in large part to technological inventions. The celebrated "four great inventions"—paper, printing, gunpowder, and the magnetic compass—were all in common use in China long before they finally reached the West.

Paper was invented in China at the beginning of the second century, and in the eighth century printing was developed, first using wood blocks and later, in the eleventh century, using moveable type. Literature and literacy flourished, along with dictionaries, histories, civil records, and even newspapers. In tenth-century China, gunpowder was being used in early guns and grenades, and later in landmines, cannons, and rockets. By the twelfth century the magnetic compass was being used for navigation.

ADVANCED IN MANY WAYS

These famous four inventions are just the tip of the iceberg. Cast iron, for example, was first used in the West in the fourteenth century. The Chinese had been using the material in a host of ways—in agriculture, weaponry, even building construction—for seventeen hundred years. Porcelain, the abacus, the mechanical clock, water pumps—the list of Chinese inventions is endless. Scientific learning, too, reached a remarkable level in fields such as mathematics, astronomy, biology, and medicine. Under successive emperors, and a well-organized government, the country's agriculture production was developed using methods that were far ahead of those of Europe at the time.

"BRIGHT" DYNASTY

After a period of deep social unrest under the Mongol-led Yuan dynasty (1271–1368), order and stability within the country were restored under the Ming (meaning "bright") dynasty. The third Ming emperor, the Yongle emperor (born

> The celebrated "Four Great Inventions"—paper, printing, gunpowder, and the magnetic compass—were all in common use in China long before they finally reached the West.

Zhu Di), made Beijing his capital and oversaw the building of the Forbidden City there as the seat of government and the imperial family. Using military might, he extended China's influence over Mongolia and Tibet in the north, and over Korea and Vietnam in the south. The Yongle emperor also looked farther afield, and in 1405 he sponsored the first in a series of voyages, the most remarkable seafaring expeditions the world has ever known in terms of their scale and duration.

GIGANTIC SHIPS

Overall command for the voyages was entrusted to the eunuch Zheng He, an experienced mariner and the commander of the imperial navy. The fleet that set off in 1405 is said to have consisted of more than 250 vessels, 60 of them being gigantic "treasure ships," more than 400 feet (120 m) long (more than five times the length of the *Santa Maria*, the ship of the Italian explorer Columbus), each accommodating 500 passengers.

FIRST EMPEROR

The Hongwu emperor, who was the emperor of China from 1368 to 1398, was the founder of the Ming dynasty.

Supporting ships carried troops, horses, food and supplies, and water. When one considers the size of the fleets of such explorers as Columbus in 1492 (three ships and ninety men), Vasco da Gama in 1498 (four ships and one hundred and fifty men), or Magellan in 1521 (five ships and less than three hundred men), this was exploration on an epic scale.

MIGHTY MING

The purpose of the voyages—of which there were seven altogether between 1405 and 1435—was to demonstrate to the world the might and splendor of the Ming dynasty. It was essentially a diplomatic public relations exercise, and no doubt it succeeded. The sight of such a fleet must have inspired terror and admiration everywhere it went. Although the fleet carried its own army, force was rarely used, and Zheng He and his floating community peacefully visited the coasts of some thirty countries throughout the Indian Ocean, from Thailand, Java, and India to the Arabian Peninsula and East Africa. They may even have rounded the Cape of Good Hope and traveled some distance up the Atlantic coast of Africa. To each country they brought gifts of precious metals, porcelain, and silk, and they returned to China with exotic tributes for the emperor (including the first giraffe ever seen in China), and even envoys sent by the countries they had visited.

Poised on the brink of becoming a world-class maritime power, China returned to self-imposed isolation.

DEFENSIVE WALL
The Great Wall of China as it exists today was mainly built by the Ming dynasty. It was built to protect China's northern border.

BUILDING BOOM

As the Dark Ages gripped Europe, China was experiencing something of a building boom, constructing well-maintained roads to connect their large urban centers and allowing for easy movement of goods, troops, and government officials. The Great Canal of China, a major transport highway running more than 1,000 miles (1,600 km) from Beijing to Hangzhou, was completed in the seventh century, and it is still the world's longest canal. A series of defensive walls, with a total length of almost 4,000 miles (6,500 km), was built and maintained to protect China's northern border.

CLOSING THE DOOR

Although the voyages were not intended as trading missions, the contacts and information that were gathered by Zheng and his entourage would have enabled

ADMIRAL ZHENG HE

The exploits of the admiral, who died during a voyage in 1433, were kept quiet by the authorities, but they lived on in popular writings and are now celebrated by the Chinese.

China to dominate the region, but it was not to be. After the end of Zheng He's final voyage in 1435, the Ming rulers placed a ban on maritime trading, partly because government funds were needed to improve fortifications in the north and to repel the invading Mongols. What also led to the ban was a fundamental return to an inward-looking national philosophy that regarded China as complete in itself, with no need to look beyond its borders.

The greatest civilization on earth, poised on the brink of becoming a world-class maritime power, returned to self-imposed isolation. While the pace of change in Europe accelerated, especially through the Industrial Revolution of subsequent centuries, technological innovation in China ground to a halt. Although a certain amount of trade continued, it was the up-and-coming trading nations—Portugal, Japan, Spain, the Netherlands, Britain, and later the US—that came to dominate the region around the eastern seas and even the Chinese coast.

> "We, Zheng He and his companions…received the Imperial Commission as envoys to the barbarians. Up until now seven voyages have taken place and, each time, we have commanded several tens of thousands of government soldiers and more than a hundred oceangoing vessels. We have…reached countries of the Eastern Regions, more than thirty countries in all… We have set eyes on barbarian regions far away…"
>
> —Zhou Man, Chinese admiral, 1431

THE EXCOMMUNICATION OF MARTIN LUTHER

1521

Main Culprits: Pope Leo X

Damage Done: Led to the Protestant Reformation, and half of Europe rejecting the Roman Catholic Church

Why: The pope refused to listen or respond to the criticisms directed at the papacy or the Roman Catholic Church

The fifteenth century saw the Roman Catholic Church in Europe acquire ever greater political power and wealth, sometimes by questionable means. As a result, an increasing number of voices expressed their objections. The English theologian John Wycliffe, whose followers were known as Lollards and who in the previous century had written against the corruption of the papacy, was declared a heretic and his remains dug up and burned forty-four years after his death. In Prague, the Czech reformer Jan Hus was burned at the stake in 1415 for his criticisms of the Catholic Church, but the vast majority of the Czech people followed his teachings and broke away from Roman Catholicism. When, a century later, Martin Luther published his list of criticisms of the Church's doctrines and practices, and questioned papal authority, the pope refused to discuss the issues and ultimately

CIO ET SPE ERIT   FORTITVDO VESTRA

MARTIN LUTHER
The German priest believed that knowledge of God was a matter of direct and personal experience.

excommunicated him (officially barred him from the Catholic Church). The result was the Protestant Reformation, a series of religious wars, a second major schism in the Church, and the loss of papal authority over half of Europe.

EARLY STUDIES

Born in Germany in 1483 and baptized a Catholic, Martin Luther attended several schools where he was educated in the Latin staples of grammar, rhetoric, and logic, as his father was keen for him to become a lawyer.

After receiving his bachelor's and master's degrees from the University of Erfurt, he enrolled in the school of law, but then became more interested in philosophy and theology (the study of religious belief). Already the young Luther had a strong conviction that knowledge of God could only be achieved through religious revelation (from a force beyond scientific understanding), and not through logic, philosophy, or reason. He soon left the university and joined a closed Augustinian order (much to his father's disappointment), where he devoted himself to reading the scriptures, praying, fasting, confessing his sins, and becoming increasingly inward-looking.

After being advised by his superior at the friary that he should become a teacher, in 1507 he was ordained as a priest and the following year he joined the University of Wittenberg as a lecturer in theology. Here he continued his own Bible studies, receiving a doctorate in

PARDONS AT A PRICE

Since the eleventh century, the Catholic Church had developed the practice of selling indulgences (accepting money in exchange for the partial remission or forgiveness of sins). Over the centuries, the practice became increasingly common and increasingly abused, providing an important revenue stream for the papacy and the local Church authorities. The money raised from selling indulgences was known to fund some of the Church's more expensive projects like the Crusades (religious military campaigns) and the building of cathedrals.

1512. His studies of the scriptures led him to conclude that the structure and many of the doctrines and practices of the Roman Catholic Church were in conflict with the teachings of the Bible, if not actually sinful. High on his list of criticisms was the selling of indulgences.

BUILDING OF ST. PETER'S

The matter reached a head in 1516 when Pope Leo X sent Johann Tetzel to Germany in order to raise money through the sale of indulgences for the rebuilding of St. Peter's Basilica in Rome. Luther took exception to the practice as a whole, questioning the idea of the pope, one of the richest men in the

Martin Luther questioned the moral right of the Church to sell something that only God could dispense.

world, raising money for his projects from the poor. He particularly disliked Tetzel's sales pitch, which claimed that the purchase of an indulgence could release a deceased person from purgatory (a place between heaven and hell where those who had sinned could still be saved). Even more fundamentally, Martin Luther questioned the moral right of the Church to sell something that only God could dispense.

POPE LEO X
The pope brought considerable pressure to bear on Luther in order to bring him into line, but excommunicating him only fueled popular protest against the power of the Catholic Church.

Luther believed that justification (being righteous in the sight of God) was not a reward for good works (such as donating money to Church coffers) but

> **Pope Innocent X called the Peace of Westphalia in 1648 "null, void, invalid, iniquitous, unjust, damnable, reprobate, inane, empty of meaning and effect for all time."**

was freely given by God to all who have faith. Indulgences had come under attack from reformers in the past, but Luther had upped the ante by basing his objections on theological arguments.

NINETY–FIVE ARGUMENTS

At the end of October 1517, Luther put all his criticisms of indulgences down on paper in the form of a discussion document entitled "Disputation of Martin Luther on the Power and Efficacy of Indulgences," which he sent to Archbishop Albrecht of Magdeburg and Mainz. (History has it that he nailed this document, which became known as the "95 Theses," to the door of the Castle Church, but there is little evidence to support this.)

The archbishop did not welcome these criticisms. It was he who had initially invited Tetzel to Germany on a sales trip, and he was benefiting directly from the monies raised, using it to pay the pope for a special dispensation allowing him to be archbishop of two bishoprics at the same time. Rather than opening a debate on the matter with Luther, Archbishop Albrecht forwarded the document to the pope, the subject of much of the criticism.

OUTLAW AND HERETIC

Over a period of years, Pope Leo X set theologians against Luther, brought a case for heresy (holding a belief contrary to Church teachings) against him, and tried to force him to retract his views. Luther only became more outspoken, refusing to recognize the authority of the pope and writing further essays attacking the Church. Finally, in 1520, the pope issued a papal edict threatening Luther with excommunication unless he withdrew many of the 95 Theses. Luther responded by burning the papal edict, and in early January 1521 he was excommunicated. He was then called before a Church diet (an assembly), held in the city of Worms, at which he confirmed that he stood by what he had written and took the opportunity to take a further dig at the errors and contradictions committed by the pope and the Church. The conclusion of the Diet of Worms was that his writings

STANDING FIRM

"Since your majesty and your lordships desire a simple reply, I will answer without horns or teeth. Unless I am convinced by Scripture and by plain reason (I do not believe in the authority of either popes or councils by themselves, for it is plain that they have often erred and contradicted each other) in those Scriptures that I have presented, for my conscience is captive to the Word of God, I cannot and I will not recant anything, for to go against conscience is neither right nor safe. Here I stand; I can do no other. God help me. Amen."

—**Martin Luther refuses to recant his beliefs, Diet of Worms, 1521**

Thanks to the printing press, Luther's criticisms of the Church were distributed throughout Europe.

should be banned and Luther declared an outlaw and a heretic. However, if the Holy Roman Church thought that this would put an end to the matter, it was sorely mistaken.

WIDELY DISTRIBUTED

This was no local quarrel between the Church and one upstart theologian. In 1518, a friend and supporter of Luther had translated his 95 Theses from Latin into German and within weeks, benefiting from the recently developed printing press, they had been distributed throughout Germany. Within a year his criticisms were to be found throughout Europe, and they met with a broad popular response.

As various reformers threw their weight behind Luther's central aims, several different Protestant groups came into being, many of them supported by state leaders and institutions anxious to be free of papal political power. These denominations included the Lutheran Church in Germany and Scandinavia, and the Calvinist Reformed Church in Switzerland and France, as well as more radical groups.

PERMANENT BREAK

Despite a successful Counter-Reformation (measures to oppose the

spread of Protestantism) by the Roman Catholic Church in Spain and Italy, Protestantism dominated northern and eastern Europe by the middle of the seventeenth century. The Peace of

WAR SPARKED BY RELIGION

The Thirty Years' War was one of the most destructive wars in the history of Europe. The peace treaties that ended it ensured that Protestantism was here to stay.

> *"The Gospel cannot be truly preached without offense and tumult."*
> —**Martin Luther**

Westphalia in 1648, which ended the bloody Thirty Years' War, asserted the rights of European leaders to determine the state religion (choosing between Catholicism, Lutheranism, and Calvinism). Protestantism represented a permanent break from the Catholic Church, rejecting the doctrine that it is the one true church. Christians of all denominations were free to practice their chosen religion, and papal dominance over Europe was at an end.

THE INCA ATAHUALPA MEETS PIZARRO THE CONQUISTADOR

November 15, 1532

Main Culprit: Francisco Pizarro

Damage Done: The total destruction of an entire civilization

Why: To convert pagans to the Christian faith and obtain unimagined wealth for king and country

When a small expeditionary Spanish force, led by Francisco Pizarro, made its way from the Pacific coast into the interior of what is now Peru, in 1532, they found a complex and highly organized society. During the previous century, the ruling Inca dynasty had brought under their control an empire that extended from Colombia in the north to Chile in the south—a distance of almost 3,000 miles (4,800 km)— and encompassed Ecuador, Peru, and parts of what are now Bolivia and Argentina.

The terrain was enormously varied, from the jungle of the west, through the Andean highlands to the coastal plains and the desert of the south. Cities built from huge blocks of meticulously cut rock displayed a high level of architectural and engineering skill. A form of civil service regulated community life, and agriculture thrived under a feudal system that demanded labor and taxes from the work force.

Along a system of well-maintained footpaths, messengers carried imperial instructions quickly throughout the territory, and pack animals transported food and goods between settlements. A rich material culture included beautiful textiles, ornate pottery, precious stones, and—of particular interest to the Spaniards—finely worked objects of gold and silver.

TIMELY ARRIVAL

Given that the Spanish force was small—less than 170 men and some 27 horses—and that their goal was nothing less than to take over the Inca Empire in the name of King Charles I of Spain, the timing of their arrival was fortunate. Upon the death of the former ruling Inca, Huayna Capac, some five years earlier, control of the empire had been divided between his two sons— Atahualpa in the north and Huáscar in the south—and the result had been civil war. The majority of Atahualpa's troops, and

> **The Spanish force was small—less than 170 men and some 27 horses. Their goal was to take over the Inca Empire in the name of King Charles I of Spain.**

FRANCISCO PIZARRO

Hailed by the Spanish as a great explorer and hero, Pizarro is regarded by many Peruvians as the destroyer of their native culture, language, and religion.

The nobleman stayed with the Spaniards for two days, no doubt impressed by the Spaniards' armor, weapons, and horses, never before seen in South America, and reported back to Atahualpa.

MEETING WITH ATAHUALPA

Pizarro and his band accepted the invitation and entered the city, which was largely empty, on November 15.

two of his finest generals, were still in the region of Cuzco, a long way to the south. Furthermore, some of the tribes on the fringes of the empire had begun to rebel against the central power, and the first effects of a smallpox epidemic in the far north may have begun to be felt by the Incas. Atahualpa had just defeated his brother and he was camped with some of his army close to the town of Cajamarca, not far from the coast. On learning that a party of foreigners was making its way inland, Atahualpa sent one of his noblemen to meet them and to invite them to meet him in Cajamarca.

Sending a messenger to Atahualpa asking him to come to the town square the following day, Pizarro set about formulating a plan to capture the Inca, by force if necessary.

Before the appointed time, Pizarro positioned his men in three long buildings around the main plaza so that they, the horses, and the artillery were out of sight. Atahualpa arrived borne on a litter (a type of sedan-chair) carried by eighty of his men and accompanied by several thousand of his soldiers, probably unarmed. There is little doubt that he felt in command of the situation—not

INCA DESTROYED

Following the destruction of the Aztec and Mayan cultures by the Spanish in Central America, the demise of the Incas marked the end of several thousand years of indigenous culture. The Inca temples were torn down and replaced with Spanish-style buildings on Inca foundations. The region's gold and silver were systematically seized, its languages disappeared, and the population declined by more than 90 percent. This decimation of the population was not caused by Spanish force, although this was used, but as a result of diseases such as smallpox and measles that the Europeans brought with them.

surprisingly, given that he had lured the Spanish into the heart of his territory and had eighty thousand of his troops positioned on the high ground around the city. Indeed, there is evidence that he intended to capture or even destroy the small Spanish force—but that's not the way it panned out.

SPANISH GUNS

Atahualpa was met by a small group of Spaniards, including Pizarro, or even, according to some accounts, by just a Spanish missionary who explained the truth of Christianity and ordered the Inca to convert to Catholicism.

The friar then gave him a Bible or a prayer book, which Atahualpa (probably confused, certainly unable to read, and possibly anxious to maintain his dignity)

dropped on the ground. Pizarro immediately took this perceived slight against the Church as an excuse to order his army to attack, and they promptly opened fire with muskets and four small cannons on the Inca soldiers. Many of the Incas were killed (as many as two thousand) and injured by gunfire or cut down by the charging Spanish cavalry, the remainder fleeing from the square in shock and panic. It is said that Atahualpa's bearers continued to protect and support their leader's litter even when their hands had been cut off by Spanish swords. When the litter was finally dropped, others barred the way and allowed themselves to be killed by the Spanish soldiers, but eventually Pizarro himself reached the litter. He seized Atahualpa just as one of his own soldiers attempted to kill the Inca with his sword, and Pizarro was wounded warding off the blow with his hand. Pizarro needed a captive ruler, not a dead one.

GOLD AND SILVER

Atahualpa was held prisoner and treated well by the Spanish, and through him Pizarro effectively had control of the Inca Empire. The abandoned army camp outside the city was ransacked and the Spanish took large quantities of gold and silver, aware now that this land held considerable treasure. Atahualpa bargained with them and agreed to half fill a specific room in Cajamarca with gold and to fill it twice over with silver in return for his freedom or, more probably, for his life.

On Atahualpa's orders, enormous amounts of gold and silver works of art and religious objects were brought from temples and palaces all across the empire,

Atahualpa agreed to half fill a room in Cajamarca with gold and to fill it twice over with silver in return for his freedom.

and by May of 1533 he had fulfilled his part of the bargain. Estimates put the weight of the Inca gold at more than 11 tons (10 tonnes), and the weight of silver at more than twice that. These precious items were then melted down by the Spanish and cast into blocks, and the wealth was shared out evenly. Approximately one fifth was sent back across the Atlantic to the king of Spain and the rest was divided among the soldiers.

CAPTURED INCA

This engraving shows Pizarro and his men arresting the Inca emperor Atahualpa. He was later strangled.

FATE SEALED

In the meantime, fearing that his brother might fall into the hands of the Spanish and replace him as puppet emperor, Atahualpa had arranged to have Huáscar killed. When Pizarro decided that Atahualpa had become more of a liability than an asset, he set about accusing Atahualpa of various crimes. These included polygamy (having more than one wife) and plotting against the Spanish. To no one's surprise, the Inca emperor was found guilty and he was sentenced to be burned at the stake. This type of execution conflicted with the Incan belief in the afterlife, when he would need his body to be intact, and Atahualpa therefore agreed to be baptized into the Christian faith if he could be strangled instead.

On August 29, 1533, after being given the name of Francisco, he was strangled as per his wishes and was buried as a Christian. His death sealed the fate of the Inca Empire.

Although there were several Inca uprisings against the Spanish in the years that followed, within sixty years the Conquistadors (the Spanish invaders) had subdued and Christianized the people of this vast portion of South America. Whether the outcome would have been different had Atahualpa used his enormous army to stop a handful of Spanish soldiers in their tracks we shall never know. We do know, however, that his decision to meet Pizarro in Cajamarca plaza handed the Inca Empire to the Spanish on a plate.

HENRY VIII WANTS A SON

1534

Main Culprit: Henry VIII

Damage Done: The development of the Christian Church in England was changed forever

Why: Henry could not gain the pope's approval to nullify his first marriage and marry again, so he denied the authority of the pope and became head of the Church in England

While the Protestant Reformation was in full swing in Germany, England was being ruled by King Henry VIII, who had come to the throne in 1509. A few days before his coronation Henry was married to Catherine of Aragon, the widow of his elder brother Arthur, who had died after being married to her for only five months. According to the law of the Catholic Church, a man may not marry his brother's widow. However, Pope Julius II gave Henry a special dispensation to marry Catherine on the grounds that her marriage to Arthur had never been consummated and the marriage had not, therefore, been valid.

FIRST QUEEN

Catherine was, by all accounts, a remarkable woman. Five years Henry's senior, she was attractive, intelligent, and well educated, and she impressed all who met her. Before her marriage to Henry, she had acted as the Spanish ambassador to England (becoming Europe's first female ambassador), and as Henry's queen consort she was appointed regent in 1513 while Henry was in France. During that time the Scots invaded England and Catherine rode north in full armor, despite being pregnant, and oversaw the English victory at the Battle of Flodden Field. She had only one fault in Henry's eyes—she didn't bear him a son that survived infancy. After six unsuccessful pregnancies, their only child to survive infancy was a girl, christened Mary, who was born in Greenwich in 1516. Henry, however, was determined to have a male heir so that there could be no dispute over the succession to the throne or the continuance of the Tudor line.

> Catherine of Aragon was a remarkable woman and had only one fault in Henry's eyes—she didn't bear him a son that survived infancy.

NEW ROMANCE

In 1525, when Catherine was forty years old and unlikely to bear further children, Henry VIII found himself strongly attracted to one of his wife's maids of honor, the young Anne Boleyn. He pursued her enthusiastically, although she refused to follow in the footsteps of her elder sister, Mary, with whom the king had already had an affair lasting several years. (Mary may even have borne him two children, including a son, whom the king did not acknowledge.) For Anne it was marriage or nothing, and so the king put into operation a plan that he may have had for some time. He would apply to Pope Clement VII to have his marriage to Catherine of Aragon annulled on the grounds that Catherine's marriage to Arthur (Henry's late brother) had in fact been consummated and that the dispensation from Pope Julius II had been obtained under false pretenses.

As the Bible warned, their union had been "blighted in the eyes of God." This would mean that Catherine and Henry had been living in sin since 1509 and that their daughter Mary was illegitimate, but that was a small price to pay for being able to marry Anne and produce a male heir to the throne.

THE KING'S GREAT MATTER

As it turned out, however, obtaining an annulment was not to prove so easy. In 1527, Henry VIII sent an envoy to Rome to petition Pope Clement VII for an annulment of

KING HENRY VIII

Although he was critical of Martin Luther, when it suited his personal ambition Henry was willing to reject the authority of Rome.

his marriage to Catherine. Unfortunately, when the king's envoy reached Rome the city had just been sacked by the forces of Emperor Charles V and the pope was effectively a prisoner, so he was in no position to give a definitive answer.

The envoy returned to England, and Henry then passed the matter over to Cardinal Thomas Wolsey, the pope's representative and an important figure in matters of state in England. He made a strong case to the pope and suggested that a papal representative attend an ecclesiastical court in England to resolve the question there. The pope refused, and forbade Henry from remarrying until a decision had been made in Rome. Angry at Thomas Wolsey's failure, the king dismissed the cardinal from public office. (Wolsey was later arrested for siding with the pope and plotting against Anne, and he would probably have been executed had he not died of natural causes in 1530.)

NEW CHANCELLOR AND ARCHBISHOP

Still without an answer from the pope, Henry then began to take matters into his own hands, banishing Catherine from court and bringing in Anne Boleyn in her place. He appointed Sir Thomas More, who supported Henry's contention that his marriage to Catherine had been invalid, as Lord Chancellor in place of Thomas Wolsey. The Boleyn family's own chaplain, Thomas Cranmer, was

Refusal to accept Henry's Act of Supremacy became a crime under the Treason Act and Thomas More lost his head as a result.

TRICKY POSITION

Henry's petition for an annulment to his marriage put Pope Clement VII in a difficult position. Emperor Charles V held considerable power over him and, as the nephew of Catherine of Aragon, Charles was opposed to the annulment. Furthermore, overturning the earlier dispensation and stating that Pope Julius II had made an error would only provide further ammunition to the Protestant reformers who were critical of all papal decisions. Equally anxious not to anger Henry VIII, the pope delayed making any decision.

appointed as the new archbishop of Canterbury, with the pope's approval.

BREAK WITH ROME

Henry VIII had been a devout Catholic and had even written a book criticizing Martin Luther's attacks on the Church, but now he was no longer willing to submit to the authority of Rome. In 1532, several acts were brought before parliament by the pro-Reformation (and pro-Anne Boleyn) lawyer Thomas Cromwell (Thomas was clearly a very popular name in the late fifteenth century). These acts recognized the king's supremacy over the Church, and at the end of that year Henry and Anne were married in secret. A few weeks later they were married in public, and in May 1533 a special court, headed by Archbishop Cranmer, declared Henry's first marriage to be null and void. This annulment was itself declared null and void by Pope

> *"If a man takes his brother's wife, it is impurity. He has uncovered his brother's nakedness; they shall be childless."*
>
> —**Leviticus 20:21**

Clement VII, and he excommunicated (barred from the Church) both Henry and Cranmer. In June, Anne was made queen consort in Catherine's place, and three months later she gave birth to a girl, the future Queen Elizabeth I.

SUPREME HEAD

Henry's formal rejection of the authority of Rome occurred in November 1534, when the English Parliament passed the Act of Supremacy. It declared the monarch to be "the only supreme head on earth of the Church in England." Henry had abandoned Rome completely and refusal to accept the act and to deprive the king of his "dignity, title, or name" became a crime under the Treason Act. Sir Thomas More, who refused to deny the authority of the pope, lost his head as a result.

His was not the only blood to be shed over the issue of religion in England in the years that followed. The Church of England became strongly Protestant under King Edward VI (Henry's son by Jane Seymour, his third wife). Roman Catholicism was restored for a short time under Catherine's daughter, Queen Mary, who became known as "Bloody Mary" for her persecution of the Protestants (almost three hundred of whom were burned at the stake).

Under Queen Elizabeth I, the Act of Supremacy and the Act of Uniformity established the independence and the form of the Church of England. The authority of the Holy Church of Rome over England was permanently ended, as a direct result of Henry VIII's insistence on marrying Anne Boleyn and the pope's refusal to grant him an annulment. The Anglican Communion, of which the Church of England is the mother church, now has some eighty million worshippers across the world, and is the third largest church after the Roman Catholic and Eastern Orthodox Churches.

ANNE BOLEYN

Despite his original infatuation, when Anne failed to produce a male heir, Henry had her convicted of high treason and beheaded on May 19, 1536.

PHILIP II OF SPAIN LAUNCHES THE ARMADA

1588

Main Culprit: King Philip II of Spain

Damage Done: The sinking of half the Spanish fleet and the deaths of some sixteen thousand Spanish sailors and soldiers

Why: King Philip's planned invasion of England was ill considered and poorly planned

If there's one thing we can learn from our journey through history's disasters, it is that when a person in total authority gets a bee in his bonnet (and it usually is a he), there is little that anyone can do, no matter how predictable the unfortunate outcome may be. The defeat of the Spanish Armada by the English navy in 1588 has been hailed as a glorious event in British history and as Queen Elizabeth I's finest hour, but King Philip II of Spain's planned invasion of England was flawed from the outset. Bad management and even worse weather merely added to the problem.

ENEMIES OF GOD

Since the death of his wife, Queen Mary (with whom Philip had been the joint ruler of England) in 1558, and the coronation of Mary's sister, the Protestant queen Elizabeth I, relations between England and Catholic Spain had deteriorated considerably. Catholics did not recognize Elizabeth's right to the throne, since she was the daughter of Henry VIII and Anne Boleyn, a union that the Catholic Church deemed

illegitimate. Elizabeth had further angered the Catholics by declaring the Church of England to be the official church, and by supporting Protestantism in France and in the Netherlands. The signing of the Treaty of Nonsuch in 1585, which pledged England's financial and military support for the Protestant Dutch against the Spanish, was seen by King Philip as a declaration of war.

The restoration of a Catholic monarchy was undoubtedly one of the principal motives behind King Philip II's plan to invade England, and in this he had the support of Pope Sixtus V. It would also put an end to the piracy of such sea captains as Sir Francis Drake, who had repeatedly raided Spanish ships in the West Indies and in the Atlantic, seizing goods, gold, and treasure.

SPANISH ARMADA

Queen Elizabeth was aware of Philip's planned invasion, and in the spring of 1587 Drake sailed to the Atlantic coast of Spain with four naval ships, and some twenty merchant ships, and small armed sailing boats. They inflicted such heavy damage on the Spanish fleet assembled at Cadiz harbor that the Spanish invasion had to be postponed for a year, during which time England was able to prepare. Drake referred to the attack as "singeing the king of Spain's beard."

King Philip had wanted the renowned admiral the Marquis of Santa Cruz to command the campaign, but he died in February 1588. The king had already chosen his replacement—the Duke of Sidonia Medina, a strongly Christian aristocrat with little military experience who had never been to sea, but a man who could be expected to comply with the king's wishes. The Armada, made up of more than one hundred and thirty ships, and carrying eight thousand sailors and eighteen thousand soldiers, left the Portuguese port of Lisbon at the end of May 1588. The fleet was to sail to Flanders off the coast of Belgium and escort an army of thirty thousand soldiers across the Channel and up the River Thames to land near London. The Duke of Parma would have the men ready and waiting to meet up with the fleet.

ADVERSE WINDS

Held back by adverse winds, it took the Armada almost eight weeks to reach the southwest tip of England, where they were spotted by lookouts on July 19. Part of the English preparations had been the construction of a series of beacons along the south coast and then north to London.

Sir Francis Drake is said to have remarked just before the battle that he had time to finish his game of bowls and still beat the Spanish.

PHILIP II OF SPAIN
Philip was a staunch defender of Catholicism in Europe, and throughout his reign Spain was at war with various countries. He also extended Spanish influence around the globe.

The first beacon was lit and then each one in turn, alerting Sir Francis Drake, whose fleet was stationed in Plymouth, and, soon after, the queen herself. Held in the harbor by a flooding tide, the British fleet could not put to sea for a few hours, giving Drake, it is said, time to finish the game of bowls that he was playing. The Spanish considered attacking the English ships in the harbor, but as the king had expressly forbidden tackling the British navy, Sidonia Medina rejected the plan. A little initiative might have been a good thing at this point.

HEART AND STOMACH

"My loving people...I am come amongst you, as you see, at this time, not for my recreation and disport, but being resolved, in the midst and heat of the battle, to live and die amongst you all; to lay down for my God, and for my kingdom, and my people, my honour and my blood even, in the dust. I know I have the body but of a weak and feeble woman; but I have the heart and stomach of a king, and of a king of England too, and think foul scorn that Parma or Spain, or any prince of Europe, should dare to invade the borders of my realm. Not doubting but by your obedience to my general, by your concord in the camp, and your valour in the field, we shall shortly have a famous victory over those enemies of my God, of my kingdom, and of my people."
—Queen Elizabeth I's rallying speech to her forces gathered at Tilbury, in August 1588

SEA BATTLE

The two navies engaged in battle twice as the Spanish made their way eastward, first on the morning of July 21 and again on July 23. Little damage was inflicted on either side, but the weaknesses of the Spanish force were obvious. First, the Spanish fleet was not designed to do battle. The large galleons, whose purpose was to act as troop transporters, were slow and cumbersome. In order to protect them, the fleet had to travel in a crescent formation with the larger ships at the center protected by the smaller vessels at the horned tips of the crescent.

The Spanish fighting tactics traditionally involved bringing their ships alongside the enemy vessels, boarding them, and then fighting at close quarters. The faster and more maneuverable English ships were able to avoid being boarded. Instead, they darted in and out of range of the Spanish ships, firing at them when they came close.

On July 27 the Spanish fleet reached Calais and, as there was no harbor deep enough for the ships to enter, they waited off the coast in their defensive formation. The Spanish, however, had not thought through how to communicate with the forces on land, and only now did Sidonia Medina learn that Parma's army and their transport barges were not ready. It would be several days before they could meet the Armada and make the crossing, which was a long time for the fleet to remain vulnerable.

BLAZING FIRESHIPS

In the middle of the night the English, who were upwind of the Spanish, sent blazing fireships to drift into the moored ships of the Armada. The Spanish cut their anchor ropes and scattered, and although no ships were burned, the fleet had lost its protective crescent shape as the wind blew them farther along the coast. The English ships followed and, in what is now known as the Battle of

"He blew with His winds, and they were scattered."
—English commemorative medal

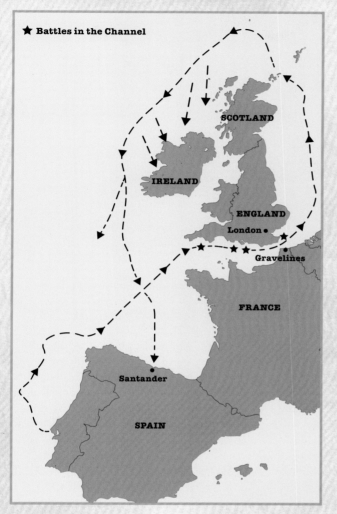

★ **Battles in the Channel**

SCOTLAND

IRELAND

ENGLAND

London •

Gravelines

FRANCE

Santander •

SPAIN

DOOMED VOYAGE

With their passage south blocked by the English navy, the Spanish ships made their way around the British Isles, and many were wrecked by storms on the rocky west coast of Ireland.

It was clear to Sidonia Medina that all hope of meeting up with Parma's army was lost and that the only option was to head back to Spain. However, the English navy now stood in the way of a return journey southwestward along the Channel and into the wind. The Armada headed north on a route that would ultimately take them around the top of Scotland and then south past the west coasts of Scotland and Ireland. Unfortunately, a combination of the North Atlantic current and exceptionally severe westerly winds drove the ships toward land, and many were unable to prevent themselves being wrecked on the rocky and treacherous coast. Of the 130 ships and twenty-six thousand men that had set sail from Lisbon, only sixty-seven ships and ten thousand men returned.

Gravelines, they fired on the Spanish fleet throughout the day, sinking or grounding five ships and damaging many more.

The faster and more maneuverable English ships were able to avoid being boarded. Instead, they darted in and out of range of the Spanish ships, firing at them when they came close.

CHARLES I'S CAVALIER ATTITUDE TO PARLIAMENT

1625–1649

Main Culprit: Charles I

Damage Done: He involved England in a bitter civil war, was found guilty of treason for overstepping the limits of his authority, and was beheaded by the English Parliament

Why: He believed that the divine right of kings gave him the power to overrule the wishes of the people

During the 1700s in England, struggles over religion were still ongoing, and there were fears that King Charles I might return the country to Catholic influence. His ambition to rule as absolute monarch with unrestricted power, his high-handed disregard for the will of Parliament, and his secret plotting with the Scots to overthrow the government backfired completely. Found guilty of treason, Charles was executed, and for a few years England abolished its monarchy and became a republic for the only time in its history.

CATHOLIC INFLUENCE

Charles inherited the crown of England, Scotland, and Ireland in 1625. Shortly afterward he married Princess Henrietta Maria, the youngest daughter of King Henry IV of France, and a Catholic. The strongly Protestant English Parliament agreed to the marriage only on condition that restrictions placed on Catholics would not be eased. Charles, however, secretly promised they would be eased and he also pledged to help France suppress the Protestant Huguenots, whom England had supported since the reign of Queen Elizabeth I. These and other actions by the king led members of the House of Commons, among whom there were several Puritans (members of an extreme Protestant group), to fear that Charles was leading the English Church in the direction of Catholicism.

MONEY FOR WAR

When the king asked Parliament for money to fund a war against Spain, the House of Commons voted to grant him far less than he wanted and also to impose restrictions on the king's right to customs duties (money collected on goods imported into the country), restrictions

Charles's ambition to rule with unrestricted power and his high-handed disregard for the will of Parliament backfired completely.

The king appointed Buckingham as Admiral of the Navy, but the expedition was a dismal failure, and Buckingham was more unpopular than ever when he returned to England. Very shortly afterward, Buckingham was assassinated.

PARLIAMENT DISSOLVED

In 1629 many members of Parliament wanted to pass a resolution and also discuss issues of religion. The king, however, tried to cut the debate short by calling for a postponement. The members then spoke out about their criticisms of the king, which met with broad approval. Outraged by this, the king not only dissolved Parliament but also had eight of the members arrested, including his chief opponent, Sir John Eliot, who spent the rest of his life in the Tower of London.

PERSONAL RULE

This time the king had no intention of recalling Parliament. He would rule alone, as was his right. Although he did a fairly good job over the next eleven years,

that he then ignored. The war against Spain was led by George Villiers, the Earl of Buckingham, a close friend of James I, who had considerable influence over the king. When he returned to England after a disastrous campaign, Parliament sought to remove him from office, but instead Charles appointed him Chancellor of Cambridge University. When Parliament protested that Buckingham was an unsuitable adviser to the king, Charles simply dissolved Parliament. Ignoring his earlier promise to the king of France, Charles was now persuaded to go to war against the French in order to protect the Huguenots.

DIVINE RIGHT OF THE KING

During the Long Parliament, John Pym had Charles' adviser the Earl of Strafford arrested, charged with high treason, and imprisoned in the Tower of London. He was found guilty and sentenced to death, but the death warrant had to be signed by the king, who refused to do so. However, with threats being made against his wife and children, the king had no choice and finally signed it. Strafford was duly executed. Parliament now gave the king a list of grievances, which included a call for the king to dismiss any ministers who were providing the king with poor advice. Asserting his divine right, the belief that the king derives his authority from God, Charles refused to be told that he could not choose his own counsel. When Parliament threatened to put the queen on trial, Charles ordered the arrest of five members of Parliament, including the man he considered to be the ringleader, John Pym. Parliament refused to hand them over and, when the king ordered their arrest, they fled.

his lavish spending on works of art and flashy architectural projects smacked of arrogance and a waste of public money, and ill feeling toward him grew. As usual, religion and money were the two main causes of discontent. In the absence of Parliament, King Charles needed revenue of his own, and so in 1634 he demanded that English seaports pay ship money, a tax usually levied only during wartime. When he extended this tax to properties inland in 1635, it met with considerable resistance. On the religious front, William Laud, the Archbishop of Canterbury, wanted to unite the Scottish and English churches, and so he imposed upon the Scots the Church of England's *Book of Common Prayer*. Seeing this as a move toward Catholicism, the Scottish Presbyterians called for the Scottish bishops to be removed and the new prayer book to be abolished.

SHORT AND LONG PARLIAMENT

In 1640, the Earl of Strafford, who had replaced Buckingham as the king's chief adviser, encouraged Charles to put down the Scottish rebellion. But in need of funds to do this, Charles was forced to recall Parliament. Led by John Pym, Parliament refused to cooperate until the king put an end to the ship tax and implemented a number of other reforms. After just three weeks King Charles dissolved Parliament yet again (this was known as the Short Parliament), but having no other options, he had to back down and recall Parliament six months later. It was the start of the "Long Parliament."

PARLIAMENT VERSUS KING

Parliament and the king were at loggerheads, with Charles asserting his divine right as king, whereas the English Parliament was determined to place limits on the king's power. In 1642, fearing that the king might use the county militia against Parliament (there was no standing army), the House of Commons passed laws that enabled them to take control of the army from the king. It was the first step toward civil war.

CIVIL WAR

By the fall of 1642, both Parliament and the Royalists (called Cavaliers) had raised and armed their own armies, and the First Civil War was fought over the next three and a half years, with the Cavaliers doing better. During this period, the parliamentarians (called Roundheads) formed the New Model Army, a full-time professional army, which crushed the Royalists at the Battle of Naseby. Charles eventually surrendered to the Scottish Presbyterian army, which handed him over to Parliament in 1647. He was then kept in a series of locations, ending up on the Isle of Wight, where he arranged a deal with the Scots promising to establish Presbyterianism in return for the Scots invading England and restoring him to the throne. The Second Civil War began in July 1648, and the Scots duly played their part, but they were defeated at the Battle of Preston in August and the Royalist cause was lost.

SENTENCED TO DEATH

Left to its own devices, the Long Parliament would have voted to accept the king's proposals for reform and the terms which would have returned him to the throne. However, the commanders of the New Model Army—notably Oliver Cromwell—stepped in and took control. In January 1649, the House of

> **The commanders of the New Model Army—notably Oliver Cromwell—stepped in and took control.**

THE KING'S ADVISER
Thomas Wentworth was a strong supporter of the king, but Charles could not prevent Parliament from sentencing him to death.

Commons agreed to set up a court to try the king for treason. He was held personally responsible for the two civil wars and for all the death and suffering that they caused. Still convinced of his authority under the divine right of kings, Charles refused to acknowledge the right of the court to bring a king to trial, and on January 27, 1649, he was found guilty and sentenced to death. He was beheaded three days later. The monarchy was at an end…at least for the next eleven years. The Commonwealth of England, and later the Protectorate under Oliver Cromwell and then his son Richard, gave way to the election of a predominantly Royalist Parliament in 1660, and the following year Charles II, eldest son of Charles I, took his place on the throne. The monarchy was back, although in a less powerful form.

NAPOLEON AND THE LOUISIANA BARGAIN

1803

Main Culprit: Napoleon Bonaparte

Damage Done: Deprived himself of money that would have helped to fund his ambitions in Europe

Why: Probably because he was so anxious to get one up on England

When French First Consul Napoleon Bonaparte sold the Louisiana Territories to the United States of America in 1803, it was the first time that land on this scale had changed hands as the result of negotiation rather than war. Napoleon had good reasons for giving up the territory to the US, but he misjudged badly when he set the price.

LA LOUISIANE

The Louisiana Territories in what is now the central US were first claimed by the French in the late 1600s, and the region was named "la Louisiane" in honor of King Louis XIV. The territory was handed over to the Spanish in 1762 but returned to France in 1800. La Louisiane was much bigger than the current state of Louisiana. The territory stretched from southern Canada in the north to the Gulf of Mexico in the south, and from the Mississippi in the east to the Rockies in the west, occupying almost a quarter of the area of the US today. It contained the whole of the present-day states of Arkansas, Iowa, Kansas, Missouri, Nebraska, and Oklahoma, as well as parts of what are now Colorado, Minnesota, Louisiana, Montana, New Mexico, North and South Dakota, Texas, and Wyoming, not to mention parts of the Canadian provinces of Alberta and Saskatchewan. This gigantic area, more than 800,000 square miles (2 million square km) had tremendous potential for settlement and agriculture, but the Mississippi and the port of New Orleans were of particular strategic importance for the Americans. In 1795, the United States had negotiated an agreement with the Spanish—Pinckney's Treaty—allowing US vessels to use the port and to store goods there ready for shipment.

"... the pride of France, and the envy of every imperialist nation..."
—Thomas Jefferson on the acquisition of Louisiana, 1803

The Louisiana Territories occupied a gigantic area of more than 800,000 square miles. It had huge potential for settlement and agriculture.

The treaty also gave the Americans the right to use the Mississippi River to transport agricultural produce and supply the most westerly US territories.

FRENCH INVASION

When the news leaked out that France once again had possession of the territory, and especially when Napoleon sent soldiers to New Orleans in 1801, it sparked deep concern throughout the American people. They feared a French invasion might lead to the freeing of their slaves in the south.

President Thomas Jefferson immediately took steps to secure US access to the Mississippi, sending lawyer and diplomat Robert Livingston to Paris with authority to negotiate the purchase of New Orleans and the land around it for the sum of $10 million. Livingston was later joined in this mission by US founding father and later president James Monroe, and by Pierre du Pont, a French colleague of Jefferson. It was du Pont who first raised the possibility of buying more than just New Orleans.

SLAVE REBELLION

Napoleon had his own strategic reasons for wanting to control New Orleans, which is why he had negotiated its repossession from the Spanish. He had a vision of rebuilding France's empire in the New World, centered on the Caribbean island colony of Saint-Domingue, and he needed a mainland

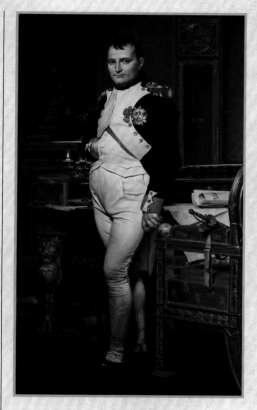

NAPOLEON BONAPARTE
Aware that war with Britain was imminent, and unable to defend the Louisiana Territory, Napoleon sold the land to the US at a bargain basement price.

base. However, he first needed to reclaim Saint-Domingue, which had been free of French control since a widespread slave rebellion in 1791. Napoleon's forces succeeded in regaining the colony in 1802, but when it became clear that they intended to reintroduce slavery, rebellion broke out again. The French army, already ravaged by yellow fever, was finally defeated in 1803, and Napoleon abandoned his dream of a French empire in the west. The revolt of the slaves of

PROUD ACHIEVEMENT

US diplomat Robert Livingston was justifiably proud of the bargain-basement purchase of the Louisiana Territories, saying, "We have lived long, but this is the noblest work of our whole lives… From this day the United States take their place among the powers of the first rank." Napoleon showed similar foresight when he said, "This accession of territory affirms forever the power of the United States, and I have given England a maritime rival who sooner or later will humble her pride."

Saint-Domingue—the only such rebellion ever to succeed—led to the establishment, in 1804, of the New World's first independent black state: Haiti.

GOOD TIMING

Napoleon no longer needed to control New Orleans and he also feared that the US (and/or Great Britain) might be willing to fight for control of the territory, so Jefferson's approach was both timely and welcome. Jefferson was, in fact, equally unwilling to go to war with France, but in Europe war between Britain and France was imminent. Napoleon was already planning an invasion of Britain and he needed cash to fund it, which was an additional reason to sell the Louisiana Territories.

SPEEDY NEGOTIATION

In fact, the land was not technically France's to sell, as Spain had not finalized arrangements for the transfer, which gave Napoleon an added incentive to resolve the matter quickly. On April 11, 1803, against the advice of his foreign minister, Napoleon instructed his treasury minister to offer the Louisiana Territories to the Americans for the sum of $15 million. When he received the offer, Livingston was stunned. He only had the authority to spend $10 million on New Orleans and its surroundings, and he had no way of communicating with America quickly. However, he had no doubt that Jefferson and the US government would be more than happy to spend 50 percent more to gain such a vast tract of land—530 million acres (an area greater than the United States at that time) at a cost of less than three cents an acre! It was too good to be true, and Livingston accepted before Napoleon could reconsider. On April 30, Livingston, Monroe, and the French treasury minister Barbé-Marbois signed the Louisiana Purchase Treaty. As well as being the largest land deal in history it was also the greatest bargain (at least until Russia sold Alaska to the US in 1867 for about two cents per acre).

TREATY APPROVAL

Surprisingly, the treaty that Livingston and Monroe sent back to the US for approval was not received enthusiastically by everyone (although no one quibbled about the price!). Jefferson himself felt

The purchase of the Louisiana Territories more than doubled the size of the United States—at a cost of just three cents an acre.

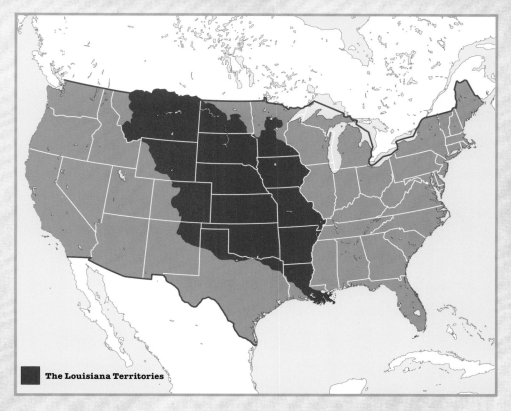

The Louisiana Territories

that an amendment to the United States' Constitution might be needed. There were concerns that the purchase might anger the Spanish and start a war. In fact, the Spanish did raise objections, as the region had not been properly surveyed and its borders were therefore unclear. There was also the question of whether the hundred thousand or so people who lived in the territories, many of them French speaking, should be given all the rights of US citizens. Nonetheless, Jefferson pressed ahead, the US Senate approved the treaty in October 1803, expeditions to survey the land were sent out, and Spain and the US came to an agreement about the borders. The rest, as they say, is history.

EXPANDING WEST

The Louisiana Territories are shown here in darker red. The US at the time occupied only the area to the east of this, and the western part was under Spanish control.

NATIVE AMERICANS

One very fundamental question that was not raised at the time was whether France had any rights of ownership to land occupied for thousands of years by Native Americans, or whether the US had in fact only bought the right to claim the land. In any event, the United States gained land rights in the region from the native people gradually over time, through military force, relocation, and treaty negotiation.

NAPOLEON'S SECOND BITE AT THE APPLE

1815

Culprit: Napoleon Bonaparte

Damage Done: Landed himself in permanent exile in a very bleak place

Why: Couldn't resist attempting to regain power in France, and misjudged the political climate

In 1804, the year after the Louisiana Purchase, Napoleon succeeded in restoring the hereditary monarchy in France, with himself as Emperor Napoleon I and his wife Josephine as empress. In the following years, through a combination of wise political alliances and superb military strategy he extended French influence throughout Europe and beyond. However, the Peninsular War against Spain and Portugal, the disastrous French retreat from Russia, and the capture of Paris by the Sixth Coalition of allied forces in 1814 led to his defeat. King Louis XVIII ascended to the throne as the constitutional monarch, and Napoleon was exiled to the island of Elba, off the northwest coast of Italy. He was given authority over the small Mediterranean island and its twelve thousand inhabitants and he retained the title of emperor and his personal guard.

EMPEROR OF ELBA

For most people this would have spelled the end of any aspirations to be the ruler of the French Empire, let alone the world. Napoleon, however, wasn't most people. Neither his ambition nor his ego would allow this to be the end. Within a few months of his arrival on Elba Napoleon had reorganized the government administration on the island, improved agriculture and mining, and assembled a small army. The news that was reaching him from France, of general dissatisfaction with the rule of the new Bourbon king, convinced him that if he could return home then the people and the army would rally to him. The waters around the island, however, were being patrolled by the British and the French, preventing his escape.

GREAT ESCAPE

The opportunity for escape arose on February 26, 1815, when the guard ships were absent, and Napoleon and six hundred of his soldiers sailed from Elba on ships that had been made ready in the

Napoleon would not allow his exile to Elba to be the end of his ambition to rule Europe—and the world.

PRUSSIAN ATTACK
In the fighting between the French and Prussian forces, the village of Plancenoit changed hands five times. Almost all of the French Young Guard were killed or injured during the fighting.

preceding weeks. On March 1 they disembarked on the south coast of France close to Cannes and marched northward, gathering new recruits as they went.

BACK IN CONTROL
On March 20, 1815, Napoleon and his army entered Paris, from which King Louis XVIII had fled the previous day, and he resumed his position as the country's leader without a shot being fired. So far, so good, but his enemies were on the warpath. A week earlier, on hearing that Napoleon was on his way to Paris, the countries represented at the Congress of Vienna (Russia, Prussia, Austria, Britain, Portugal, Spain, Sweden, and Bourbon France) had declared him to be an outlaw.

Effectively, this was a declaration of the War of the Seventh Coalition. An invasion of France was planned for July 1, although a British-allied force, under the command of the Duke of Wellington and Prussian armies under Field Marshall von Blücher, would be ready sooner. The downside of the delay was that it would give Napoleon, who could only muster a much smaller army, three months to prepare and swell his ranks.

DECISION TO ATTACK
In any event, Napoleon chose to take the initiative and attack before the Austrian and Russian forces were ready. His strategy was to drive his forces between the armies of Wellington and Blücher, which were located in the Netherlands, and prevent them from combining and

LONG LIVE THE EMPEROR
Following his escape from Elba, Napoleon's troops headed from the south coast of France toward Paris. Avoiding the most obvious route by marching through the Alps, their numbers swelled as they progressed. When they encountered the supposedly royalist 5th and 7th Infantry Regiments, the soldiers all joined Napoleon's forces. When confronted by troops at Lyon, it is said that Napoleon walked to within firing range, ripped open his coat, and challenged the soldiers to shoot their emperor. To cheers of "Long live the emperor," the men joined him.

outnumbering his own troops. He would
then inflict such heavy losses on each of
them that the coalition would come to the
negotiating table. Well, that was the plan.

With his army divided into three
parts—left and right wings, commanded
by Marshals Ney and Grouchy
respectively, and a reserve force under
his own command—Napoleon crossed
the border into the Netherlands on the
morning of June 15. On the following
day Grouchy's right wing and part of
the reserve attacked the Prussians at
Ligny. Although the French troops won
the battle (with great losses on both
sides), a substantial part of the Prussian
army had to retreat toward the north.

Ney's left wing, meanwhile, was
ordered to take the crossroads at Quatre
Bras, to the west of Ligny, which was
being held by Dutch forces under the
command of William, Prince of Orange.

The Dutch were greatly outnumbered
and were gradually being pushed back
until reinforcements arrived and
Wellington took command, regaining
Quatre Bras. It was clear to Wellington,
however, that without the help of the
Prussians they could not hold Quatre
Bras, and so he ordered his troops to
fall back also to the north.

When Napoleon's troops advanced
on Quatre Bras the following afternoon,
there was no one there. Wellington and
his Anglo-Dutch army were close to the
town of Waterloo—a name that
Napoleon would come to remember—

and his men were drawn up along a
2.5-mile (4-km) battle front, largely
hidden by a long, low ridge. Blücher's
army was a few miles to the east at
Wavre, and early on the morning of the
18th he was able to promise Wellington
that he would send reinforcements.

BATTLE OF WATERLOO
The Battle of Waterloo did not begin
until midday, because Napoleon needed
the ground to dry out before he could
move his heavy guns onto it. Wellington's

*"Nothing except a battle lost can be half so melancholy
as a battle won."*
—Duke of Wellington, 1815

WATERLOO
British troops in square formation are
charged by French cuirassiers, armored
cavalrymen, during the Battle of Waterloo.

men withstood the onslaught of the
French throughout the afternoon,
with both sides launching infantry
and cavalry attacks.

In the meantime, Grouchy's troops
were battling against the Prussian army
at Wavre. Although the French overcame
them, a substantial part of the French
forces were occupied fighting the battle,
which enabled the Prussian commander
Blücher to move the promised
reinforcements to the west.

In the evening they reached Waterloo
and broke through the French right
flank. Wellington then responded with
an attack from the front and the French
army fled southward in confusion,
pursued by the coalition forces.

The Battle of Waterloo, in which more
than a hundred thousand soldiers died,
was Napoleon's last battle and the end of
his career. He reached Paris on June 21
and attempted to rally support against
the approaching coalition forces, but the
country was in no mood to listen. The
following day he abdicated in favor of his
four-year-old son (who was in Austria),
and on June 25 the provisional government
asked him to leave the city, which he did.

He made his way to Rochefort on
the Atlantic coast, intending to escape
to the US, but there he found a British
naval blockade in place. Caught between
the devil and the deep blue sea, he finally
surrendered to Captain Frederick Lewis
Maitland of the Royal Navy aboard
HMS *Bellerophon* on July 17, 1815.

CRAGGY ROCK

Napoleon was taken to the UK, where
he was imprisoned and then transported
to exile on the island of St. Helena.
If Elba had been rather small and a little
unexciting, St. Helena was a hundred
times worse. Located 1,200 miles
(2,000 km) off the west coast of Africa
in the middle of the South Atlantic, this
craggy volcanic rock, with an area of just
50 square miles (130 square km), was
Napoleon's open prison for the rest of
his life, which proved to be less than six
years. He died on May 5, 1821.

> **If Elba had been rather small
> and a little unexciting,
> St. Helena was a hundred
> times worse.**

BRITISH TROOPS MASSACRE WORKERS AT "PETERLOO"

August 16, 1819

Main Culprits: The magistrates of Manchester, England

Damage Done: Fifteen killed, hundreds injured

Why: The ruling class protecting its interests and privileges

In the early nineteenth century, the living and working conditions of the working-class people of Manchester were undeniably grim. Southern Lancashire had long been the country's main center of textile production, based on a cottage-based industry which saw families spinning wool and cotton into yarn, which they would then weave into cloth on hand-operated looms. But during the second half of the nineteenth century, all that changed thanks to the development of a range of technological innovations that led to the first wave of the Industrial Revolution.

Most notable of these innovations were John Kay's flying shuttle, which speeded up the weaving process, Richard Arkwright's water-powered spinning frame, and James Hargreaves's multispindled "spinning jenny." Together with the introduction of water and steam power and improvements in iron smelting, these inventions spelled the end of the domestic textiles industry in northwest England. The cottage workers of the area—unable to compete with mass-produced goods—flooded into the growing industrial towns of northwest England. Here, they worked the machines in the cotton mills under poor conditions and for low pay. In towns such as Rochdale, Blackburn, and especially Manchester—the first truly industrial city, second in size only to London in the early 1800s—workers were crowded into low-quality housing built by the factory owners.

SIMMERING DISCONTENT

The price of grain and bread had remained high after the end of the Napoleonic Wars and unemployment was on the increase. With no further need to clothe and supply a large army or navy, the end of the war had meant a

> "Everything is almost at a standstill, nothing but ruin and starvation stare one in the face. The state of the district is truly dreadful."
> —Joseph Johnson, *Manchester Observer*, 1819

SMOKING CITY

William Wylde's *View of Manchester from Kersal Moor* captures the contrast between the countryside and the smoking chimneys of the world's first industrialized city.

dramatic decline in demand for cotton goods, and many workers found themselves without jobs as the cotton mills reduced their output. The Combination Acts of 1799 and 1800 forbade workers to form trade unions (organizations that protected workers' wages and rights). This angered many British workers and there were calls for parliamentary reform to give working people real representation in government. Between 1815 and 1818 these many grievances found expression in large-scale political rallies, marches, and pickets that took place throughout Yorkshire and Lancashire. Many of these were broken up by police and local yeomanry (volunteer regiments used to support the authorities). As a result, there was a growing feeling among the ruling classes—already shaken by the overthrow of the monarchy during the French Revolution—that a similar public revolt was in the air.

PRICE OF BREAD

As the Industrial Revolution took hold, traditional social relations were being rapidly swept aside. After Waterloo and the end of the Napoleonic Wars, many thought that conditions would improve, but if anything they worsened. During the war, with the doors effectively closed on imports of grain, the large landowners had experienced a period of great profits as wheat prices reached an all-time high, making bread, a staple of the working-class diet, expensive to buy. Fearing that the return of imported grain would bring down the price, the landowners successfully persuaded the British government to pass the Corn Laws. This put high taxes on imported grain and kept prices artificially high once the war was over.

PEACEFUL RALLY

It was under these circumstances that an invitation was sent to a well-known radical speaker Henry Hunt to speak at a very large outdoor gathering in St. Peter's Field in the center of Manchester on August 16, 1819. The primary purpose of the rally was to call for parliamentary reform, and the organizers—the Manchester Patriotic Union Society—were adamant that it should be peaceful. They made it clear that no one should bring a weapon and that "Cleanliness, Sobriety, Order and Peace" was the order of the day. Even the Home Office had issued instructions that the meeting should not be broken up by violence, and that legal means should be used to arrest the speakers and ringleaders. This was not, however, how the city's magistracy—charged with the administration of civil law and made up of members of the landowning families—saw the situation.

STOKING THE FIRE

Fearing possibly for their personal safety and certainly afraid of the long-term threat that such gatherings posed to their wealth and privilege, "the great and the good" of Manchester made sure they had as many police and soldiers on hand as possible. The magistrates' plan was to arrest Henry Hunt and the rest of the "rabble rousers" and to use whatever force might be needed to do so. To this end, in addition to four hundred special constables, they brought in four squadrons of cavalry of the 15th Hussars (six hundred men), several hundred infantrymen, a detachment of the Royal Horse Artillery with two small cannons, four hundred men of the Cheshire Yeomanry cavalry, and 120 cavalrymen of the Manchester and Salford Yeomanry. This latter regiment had been formed following political riots a couple of years earlier and it comprised local shopkeepers and small business owners (including several publicans) who were generally young, inexperienced, and strongly opposed to the political views held and being advocated by the Radicals and the working people.

There was a growing feeling among the ruling classes that revolution was in the air.

SPEECHES

Henry Hunt and several other speakers, as well as a number of newspaper reporters, made their way to the platform at about 1:20 pm to loud applause and the speeches began. Within ten minutes, however, the chairman of the magistrates, William Hulton, decided that "the town was in great danger" and instructed the chief constable to move his forces in and arrest the speakers. In response, the chief constable replied that he would need help from the military. Hulton then penned two messages calling for military assistance, sending one to Manchester's military commander, Lieutenant-Colonel George L'Estrange, and the other to Major Thomas Trafford, commander of the Manchester and Salford Yeomanry.

THOUSANDS GATHER

The sky on August 16 was cloudless, and throughout the morning thousands of people from Manchester and the surrounding towns, dressed in their best clothes, made their way to St. Peter's Field in organized groups. It has been estimated that by 11:00 am the throng, by now pressed shoulder to shoulder, numbered at least sixty thousand — probably the largest gathering that England had ever seen. Fearing that it would be impossible to move through the crowd to arrest the speakers, the magistrates sent in the four hundred special constables to form two lines and create a corridor between the speakers' platform and the house where they were staying.

VIOLENCE ERUPTS

Trafford received the message first and set off with his troops at a gallop, knocking down a woman in the street and causing the death of her two-year-old son when he was flung from her arms. After speaking with Hulton, Trafford ordered his second in command, a Manchester factory owner named Hugh Birley, to lead sixty of the mounted yeomanry along the police corridor and clear the way to the speakers' platform. When the horses became hemmed in and began to rear, the inexperienced cavalrymen—some of whom may well have been drinking in the nearby inn— began to strike out at the protesters with their sabers. Finally reaching the platform, Captain Birley and the deputy constable, Joseph Nadin, proceeded to arrest everyone there—speakers, organizers, and members of the press. As they attempted to make their way back to the edge of the field, the angry crowd tried to bar their way.

Hulton then told L'Estrange, who had arrived with the 15th Hussars, that the yeomanry were under attack and ordered him to disperse the crowd. The mounted Hussars formed a line and charged into the crowd, sabers drawn, from the east side of the field while the Cheshire Yeomanry Cavalry did the same from the south side. The crowd attempted to flee, but the main route out of the area was blocked by soldiers standing with fixed bayonets and panic ensued. The men of the Manchester and Salford Yeomanry were by now completely out of control and were hacking at the crowd with their swords.

By the time the people had managed to leave, at least eleven men, women, and children lay dead on St. Peter's Field, and more than four hundred were injured, many of them seriously. There followed a night of riots and clashes as the once-peaceful protesters vented their rage.

PRICE TO PAY

For those who had attended the rally, there was a price to pay. Many lost their jobs as a result of having been present. Some of the wounded were even turned away from hospitals by doctors who disagreed with their politics. Several of the speakers, including Henry Hunt,

For those who had attended the rally, there was a price to pay. Many lost their jobs as a result of having been present. Some of the wounded were even turned away from hospitals by doctors who disagreed with their politics.

BLOODSHED
Published shortly after the massacre, this depiction of the Hussars attacking the protesters was dedicated to Henry Hunt and to the many casualties.

were imprisoned. The Prince Regent (soon-to-be King George IV) expressed his gratitude to the Manchester magistrates for the way they had handled the matter. The government also soon introduced the Six Acts—intended to prevent further mass meetings and to suppress left-wing newspapers.

Nonetheless, if the heavy-handed response of the ruling class and the military was meant to put an end to working-class demands, it did not actually achieve its goal. Indeed, news of the Peterloo Massacre provoked widespread anger across the country and served to draw members of the middle class toward the cause of the working people. The events in St. Peter's Field can be seen as an important milestone on the road that ultimately led to a more representative and democratic form of Parliament in Britain.

REPORTS OF MASSACRE

The day after the massacre, the people of London learned what had happened, thanks to a journalist, Richard Carlile, who had avoided being arrested and had made his way to London overnight. The authorities responded by confiscating all remaining copies of his report and eventually imprisoning him. In Manchester, James Wroe published an account of the attack and, in reference to the fact that the 15th Hussars had been at the Battle of Waterloo, described the event as the Peterloo Massacre. His pamphlet on the subject remained in circulation for many weeks and he, too, ended up in prison.

SANTA ANNA ATTACKS THE ALAMO

February 23–March 6, 1836

Main Culprit: Antonio López de Santa Anna, commander of the Mexican army

Damage Done: His army slaughtered hundreds of US settlers at the Alamo, raising support for the settlers' cause and leading to independence for Texas

Why: To enforce Mexican government authority over the "Texian" settlers

The "Mexican Empire" gained its independence from Spain in 1821, and the new government was soon encouraging settlers to move into the northeastern part of the Mexican state of Tejas, or Texas. With the offer of land and tax concessions, many Americans seized the opportunity, and by the mid-1830s US settlers, who went by the name of "Texians," outnumbered Mexicans by a ratio of four to one. The Mexican government soon introduced a range of measures to put an end to this imbalance, banning further immigration and ending tax concessions. These added to the settlers' growing list of grievances against the Mexican government, which included having to swear allegiance to, and pay money to, the Catholic Church. They were also prohibited from using

> **The Texian settlers began to call for greater control over their own affairs.**

slave labor, which the settlers regarded as essential for the profitable growing of cotton. Mexico's government was also becoming increasingly centralized, which went against the Mexican constitution of 1824. Soon the settlers began to call for greater control over their own affairs (though not for actual independence from Mexico).

GROWING HOSTILITY

Hostility between the settlers and the government escalated as the Texians formed committees to organize their activities and began to raise their own militia. At the beginning of October 1835 the first skirmish of the Texas Revolution took place between the Texian and Mexican armies at Gonzales. Over the following weeks, the Texians had several military successes, culminating in the siege of San Antonio de Béxar. Forced to withdraw from the town to the nearby Alamo mission (a former Franciscan building), the Mexican troops subsequently surrendered on terms that had in the meantime quit his post and taken command of an "Army of Operations" to put down the rebellion once and for all. He had also pushed through a resolution stating that foreigners found taking up arms against the Mexican authorities would be treated as "pirates." This meant that the Mexican army would be taking no prisoners and would execute any Texian soldiers it captured.

By the end of 1835 the Mexican army was more than six thousand strong, and through January and February the Mexican troops made their way northward in exceptionally wintry conditions, some of the soldiers succumbing to disease and hypothermia (a condition caused by extreme cold weather). While part of the army traveled up the coast, fighting off detachments of the Texian army, some fifteen hundred troops headed directly for San Antonio de Béxar, the scene of the Mexican army's earlier embarrassing surrender, in the last week of February.

HOPELESSLY UNDERMANNED

The fifteen-hundred-strong Mexican contingent took the town of San Antonio de Béxar on February 23, 1836. The Texian garrison at the Alamo, woefully undermanned by less than two hundred men led by the pioneer soldier Jim Bowie and Lieutenant Colonel William B. Travis, were taken by surprise. They quickly made preparations for a siege, knowing they were surrounded and that essential supplies could be cut off. What cattle they could find were brought into

SANTA ANNA
Antonio López de Santa Anna stood down from his position as President of Mexico in order to lead a force against the rebellious Americans.

included leaving Texas. The Texians then stationed a garrison there and increased the fortification of the sprawling mission by mounting cannons left behind by the Mexican army and building walkways inside the high surrounding walls from which rifles could be fired.

To the Texians, it appeared as though they had succeeded, but the Mexican president, Antonio López de Santa Anna,

"I am besieged...I shall never surrender or retreat..."
—William B. Travis, February 24, 1836

the compound, as were the families of Texian volunteers living in Béxar itself. Bowie and Travis sent out envoys to Santa Anna to discuss terms for a surrender. When they learned that he would only accept a surrender that had no conditions attached, they fired the largest cannon in reply.

OVERWHELMED AND SLAUGHTERED

During the first week of the siege, the Alamo was subject to a steady bombardment from the Mexican cannons, and many of their own balls were fired back at Santa Anna's troops, but the Texians had too little powder to keep up constant cannon fire. Two groups of reinforcements reached Santa Anna, more than doubling Mexican troop numbers to over three thousand, while only a handful of Texians managed to reach the Alamo. On the night of March 5, the Mexican bombardment ceased and the exhausted Texians rested, but at 5:30 am, under cover of darkness, the Mexicans launched their attack. Initially the Texians held them off valiantly, but they were overcome by sheer force of numbers, and once the walls were breached they retreated to the fortified barracks while the women and children sought refuge in the chapel. The Mexicans turned the Texian cannon on the barracks and blew the doors in before firing on the trapped soldiers. True to Santa Anna's word, within an hour of the initial attack the Mexican soldiers had killed every one of the men, including seven who were captured and ordered to be executed by Santa Anna. The bodies that littered the mission compound were repeatedly bayoneted and shot. The women and children were

BOWIE, TRAVIS, AND DAVY CROCKETT

At the start of the year, the Texian garrison at the Alamo, under the command of Colonel James C. Neill, had numbered fewer than a hundred men. In mid-January Neill had sent out a request to Sam Houston, one of the Texian army commanders, asking for reinforcements, ammunition, and supplies. Unable to provide what was needed, and acknowledging that the Alamo would be unable to hold out for long against the Mexicans, Houston decided that the post should be abandoned and sent thirty men, headed by the pioneer Jim Bowie, to remove the cannons and destroy the "fort." Unfortunately, when they reached the Alamo there were no animals there to haul the guns and so, recognizing the importance of preventing San Antonio from falling to the Mexicans, Bowie decided to remain at the fort with his men. He, too, requested troops and supplies, but little came. In early February a further thirty men under Lieutenant Colonel William B. Travis arrived, and Davy Crockett turned up with a few more volunteers a few days later, but the garrison still numbered less than two hundred men. When Neill left the Alamo on February 11 to get further supplies, he put Travis in command, but the garrison overruled the decision and put Bowie in charge instead. In the end the two shared command.

slaughter of their countrymen, volunteers flocked to join Houston, and the army's numbers swelled as Santa Anna pursued northeastward toward Louisiana.

The two armies met on April 21 at the San Jacinto River, in what is now Harris County, Texas. Confident that Houston would not attack the much larger Mexican force, Santa Anna stood his men down before noon prior to launching his own attack, but he was mistaken. The Texian army charged the Mexican camp in the afternoon with a battle cry of "Remember the Alamo!" and in less than half an hour they had killed or captured the entire Mexican army. Santa Anna was taken prisoner and forced to sign what were later to become known as the Treaties of Velasco. It was the beginning of the road to independence for Texas.

spared, apart from one boy who was mistaken for an adult. Casualty figures for the Mexican troops are hard to estimate, but it is thought that some five hundred of Santa Anna's soldiers were killed in the storming of the Alamo Mission.

REMEMBER THE ALAMO!
It was now Santa Anna's intention to demolish the rest of the Texian army, under the command of Sam Houston. He assumed that the size of his own army, together with his reputation after the massacre at the Alamo, would persuade the Texian army and the settlers to abandon their rebellion, but in fact the opposite occurred. Incensed by the

Incensed by the slaughter of their countrymen, volunteers flocked to join the Texian army.

BRITAIN INVADES AFGHANISTAN

March 1839

Main Culprit: Lord Auckland, Sir William Hay Macnaghten

Damage Done: More than sixteen thousand soldiers and civilians were massacred by Afghan tribesmen as they tried to flee the country

Why: Britain wanted to prevent Russia from gaining influence in Afghanistan

The first half of the nineteenth century saw the gradual development of what was to become known as the "Great Game," as Britain and Tsarist Russia played political chess on the map of Central Asia. With Russia growing in influence, Britain feared that India could be the ultimate target. Considered the "jewel in the crown" of Queen Victoria, India was Britain's greatest colonial possession and control of nearby Afghanistan was thought vital to keeping hold of it.

In 1838 the British received news that the Russians were in discussions with the Afghan ruler, Dost Mohammad. Seeing this as a significant threat, the governor-general of India, Lord Auckland, sent a messenger to Dost Mohammad with a request to distance himself from the Russians. The request was refused. Lord Auckland, on the advice of diplomat Sir William Hay Macnaghten, decided to take military action and to put former Afghan leader Shuja Shah Durrani back on the throne. This was against the advice of another

political officer, Sir Alexander Burnes, who believed the best policy would be to support Dost Mohammad and keep him on the British side.

DIFFICULT MARCH

In late 1838, some twenty thousand East India Company British and Indian soldiers, together with almost twice as many support staff and families of the soldiers, made the difficult march from India through the Bolan Pass into Afghanistan. Taking the Afghan cities Kandahar in April and Ghazni in June, and leaving garrisons in both cities, the army reached the Afghan capital Kabul in August 1839. Dost Mohammad fled and Shuja Shah Durrani returned to the throne, a puppet leader who would protect British interests with guidance from William Macnaghten and Alexander Burnes. Dost Mohammad later gave himself up to the British and went into exile in India.

STIRRINGS OF REBELLION

The operation appeared to have gone smoothly, and there had been very few

ALEXANDER BURNES
The Scottish aide, seen here dressed in Bukhara costume, advised against reinstating Shuja Shah. He was killed in the insurrection.

casualties. Macnaghten sent the majority of the troops back to India and the rest settled down to a comfortable British colonial lifestyle. But within a year things started to go wrong. It became clear that Shuja Shah was far less popular than Dost Mohammad, and that the British presence was seen as the occupation of an invading force. Akbar Khan, the son of Dost Mohammad, was encouraging rebellion against the British among the rural tribespeople and a guerrilla war was breaking out. When the British government stopped paying money to various tribal leaders to keep the peace, matters got even worse. During the spring and summer of 1841 the situation became increasingly tense. Surprisingly, command of the army was handed over at this point to the aged

> Surprisingly, command of the army was handed over to the aged General William Elphinstone, who was both inept and unwell.

TREATY WITH AFGHANS

In 1809, fearing an invasion of India by the French emperor Napoleon and Tsar Alexander I of Russia, the British signed a treaty with the Afghan leader Shuja Shah Durrani. This prevented other foreign powers passing through Afghanistan. Subsequent Afghan leaders, however, were less willing to observe the terms of the treaty.

BRITAIN

London

RUSSIA

KAZAKHSTAN

UZBEKISTAN

AFGHANISTAN

Kabul

Kandahar

INDIA

Relative locations of Britain
and Afghanistan

General William Elphinstone, who was both inept and unwell.

COLD MURDER

On November 2, 1841, on the instructions of Akbar Khan, who now had considerable support, a nationwide uprising began. In Kabul, the home of Sir Alexander Burnes was stormed and he and his advisers were murdered. The following week the fort holding the army's supplies was taken by rebels. In an attempt to rescue the situation, Macnaghten offered Akbar Khan the throne of Afghanistan in return for allowing the British to remain in the country. At the same time he paid out money to have Akbar Khan assassinated, a trick that, unfortunately, Akbar Khan discovered. When Macnaghten and three officers met with Akbar Khan close to

GATEWAY
Afghanistan offered access to India from the north through Kazakhstan and Uzbekistan. To Russia and Britain it was a pawn in the "Great Game."

the British army compound outside Kabul on December 23 they were killed by Akbar Khan himself. Macnaghten's body was then dragged through Kabul market, as Burnes's body had been.

TRAGIC RETREAT

To the dismay of his officers, General Elphinstone ignored the murders of Burnes and Macnaghten and instead agreed to hand over the British army's gunpowder, muskets, and cannons to the tribal chiefs. In return the Afghans promised the British and Indian troops and their followers a safe exit out of

Afghanistan. On January 6, 1842, about 4,500 British and Indian soldiers, together with twelve thousand camp followers, departed from Kabul in the direction of Jalalabad, 90 miles (145 km) to the east over several high passes. It was the middle of winter. The Afghans reached the first snowy pass before them, and on January 9, one-quarter of the British and Indian soldiers and civilians were gunned down. Over the succeeding days, with the exception of a few officers' wives who were taken hostage, almost the entire group of 16,500 people was steadily massacred as they struggled through the rocky, freezing terrain. On January 13, the last forty men, mainly members of the 44th Regiment of Foot, were surrounded on a hill close to the village of Gandamak. It is said that they were offered a chance to surrender,

GHAZNI CITY

The British garrison in Ghazni was defeated by Afghan forces, but the city was retaken when the British returned and its fortifications were demolished.

to which one of the soldiers replied, "Not bloody likely." Nine were taken prisoner, and the rest were slaughtered.

Only one British soldier, Assistant Surgeon William Brydon, reached Jalalabad, having been hidden by an Afghan shepherd who had then given the severely injured man his horse.

TIME FOR REVENGE

The murder of the retreating regiments by Afghan tribesmen was the most humiliating and tragic episode in British colonial military history. The British were determined to get their revenge. Akbar Khan was now in power, and in April Shuja Shah was assassinated. British relief forces were sent to the garrisons still holding Jalalabad and Khandahar, and Akbar Khan's rebels were defeated in a battle near Jalalabad. In August, a British force retook Ghazni from the rebels and another inflicted a final defeat on Akbar Khan. In September, Kabul was captured, the British and Indian prisoners being held there were released, and the city's market area was destroyed as a punishment.

Freed by the British, Dost Mohammad returned to power in Afghanistan, and in 1845 Akbar Khan died, probably poisoned by his father. For the time being, Britain backed away from playing an active role in the politics of Afghanistan, but this was not the last time that a foreign invader would come to grief in this wildly inhospitable and fiercely independent country.

> **A humiliating and tragic episode in British colonial military history.**

TRAGEDY IN THE VALLEY OF DEATH

October 25, 1854

Main Culprits: Lord Raglan and Captain Nolan, and a feud between Lords Lucan and Cardigan

Damage Done: 118 men of the Light Brigade were killed and 127 were wounded

Why: The initial order to attack was vague, and personal disagreements among officers caused further confusion

The Charge of the Light Brigade, which took place on October 25, 1854, has been hailed as an example of supreme military bravery in the face of extreme danger. It was also the result of a blind following of orders and a monstrous blunder brought about by an obscure command and personal disagreement between key officers. It cost the lives of hundreds of men.

In September 1854, French, British, and Turkish troops landed on the west coast of the Crimean Peninsula, which juts into the Black Sea from the coast of the Ukraine. Their aim was to take the important naval base of Sevastopol from the Russian Imperial Army. After defeating the Russians at the River Alma, the British set up their supply base in the coastal town of Balaclava, a few miles to the south of Sevastopol, before laying siege to it.

On October 25 the Russian commander Prince Menshikov, with an army of twenty thousand infantry and three thousand cavalry, advanced on Balaclava and threatened to cut off the only supply route between Balaclava and Sevastopol. This route, the Woronzoff Road, ran along the top of a ridge known as the Causeway Heights. The North Valley, to its north, separated it from the Fedioukine Hills, and another valley lay to its south with hills beyond. Work was in progress to fortify the Causeway Heights with six entrenched defensive positions (known as redoubts), equipped with naval guns, but it hadn't been completed. Five hundred Turkish soldiers were manning the first redoubt but advancing Russians took it, and the garrisons in the other redoubts soon fell back to the south, toward Balaclava.

[*"There is your enemy. There are your guns, my Lord."*
—**Captain Lewis Nolan**]

MEETING OF CAVALRIES

The Russians also took up positions along the Fedioukine Hills to the north. Three thousand of their cavalry came along the North Valley and then over the Causeway Heights just as the nine-hundred-strong British Heavy Brigade of cavalry moved east along the South Valley.

Neither knew of the other's presence until the Russians appeared over the ridge and began their descent, when they found the columns of the British cavalry crossing their path. Under the command of Major General James Scarlett, the Heavy Brigade wheeled to their left, formed a line facing the Russian cavalry, and attacked. After a short struggle, the Russian cavalry fled back over the Causeway Heights into the North Valley, where 670 cavalrymen of the Light Brigade were ideally positioned to attack

the Russians. The Earl of Cardigan, however, instructed them not to attack, claiming to have been told by his superior, Lord Lucan, that they were not to take offensive action. The Russian cavalry continued to the east end of the valley.

LORD LOOK-ON

This was not the first time that the British cavalry had been prevented from using their strengths and skills to best advantage. In the battles that had taken place the previous month on the army's march south, Lieutenant General the Earl of Raglan, the commander of the British army, had held them back. The blame for their inaction then had fallen on the cavalry commander, Lord Lucan, who had received the nickname "Lord Look-On" as a result. This was to prove an important element in the fiasco that followed.

THIN RED LINE

Meanwhile, as the majority of the Russian cavalry had been descending from the Causeway Heights only to be beaten back by the Heavy Brigade, a smaller force of their cavalry had advanced directly south toward Balaclava. The 93rd Highlanders had successfully halted their progress by forming a line and firing at them from a distance. It had been enough to turn them back, and a war correspondent with *The Times*, William Russell, later referred to this gallant defense by a row

MENSHIKOV

Prince Alexander Sergeyevich Menshikov was commander-in-chief of the Russian forces in the Crimea but was removed from his command after Russian defeats following the Battle of Balaclava.

of red-coated soldiers, rifles raised with bayonets fixed, as a "thin red line tipped with steel." It was a phrase that was to go down in history.

THE ORDER IS GIVEN

From his position on high ground at the west end of the North Valley, Lord Raglan could see that the Russians were taking the guns on the Causeway Heights, an action that would be seen as a victory for the Russians. Since no other troops were available, he decided to send the Light Brigade, still positioned at the west end of the North Valley, to attack them, and this was the order he gave. It read, "Lord Raglan wishes the cavalry to advance rapidly to the front, and try

"THE CHARGE OF THE LIGHT BRIGADE"
by Alfred Lord Tennyson

Half a league, half a league,
Half a league onward,
All in the valley of Death
Rode the six hundred.
"Forward the Light Brigade!
Charge for the guns!" he said.
Into the valley of Death
Rode the six hundred.
"Forward, the Light Brigade!"
Was there a man dismay'd?
Not tho' the soldier knew
Some one had blunder'd.
Theirs not to make reply,
Theirs not to reason why,
Theirs but to do and die.
Into the valley of Death
Rode the six hundred.

> **An unclear order, complicated by a string of petty personal disagreements, had led to the most avoidable disaster in British military history.**

to prevent the enemy carrying away the guns. Troop of horse artillery may accompany. French cavalry is on your left. Immediate." The order was carried to the Light Brigade by Captain Lewis Nolan, a strong supporter of the cavalry and a critic of Lord Lucan for that reason. Nolan galloped down and handed the order to Lord Lucan—and here the confusion began. The Russians on Causeway Heights could not be seen from the valley floor, and the order therefore made no sense to Lord Lucan. On being asked to explain which guns and what enemy were being referred to, it is reported that Nolan (who knew exactly what the order was referring to) gave a vague wave of his arm in the direction of the far end of the valley, and said curtly, "There is your enemy. There are your guns, My Lord." Giving no further explanation, he rode away.

Lucan, aware that others had previously accused him of inaction when it came to the cavalry, ordered Lord Cardigan to charge the Russian position. Had relations between Lucan and Cardigan been better, there could have been some discussion at this point. They were brothers-in-law, but Cardigan had separated from Lucan's sister and resentment had built over decades. Cardigan gave the order, and the cavalry mounted and set off down the valley, with Lord Lucan and the Heavy Brigade behind them.

HORROR UNFOLDS

Lord Raglan positioned on the Sapouné Ridge could only look on in horror as he watched the Light Brigade riding eastward and then entering the mouth of the valley rather than swinging to their right to go up the Causeway Heights. To the cavalry's left, the Russians occupying the Fedioukine Hills opened fire; to the right, the Russian troops that had taken the redoubts on the Woronzoff Road opened fire; and ahead of them the Russian guns blazed. In a hail of rifle bullets and shells, the horsemen quickened their pace as their colleagues fell all around them.

Lord Lucan and the Heavy Brigade had pulled up when the scale of the gunfire had become apparent, but the Light Brigade charged on at a full gallop, right through the heavy guns and into the Russian cavalry. They succeeded in

CHARGE FOR THE GUNS!

Fired upon from three sides, the valiant cavalrymen of the Light Brigade rode right through the Russian guns.

pushing them back, but were finally forced back down the valley, still under heavy fire from Russian cavalry that had descended from the ridges on either side.

Of the 670 men that charged down the "Valley of Death," less than two hundred made it back. Almost 250 had been killed or wounded, the rest had been taken prisoner, and 475 horses had died. An unclear order had led to the most avoidable disaster in British military history. Incidentally, the Earl of Cardigan, who had ridden at the head of the charge, survived unscathed and is said to have had a champagne dinner aboard his yacht in Balaclava harbor that evening.

THE ASSASSINATION OF TSAR ALEXANDER II

March 13, 1881

Main Culprit: The revolutionary group, The People's Will

Damage Done: Led to even greater repression by the tsarist regime and slowed the pace of political reform

Why: The People's Will were dissatisfied with the pace of change under Tsar Alexander II

Alexander, born in Moscow in 1818, became tsar of Russia in March 1855 on the death of his father, Tsar Nicholas I. The Crimean War was in its second year. Six months after his accession, Sevastopol was captured, and the following year the Treaty of Paris put an end to Russian dominance in the Balkans. The country that had considered itself a major power in Europe had been revealed as seriously backward. Its army was made up entirely of long-service soldiers and had been unable to raise new recruits as reinforcements. While western European states were benefiting from the introduction of factories and rapid industrialization, industrial output in Russia was falling. Farming and agricultural production were also stagnant. More than a third of the country's population of 62.5 million were serfs—slaves who were literally owned by the nobility who owned the land on which they worked.

FEUDAL SYSTEM

Discussions concerning the possible freeing of the serfs from slavery (emancipation) had been underway in government circles since the 1830s, but no progress had been made under tsar Nicholas I. Now three leading reformers brought their ideas to the new tsar, suggesting that changing the status of the serfs to land-owning peasants could lay the foundations of a market economy based on trade and private ownership. Although he was no forward-thinking reformer, Tsar Alexander II was a smart statesman. He understood that the feudal system of serfs acted as a brake on the

> *"It is better to abolish serfdom from above than to wait for it to abolish itself from below."*
>
> **—Tsar Alexander II, 1861**

YOUNG ALEXANDER
Alexander was tutored by the Romantic poet Vasily Zhukovsky, which may have lessened the influence of his autocratic father and made him a more liberal tsar.

landowner, and granted them the rights to buy half of the land that they worked.

LAND AND LIBERTY

In the following years Tsar Alexander oversaw the introduction of a wide range of reforms, including the creation of local councils with the power to manage transport, education, and health in their areas, a restructuring of the military, and the expansion of industry and the railroads. However, while conservatives worried about the rapid pace of the reforms, radical groups saw them as too little and too slow. A group calling itself Land and Liberty demanded the wholesale handover of lands to the peasants, and some proposed terrorism (the use of violence) as a means to achieve change.

ASSASSINATION ATTEMPTS

In April 1879, a former student, acting alone, fired a revolver repeatedly at the tsar but missed. He was arrested and later hanged. Later that year, the

development of Russia, and a committee was formed to look into improving the conditions of the peasants. The nobility were willing to free the serfs but not to see their land given away. However, they had little choice as a large proportion of their estates and the majority of their serfs (who were a form of property) had been loaned to them by the banks or the government. The Emancipation Manifesto, which outlined the legal framework for the reforms, was adopted in February 1861. It freed the serfs, giving them the right to marry or start a business without the permission of the

A STEP FORWARD

In the Emancipation Manifesto of 1861, serfs were given the right to own land. Since they could not afford to pay for it, the government advanced money in the form of government bonds to the landowners and the serfs were to pay back the money, with interest (extra money on top) over a period of forty-nine years. The transition was far from problem-free, but it was a major step forward for the country.

terrorists in Land and Liberty formed a splinter group called The People's Will, questioning the very basis of political power in Russia and calling for revolutionary change and an end to the tsarist rule. The People's Will made the assassination of the tsar a priority. In October, they attempted to blow up the train in which the tsar was traveling, but failed. The following year a carpenter in the group took a job in the tsar's Winter Palace in St. Petersburg and managed to hide a large quantity of explosives

ALEXANDER II KILLED
An assassination attempt by The People's Will finally managed to kill Alexander II as he comforted a dying man.

beneath the dining room. At 6:30 on the evening of February 17, when the tsar was expected to be dining, it exploded, but the tsar had been delayed and he escaped the blast. Sixty-seven members of the household were not so fortunate.

THE PEOPLE'S DEMANDS
The People's Will now informed the Russian government that they would call off their campaign of terror if the government introduced free elections in which everyone could vote, and put an end to censorship (control of the press and media). While the tsar was willing to consider limited social reform, this kind of major political reform was not acceptable. He did, however, order the

release of several political prisoners and instructed his minister of the interior to suggest some revisions to the constitution. The tsar also gave him the task of getting rid of The People's Will organization.

When proposed revisions to local councils and a newly created national assembly threatened to reduce his own authority, he suggested that the minister look again.

BLOWN APART

Impatient at the delays, The People's Will planned another assassination attempt, and on March 13, 1881, they succeeded. In St. Petersburg, a member of the group, Nikolai Rysakov, threw a bomb at the tsar's bulletproof carriage, which was accompanied by armed Cossacks on horseback and police officers in sleighs. When the bomb exploded, one of the Cossacks was seriously injured. The tsar ignored advice to remain in the carriage and stepped out to comfort the dying man. As he did the tsar received the full blast of a second bomb hurled by another terrorist, Ignaty Grinevitsky, who died in the blast. The tsar, his legs blown off and his body ripped apart, was taken by sleigh to the Winter Palace, where he died shortly afterward.

As it turned out, Alexander II had, the previous day, approved draft plans for the creation of an elected assembly,

> **The assassination in 1881 of Tsar Alexander II cut short a process of change in Russia that had the potential to improve the lives of millions.**

REFORMER

As Minister of the Interior, Count Loris-Melikov was the architect of a range of reforms. When these reforms were shelved by Alexander III, Loris-Melikov resigned.

or Duma. On his ascent to the Russian throne, his eldest son, Tsar Alexander III, rejected these plans and substantially reversed many of the reforms introduced by his father, including reducing the power of the local councils. The "what-ifs" of history are, of course, impossible to answer, but the assassination of Tsar Alexander II in 1881 certainly cut short a process of change in Russia that had the potential to improve the lives of millions. His death plunged the country back into a period of repression under an all-powerful tsar that was finally replaced by the political system of Communism, with all its imperfections. The Duma was finally introduced after the Russian Revolution in 1905.

AUSTRIA'S MAYERLING INCIDENT

January 29–30, 1889

Main Culprit: Crown Prince Rudolf of Austria, or did someone else shoot him?

Damage Done: Hopes of a more liberal Austro-Hungarian leadership died with Rudolf—the assassination of the new heir, Archduke Franz Ferdinand, by Serb nationalists, triggered World War I

Why: The reasons remain unknown, although it's thought that Rudolf may have feared the exposure of an affair

The facts of the Mayerling Incident are largely clouded in mystery and will probably never be known. What we do know is that Crown Prince Rudolf of Austria and his teenage lover, Baroness Mary Vetsera, died that night. The version of events made public at the time was that it was murder-suicide. If this was true, then Rudolf's final gunshot was to lead to the end of the Hapsburg dynasty and ultimately to the assassination of his cousin Archduke Franz Ferdinand, sparking World War I.

A "GOOD" MARRIAGE

Prince Rudolf was the only son of Emperor Franz-Josef of Austria-Hungary and Empress Elisabeth of Bavaria. In 1881, when he was twenty-two years old, he made a "good" marriage to Princess Stephanie of Belgium, who was not yet seventeen. Although they were initially happy together, the couple proved to be ill suited. Stephanie was extremely conventional, even boring, and, as her mother-in-law put it, "a moral heavyweight." Rudolf was far more impulsive and liberal thinking. By the time their first and only child, a girl named Elisabeth Marie, was born in 1883, the two were drifting apart.

Things got even worse between them when the promiscuous Rudolf gave his wife a venereal disease, which prevented her from having more children and, in particular, a male heir to the Hapsburg throne. She openly began an affair with a Polish count and Rudolf continued to entertain a series of mistresses, including the seventeen-year-old Baroness "Mary" Marie Alexandrine von Vetsera. It is thought that they met in the fall of 1888, but according to an account written by his sister-in-law some thirty years later, Rudolf told her the affair had actually begun at least two years earlier, when Mary was just fifteen. This might explain his decision to buy the manor house at Mayerling, in the Vienna Woods, in 1888 and to transform it into a hunting lodge. It would have provided the couple with a secluded, and rather grand, love nest.

ILL MATCHED
Crown Prince Rudolf and Princess
Stephanie, seen here at their engagement,
were married in 1881. Less than eight
years later he was dead.

MAYERLING HUNTING LODGE

Telling his family that he was planning to
spend the following day hunting, Rudolf
spent the night of January 29, 1899, at
Mayerling, but when his valet came to
wake him in the morning he found the
prince's bedroom door locked. Unable to
raise a response, the valet and Rudolf's
hunting buddy, Count Josef Hoyos, who
had also spent the night there, used an
ax to break the door. In the dim light of
the shuttered room they found Mary
lying on the bed and Rudolf sitting
(or lying) beside it on the floor. Both
were dead and, seeing a glass on the
bedside table, Count Josef concluded
that poison was the cause.

GUNSHOT WOUNDS

The count made his way to Vienna as
quickly as possible to inform the emperor
and empress of the tragedy. They were,
of course, deeply shocked by the news,
but the emperor had the presence of
mind to call the minister of police and
have Mayerling and the surrounding
area cordoned off. To cover up Prince
Rudolf's apparent suicide, the press was
told that he had died of an aneurism
(causing a heart attack). A doctor was
sent to determine the exact cause of
death, which apparently turned out to be
gunshot wounds. It appeared that Rudolf
had shot Mary in the head and then,
having sat beside the body for some
hours, shot himself. The body of the
young baroness was quickly removed
from the house by her uncles and then
hastily buried in the cemetery of a
nearby monastery.

Journalists, however, soon discovered
that the body of Rudolf's mistress had
also been found in the room and that
this was probably a murder-suicide.
Although the imperial household did
all it could to suppress the story, the
emperor had difficulty persuading the
Church to allow Rudolf's body to be
buried in the Imperial Crypt in Vienna.
The Church ruling at the time was that a
suicide could not receive a Christian
burial. However, in this case, a special
dispensation was given on the basis that
Rudolf had died while in an unbalanced
mental state.

> **Both Prince Rudolf and
> Mary were dead, and
> Count Josef concluded
> that poison was the cause.**

QUESTIONS ARE ASKED

A range of doubts has been raised concerning precisely what did happen that night and why. According to one report only one bullet had been fired from the gun found beside the prince, and according to another, six bullets had been fired, neither of which would account for two bullet wounds. The body of Mary also threw up conflicting evidence. Her coffin was opened by occupying Russian troops in 1946, and when her remains were being reburied in 1955 it was observed that there was no bullet-hole in the skull. Rather, there were signs that she may have been struck by a blunt instrument, an unlikely way for her lover to have killed her. Her skeleton was again dug up in 1991, but a medical examination at that time proved inconclusive because part of the skull was now missing.

THE MOTIVE

Then there is the question "why?" It is said that there had been an argument a few days earlier between Rudolf and the emperor, who insisted that Rudolf end the affair. Would that be a good enough reason for a suicide pact, given that their affair was widely known? Then again, it is known that a few months earlier Rudolf had proposed a suicide pact to his other mistress at the time, an actress by the name of Mitzi Kaspar. She had refused, but perhaps Mary was more romantically minded. It was also suggested that Mary may have been pregnant and had died in the process of having an abortion. Another theory had it that she took poison, the grieving prince then killing himself.

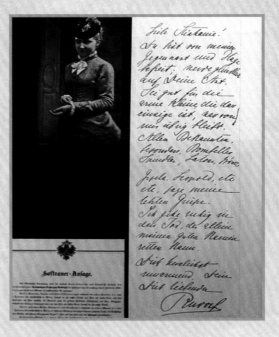

DEAR STEPHANIE
The note from Rudolf found after his death suggests he did intend to commit suicide, but it gives no reason why he felt he should take his own life.

FINAL FAREWELL

"Dear Stephanie, you are now rid of my presence and annoyance; be happy in your own way. Take care of the poor wee one, she is all that remains of me. To all acquaintances…say my last greetings. I go quietly to my death, which alone can save my good name. I embrace you affectionately. Your loving Rudolph."

—From the final letter written by Prince Rudolf to Princess Stephanie.

POLITICAL ASSASSINATION?

A wholly different scenario is recounted in great detail by a German spy writing at the time. According to him, the couple were gunned down by three men who arrived at the lodge on the evening of January 29. The tragedy, in this case, was a political assassination carried out either by the French, who (it is suggested) had tried unsuccessfully to involve the prince in a plot to overthrow his pro-German father, or by Austrian agents who were concerned that the liberal-minded Rudolf intended to give Hungary too much independence.

THE END OF THE HAPSBURGS

As the only son of the emperor and empress, Rudolf was heir to the

UNDER WRAPS

For the lying-in-state of Crown Prince Rudolf at the Hofburg in Vienna, his head was wrapped in a bandage to hide the damage caused by the bullet.

> **Had Prince Rudolf lived the course of European history may have been significantly different.**

Hapsburg throne, and he himself had no male offspring. The next in line was therefore Emperor Franz Josef's younger brother, Archduke Karl Ludwig, but he quickly gave up his right to the succession in favor of his eldest son, Archduke Franz Ferdinand. The assassination of the Archduke in Sarajevo in 1914, which triggered World War I, spelled the end of the Hapsburg monarchy. Had Rudolf lived to become emperor, he would undoubtedly have been more liberal than his father. He may have taken a more progressive approach to the countries seeking more political independence in the region, and the course of European history may have been significantly different.

THE GERMAN NAVY SINKS THE *LUSITANIA*

May 7, 1915

Main Culprit: The German navy

Damage Done: Hundreds of civilians lost their lives, and the US was ultimately drawn into World War I

Why: Germany was anxious to prevent war materials from reaching Britain and wanted to get even for the British naval blockade that was starving Germany

The sinking of the British passenger ship RMS *Lusitania*, torpedoed by a German submarine on May 7, 1915, resulted in the loss of more than a thousand lives, including more than a hundred American citizens. It sent a wave of horror and anger through the Allied countries fighting in World War 1, but especially the neutral US, which was not officially involved in the war. Despite claims by Germany that the vessel was in truth a military ship, this act of aggression against civilians undoubtedly boosted anti-German sentiment in the US and played an important role in drawing the US into the war.

WORLD'S LARGEST SHIP

The Royal Mail Ship *Lusitania*, built in Scotland for the Cunard Line, was launched in 1906 and was at that time the world's largest ship, with a gross tonnage of more than 30,000 tons (27,000 tonnes). She was also the fastest and most powerful ship in the world; her 68,000-horsepower engines were capable of propelling her at 25 knots, and on her second Liverpool to New York crossing she broke the transatlantic record, taking less than five days. The construction of the *Lusitania* was partly funded by the British government on the understanding that she be fitted with gun mounts and that in the event of a war, or other emergency, she would be turned over to the government and converted into an armed merchant cruiser. In fact the *Lusitania* remained with Cunard after the start of World War I, carrying passengers across the Atlantic between Liverpool and New York City.

NAVAL WAR ZONE

As the war progressed, Britain enforced a naval blockade against ships potentially

The *Lusitania* was at that time the world's largest and fastest ship, and on her second Liverpool to New York crossing, she broke the transatlantic record.

RMS *LUSITANIA*
One of only a small group of four-funneled liners, the *Lusitania* was highly distinctive. The U-boat captain knew what he was aiming at when he fired the torpedo.

supplying Germany. In retaliation, German naval—and particularly submarine—interventions against shipping in the Atlantic and around the shores of Britain increased. The Hague Convention, which formally established laws addressing the conduct of war, asserted that unarmed merchant ships should not be fired upon. Germany, however, in response to the British declaration that the North Sea was now a war zone, announced in February 1915 that all the waters around Britain were thereafter a war zone, that British merchant shipping would be targeted, and that it might not always be possible to warn or evacuate vessels before firing on them. The British then advised all its merchant ships to ram or fire upon any submarine sighted, making it unlikely that German submarine commanders would take the risk of surfacing and warning would-be targets.

AT THEIR OWN RISK
Transatlantic passenger services continued even though the possibility of German submarine, or "U-boat," attack was increasing. Passengers in the US were warned of the potential risk but the Cunard Line was at pains to reassure passengers that the speed of the *Lusitania*—almost twice that of a U-boat—and her watertight bulkheads (barriers between different parts of the ship) made her safe from being sunk. Although there was concern, very few passengers took the threat seriously or canceled their bookings.

Unsere Unterseeboote im Hafen.

GERMAN U-BOATS

On May 1 the *Lusitania* sailed out of New York bound for Liverpool with a crew of 694 and 1,265 passengers, of whom 159 were Americans. Her passenger list boasted a host of the wealthy and the famous, from bankers and industrialists to artists, writers, designers, musicians, and socialites. Her captain, William Thomas Turner, was under instructions to keep her speed up, to avoid sailing close to headlands, where submarines might lie in wait, and to sail a zigzag path if confronted with the immediate danger of a submarine. Her crossing of the Atlantic was uneventful, but throughout the week the British

U-20
The German submarine *U-20*, seen here (second from left) moored in Kiel harbor in 1914, was later scuttled after grounding off Jutland, Denmark.

Admiralty had been aware of a German submarine, U-20, operating in the Irish Sea. On May 5, a German U-boat sank the merchant ship *Earl of Lathom* after ordering her crew to abandon ship, and on the 6th the U-20 sank two 6,000-ton (5,400-tonne) ships and missed two others. Warnings were broadcast by the Royal Navy to all shipping, and Captain Turner took the precaution of closing the *Lusitania*'s watertight doors, doubling the

In less than twenty minutes from the time of impact, the *Lusitania* had sunk, its downdraft dragging people under the water.

lookout, and preparing the lifeboats for launching. As the *Lusitania* reached the southern coast of Ireland on the morning of May 7 she was forced by misty conditions to slow down to 15 knots, and when a further radio warning was received, the captain altered course to pass closer to the Irish coast. He did not, however, adopt a zigzag course. As the weather cleared, the ship's speed was increased to 18 knots.

FIRST TORPEDO

In the early afternoon, the submarine U-20, captained by Walther Schwieger, surfaced some 10 miles (16 km) south of the Old Head of Kinsale, a headland on the south coast of Ireland. At 1:20 pm the highly recognizable outline of the *Lusitania* was sighted approaching from the west. Submerging to periscope depth, the submarine came within 800 yards (730 m) of the oncoming liner and at 2:10 pm a single torpedo was fired.

DRAGGED UNDERWATER

Spotting the approaching telltale stream of bubbles, a lookout aboard the *Lusitania* shouted a warning, but it was too late to do anything. Seconds later the torpedo struck the ship behind the captain's bridge with a loud explosion, blowing a large hole in the hull. A second, even greater, explosion followed immediately, blasting steel and debris into the air, and within minutes the ship began to list and the front of the ship began to go down. The captain issued instructions to turn toward the land, but the ship would not respond. Nor could the engines be put into reverse to slow the ship down, which made it impossible to launch the lifeboats immediately. As the ship slowed, the severe list prevented lifeboats from being lowered properly, as they scraped down the sloping hull and caught on the protruding rivets. Those on the other side of the ship were too far from the deck for the fleeing passengers to reach them or hit the sea at such an angle that they filled with water. In less than twenty minutes from the time of impact, the *Lusitania* had sunk, its downdraft dragging people under the water. Only six of the ship's forty-eight lifeboats reached the water successfully, and the vast majority of the passengers were

WARNING TO ALL SHIPPING

In the days before the *Lusitania's* 202nd Atlantic crossing, a warning advertisement appeared in several New York newspapers. It read:

"NOTICE!
Travelers intending to embark on the Atlantic voyage are reminded that a state of war exists between Germany and her allies and Great Britain and her allies; that the zone of war includes the waters adjacent to the British Isles; that, in accordance with formal notice given by the Imperial German Government, vessels flying the flag of Great Britain or of any of her allies, are liable to destruction in those waters and that travelers sailing in the war zone on ships of Great Britain or her allies do so at their own risk."
—Imperial German Embassy, Washington, D.C., April 22, 1915

FIGHTING TALK

"This represents not merely piracy, but piracy on a vaster scale of murder than old-time pirates ever practiced…it is a warfare against innocent men, women, and children traveling on the ocean, and our own fellow countrymen and country-women, who were among the sufferers. It seems inconceivable that we can refrain from taking action in this matter, for we owe it not only to humanity, but to our own national self-respect."

— The words of former President Roosevelt. This was fighting talk, and even though neither the American public nor its leaders were willing to go to war at that time, the sinking of the *Lusitania* had certainly raised the possibility.

drowned or found themselves struggling in the cold sea. Vessels from the nearest Irish ports made their way to the scene to rescue survivors, but only 764 passengers and crewmembers out of a total of 1,959 people survived, and almost 900 bodies were never recovered. Only 11 of the 139 Americans on board survived.

APPLAUSE AND OUTRAGE

Germany and Austria applauded the actions of Kapitänleutnant Schwieger and immediately justified the sinking of *Lusitania* by claiming that she was armed, that she was carrying troops, and that her cargo included large quantities of weaponry and munitions that had caused the second explosion.

The international community, on the other hand, reacted with outrage. Although the *Lusitania* had been fitted with gun mounts, she certainly had no guns on board, and nor was she carrying troops. As far as munitions were concerned, she had been carrying more than four million rounds of rifle cartridges and over a thousand empty shell cases, as well as fuses, but neither Cunard nor US customs classified these as munitions. (The second explosion was put down to the igniting of coal dust in the boiler rooms, although it now seems more likely that it was caused by a steam explosion when high pressure steam lines ruptured.) No one in the US or among the

LOSS OF LIFE
Almost two-thirds of the *Lusitania*'s
passengers and crew drowned, largely
because the lifeboats could not be
launched properly from the listing ship.

Allied countries accepted that such a
cargo justified the killing of more than a
thousand civilians.

US ENTERS WAR

US president Woodrow Wilson—
recognizing that unrestricted submarine
warfare against the world's shipping
represented a new and ugly turn in the
war—sent several strongly worded notes
to the German government making it
clear that the sinking of merchant
shipping was unacceptable. In September
1915, fearing that the US might join the
war against them, Germany backed
down and the German chancellor and
Kaiser Wilhelm II issued instructions,
against the wishes of the German
Admiralty, forbidding U-boats to fire on
neutral ships without warning. The fear
of U-boat attacks on transatlantic
shipping subsided, and it was enough to
calm the US for the time being.

In January 1917, however, with the
war going badly for Germany on the
Western Front, unrestricted submarine
warfare was seen as vital to that country's
war effort, and the policy was reversed.
The German military were sure that this
would not cause America to declare war.
They were wrong. Woodrow Wilson broke
off diplomatic relations with Germany, but
this had no effect on their decision, and
within two months seven US merchant
ships had been sunk. On April 6, 1917,
America entered the war. It was the
culmination of a process that had started
with the sinking of the *Lusitania*—a
decision that Germany was to regret.

> "… a great steamer…carrying more than a thousand souls who had
> no part or lot in the conduct of the war, was torpedoed and sunk
> without so much as a challenge or a warning, and that men, women,
> and children were sent to their death in circumstances
> unparalleled in modern warfare."
>
> **—President Wilson's "Reply to Berlin" (No. 1803),
> Department of State, Washington, June 9, 1915**

THE TREATY OF VERSAILLES

January 18, 1919

Main Culprits: The Allied Powers

Damage Done: The terms of the Treaty of Versailles created the conditions that were to lead to the outbreak of World War II

Why: The treaty neither made Germany an equal partner in a peaceful Europe nor crushed it so that it could never again use military aggression

In the early hours of the morning of November 11, 1918, the Allied Powers of World War I (principally Britain, the US, and France) and the Central Powers (Germany, Austria-Hungary, and Turkey) agreed to end hostilities. The general terms were dictated by the Allies (the defeated Central Powers had no say in the terms) and it took a further six months for the Allies to finalize between themselves the details of a peace treaty. Britain wanted Germany to be a buffer against the political ideology of Communism taking hold in Russia, the US was looking for a long-lasting peace in Europe without American involvement, and France sought to regain its former power at the expense of Germany.

There were differences in their aims, but the Treaty of Versailles and the demands that it made on Germany appeared to be a workable compromise. Two decades later, that compromise failed: Nazism emerged; war returned, involving the US once again; and France paid a high price for its revenge.

THE BIG FOUR

The Paris Peace Conference, charged with working out the details of the peace treaty, met in January 1919. It involved representatives of twenty-five nations, but the prime movers—the "Big Four"—were France, Italy, the US, and Britain. Several months prior to the signing of the armistice, US president Woodrow Wilson had put forward his list of "Fourteen Points," which he felt were necessary in order to secure a lasting peace, referred to as a "peace without victory." These principally called for the restoration of territories to their pre-war borders, arms reductions, and freedom of navigation in the seas. When the armistice was signed, Germany had been led to believe that these would form the

Western Europe lay in tatters and the cost of the mayhem was huge. Germany needed to pay for that damage.

basis of any peace treaty, but the European members of the "Big Four" had other ideas. The Allies negotiated separate treaties with the Ottoman Empire, Austria, and Hungary, but in the Treaty of Versailles, Germany was singled out for especially harsh treatment.

TERMS OF THE TREATY

Germany was required to give up portions of its claimed territory to Poland, France, Denmark, Belgium, and Czechoslovakia. Military forces would be removed and Allied forces would occupy for the next fifteen years the industrially

GERMAN SURRENDER

From July 1918 an Allied offensive forced the worn-out German army to retreat. The collapse of the Central Powers was swift.

important coal- and steel-producing German Rhineland, which borders France. Germany's colonies in Africa and the Pacific were also shared out between several of the Allied countries.

Key elements of the treaty were designed to prevent Germany from rebuilding its military strength, and this included restricting the size of the German army to one hundred thousand troops, severely limiting the size of its navy, and forbidding Germany to have an armed air force. A ban was placed on the import and export of armaments, the manufacture of weapons was restricted, and poison gas, submarines, and tanks were prohibited. The terms might have been more severe had it not been for Britain's desire for Germany to remain strong enough to resist the spread of Communism from Russia.

WAR-TORN EUROPE

Western Europe lay in tatters. Ten million soldiers and almost as many civilians had been killed. Towns and villages had been demolished. Millions of people were displaced or homeless. Roads, railroads, bridges, farms, and industries had been destroyed. The cost of the mayhem was huge, and the question of compensation by those who had caused this devastation (known as reparation) was high on the list of priorities for many of the war-torn countries, but especially for France.

PAYBACK TIME

When it came to determining the actual amount of reparations to be paid, neither Britain nor the US wished Germany to be brought to its knees. They wanted it to remain an important trading partner and recognized that destroying its economy could lead to political and

GUILT CLAUSE

With the aim of making Germany responsible for paying for the damage, Article 231 of the Treaty of Versailles, which became known as the "Guilt Clause," read, "Germany accepts the responsibility of Germany and her allies for causing all the loss and damage to which the Allied and Associated Governments and their nationals have been subjected as a consequence of the war imposed upon them by the aggression of Germany and her allies." It was a condition of the peace terms that was to rankle above all others.

> **Germany was humiliated by the defeat and the punishing nature of the peace terms.**

social unrest. Nonetheless, the price demanded—$53.7 billion—was high, although it was reduced to $31.4 billion two years later (the equivalent of $385 billion today). Even at the time, it was acknowledged that Germany would be unable to repay the level of reparations demanded.

Prior to the signing of the armistice, the last kaiser, or emperor, of Germany, Wilhelm II abdicated. Power was handed over to a government headed by the new chancellor, Friedrich Ebert, a member of the left-wing Social Democratic Party. It was he who signed the armistice agreement, and in February 1919 he was made first president of the Weimar Republic. When the terms of the Treaty of Versailles were revealed later that year, his first question was directed to the military. If Germany were to refuse to sign, and hostilities were resumed, would its army be strong enough to respond? The answer was a resounding "no." Germany accepted the Treaty of Versailles—which became known as the Diktat (an unpopular order imposed by those in power), since Germany had had no say in its composition and no choice but to accept it.

RESTORATION OF GERMAN HONOR

Humiliated by the defeat and by the punishing nature of the peace terms, the military, the conservative right wing, and very soon the German people began to accuse the more liberal Social Democrats

The New York Times.

ARMISTICE SIGNED, END OF THE WAR! BERLIN SEIZED BY REVOLUTIONISTS; NEW CHANCELLOR BEGS FOR ORDER; OUSTED KAISER FLEES TO HOLLAND

ARMISTICE

The New York Times announces the signing of the armistice and highlights the political disorder already breaking out in Germany.

Promising the restoration of Germany's honor and dominance, and the downfall of its internal enemies — Communists, Jews, Social Democrats — Hitler rose to power during the late 1920s and early '30s. In 1933 Hitler became German chancellor, ushering in a repressive, one-party state. The process of rearmament that had already begun under the Weimar Republic (in contravention of the Treaty of Versailles) was accelerated, and on September 1, 1939, Germany invaded Poland. Two days later Britain and France responded by declaring war on Germany, and Europe was soon being torn apart again, followed shortly by much of the rest of the globe.

of having stabbed Germany in the back. Germany's loss of its raw materials and industry, and the cost of the reparations, had serious economic consequences, leading to a huge increase in prices, mass unemployment, and social unrest. This political climate was ripe for the emergence of extreme nationalistic right-wing ideologies such as National Socialism, or Nazism as it is better known. It called for the terms of the Treaty of Versailles to be revised, for Germany to rearm, for the payment of reparations to stop, and for the repossession of the Rhineland.

RISE OF NAZIS

Adolf Hitler promised to restore Germany's honor and called for the terms of the Treaty of Versailles to be revised.

"We will never stop until we win back what we deserve."

—German newspaper *Deutsche Zeitung*

STALIN'S FIRST FIVE-YEAR PLAN

1929–1933

Main Culprit: Soviet leader Joseph Stalin

Damage Done: He used a policy of collectivization to starve millions of Ukrainians to death

Why: To break the national spirit of the Ukrainian people

The implementation of large-scale change across a whole society often has unintended and damaging, even horrific, consequences for the people affected. In the case of Joseph Stalin, the leader of the Soviet Union, and his first Five-Year Plan, the dreadful consequences may not have been accidental. There was certainly no attempt to change the course of events when, in the first years of the 1930s, it became obvious that his planned collectivization of the farms of Ukraine was causing famine on an unprecedented scale. Indeed, the policy was implemented with even greater vigor, turning a very bad decision into deliberate "death by starvation," or *holodomor* in Ukrainian. Stalin's attempted genocide, the deliberate killing of a large group of people, is an unpleasant truth that the world has been strangely unwilling to discuss or even accept as fact.

INDUSTRIAL POWER

When Stalin came to power, he wanted to make the Soviet Union a global power. Central to this aim was the development of industry and the mass-production of goods in factories. His first Five-Year Plan (1929–1933) set out targets for massive increases in the production of iron, steel, coal, oil, and electricity. The year after its introduction, Stalin expanded the plan to include the collectivization of farms throughout the Soviet Union. Collectivization involved joining together the small peasant-run farms into large collectively run operations. Former Soviet leader Vladimir Lenin had distributed privately owned land among the peasants, who now grew crops and raised animals in traditional ways on a small scale. Stalin saw this as an obstacle to efficient food production and true socialism, a political ideology based on collective or community ownership. Stalin maintained that collectivization would make the introduction of machinery (mechanization) possible, reduce the number of people working on the land (and make them available as a labor force for the new heavy industries), and increase production to feed the growing urban population.

CLASS ENEMIES

Hand in hand with the policy of collectivization, Stalin announced that the kulaks—wealthier peasants who hired the labor of others, owned machinery, or sold their surplus on the market—were class enemies and must be removed. In his own words, "Now we have the opportunity to carry out a resolute offensive against the kulaks, break their resistance, eliminate them as a class and replace their production with the production of [communal and state-owned collective farms]." As a policy, this went far beyond taking their land and livestock. That was just the start. Hundreds of thousands, if not millions, of kulaks were sent to work in labor colonies, deported to areas outside the agricultural regions, shot, or imprisoned. Stalin was willing to push through the policy of collectivization at any price, and in many parts of the Soviet Union the price was very high. Ironically, the Ukraine, a huge area of fertile agricultural land, witnessed more suffering than anywhere else as a result of falling production. It was no accident.

BREAD-BASKET OF USSR

The Ukraine had been fiercely independent in spirit since the end of tsarist rule, when it had declared itself a people's republic and fought a four-year battle against both Lenin's Red Army and the pro-tsar White Army that ended in a Soviet victory. The Ukraine became

> **Stalin's Five-Year Plan led to a deliberate "death by starvation" in Ukraine, known as *holodomor* in Ukrainian.**

JOSEPH STALIN
The Soviet leader saw collectivization as an opportunity not only to get rid of "class enemies" but also a means to crush the fiercely independent Ukrainian people.

the bread-basket of the USSR, but it retained a strong nationalism and pride in its culture, language, and religion. To Stalin this was unacceptable, and in 1929 several thousand academics, intellectuals, and cultural leaders were deported or executed. Now collectivization offered a further opportunity to break the spirit of the Ukraine.

DEPORTED OR SHOT

As peasants were deprived of land and livestock, taken for the collective farms, many fought to retain what they had worked so hard to achieve. Those who resisted were labeled as kulaks and were deported or shot. Some refused to hand

over the grain they had cultivated. Others
slaughtered their animals sooner to stop
them being taken. Reprisals followed, but
there was an overall fall in agricultural
production and a drop in the number of
animals, cattle falling by 30 percent and
sheep by almost 60 percent.

MILLIONS STARVE TO DEATH

In order to put an end to the resistance,
Stalin took one simple step. He ramped
up the grain quotas demanded by the

state, increasing them by more than
40 percent in 1932. That year there
was a good harvest but until the state's
requirements were fulfilled, the peasants
were allowed no grain, and as a result
there was simply nothing for them to
eat. The grain was transported away
and much of it was sold on the world
market, the money funding the
industrialization program.

Communist Party officials, the
military, and the secret police carried out

**Ukraine was turned into a
virtual concentration camp.**

[*"Now we have the opportunity to carry out a resolute offensive against the kulaks, break their resistance, eliminate them as a class..."*]

—Joseph Stalin, 1929

a virtual war on the peasantry, executing or deporting anyone found in possession of even a handful of grain. People who were not visibly malnourished were suspected of theft or hoarding food. Military blockades were set up to prevent anyone from leaving the affected areas or food from entering, and the Ukraine was turned into a virtual concentration camp.

Between 1932 and 1933 as many as fifteen million people are thought to have starved to death throughout the Soviet Union, more than a third of these being Ukrainians. When officials within the party organization pointed out the deaths and terrible famine that were occurring, they were accused of anti-Soviet propaganda, and there was a purge of the Communist bureaucracy. The Soviet Union declared outright that there was no problem, closing the door on any possible international aid. It is even thought that some Western journalists, aware of what was happening but threatened with being denied access to Soviet news sources, chose not to cover the story. The international community was, nonetheless, generally aware of what was happening—if not the full scale of it—but took no action against the USSR, unwilling to jeopardize the lucrative trade agreements that flowed from the Soviet industrialization program.

GENOCIDE

By the end of 1933, figuring that the Ukraine was truly crushed and would offer no further obstacle to complete collectivization, Stalin eased up on food restrictions. It is estimated that between 10 and 20 percent of the population of the Ukraine had died as a result of his ruthless policy and the Five-Year Plan. Only since the break-up of the Soviet Union in 1991 and the advent of Ukrainian independence have the full facts begun to emerge.

Even now only a handful of countries has been willing to recognize Stalin's forced famine as an act of genocide.

WAR ON PEASANTS

"On one side, millions of starving peasants, their bodies often swollen from lack of food; on the other, soldiers, members of the GPU [Soviet secret police] carrying out the instructions of the dictatorship of the proletariat. They had gone over the country like a swarm of locusts and taken away everything edible; they had shot or exiled thousands of peasants, sometimes whole villages; they had reduced some of the most fertile land in the world to a melancholy desert."

—Malcolm Muggeridge, "War on the Peasants," in the *Fortnightly Review*, May 1, 1933

HITLER INVADES THE SOVIET UNION

June 22–December 5, 1941

Main Culprit: Adolf Hitler, against the advice of his military command

Damage Done: Operation Barbarossa resulted in literally millions of casualties on both sides, and Germany gained nothing by it

Why: Hitler underestimated the Red Army and was confident that the campaign would be over before winter—it wasn't

Greed and pride are woefully inadequate terms to describe Hitler's motivation for invading the Soviet Union in 1941. In his book *Mein Kampf*, written in 1925, Hitler had already made it clear that he believed Germany needed, and should take, the territories to its east in order to provide its citizens with the living space (*Lebensraum*), natural resources, and agricultural land that they deserved. When he finally put this plan into action—in Operation Barbarossa, as it was codenamed—it led to the greatest loss of human life ever seen on the planet, as well as the untold suffering of millions of survivors. It also planted the seeds of the Holocaust. In return, Germany gained absolutely nothing and

Hitler believed that Germany needed, and should take, the territories to its east in order to provide its citizens with living space (*Lebensraum*).

ultimately lost the war as a direct result of the failed invasion.

LOOKING EAST

In the two years after the start of World War II, the Axis powers (the nations fighting on the side of Germany) had taken control of almost three-quarters of Europe. Nazi Germany's next logical targets were Britain and the Soviet Union. In the second half of 1940 Britain had held off the German air force, the Luftwaffe, and the country's morale had not been broken despite extensive bombing. Hitler's next option was a seaborne invasion, but the English Channel and the strength of the British navy presented a major obstacle. Besides, Britain had little to offer in the way of materials or space.

Invading the Soviet Union was the obvious choice, given its resources (Germany was in desperate need of oil and other raw materials) and the fact that Hitler despised Communists, Jews, and Slavs, not to mention Stalin, whose political ideology was the complete

GERMAN ADVANCE

The first few days of the German invasion of the Soviet Union were rapid, with German forces smashing through the enemy's lines at speed.

---

opposite of the Nazis. (The Nazis believed in an all-powerful dictator having total control over the state with rigid class roles, whereas Communism was a system based on economic equality and a classless society.) Despite the fact that Germany and the Soviet Union had signed the Molotov-Ribbentrop non-aggression pact in 1939, Hitler had good

reason to think that Stalin would eventually choose to make his own territorial claims in a war-torn Europe. The longer he delayed, the stronger and more organized the Soviet army would be.

DECISION TO INVADE

Even the Allies could see the logic behind Hitler's decision to invade, but when it came to the details of the plan Hitler confronted opposition from within his own ranks. The military were in favor of an attack on Moscow to destroy Russia's nerve center and the heart of

> *"We only have to kick in the door and the whole rotten structure will come crashing down."*
> —Adolf Hitler, June 22, 1941

Communism. Hitler, however, proposed to attack along the entire length of the Eastern Front, from the Baltic in the north to the Black Sea in the south with a three-pronged assault. Army Group North was to move through the Baltic states (recently handed over to Russia under the Molotov-Ribbentrop Pact) to take Leningrad, Army Group Center was to advance through Belorussia and capture Moscow, and Army Group South was to cross the agricultural and

The troop numbers on both sides are almost unimaginable, with more than three million German and Axis troops and more than two million Soviet troops.

NAZI FORCES
Hitler sent a huge number of troops into Russia, but they were spread over several fronts and they met far more resistance than he expected.

mineral-rich Ukraine, taking Kiev, Stalingrad, and the oil fields of the Caucasus. Hitler got his way.

The success of Operation Barbarossa depended upon it being accomplished quickly through the famed blitzkreig ("lightning war") strategy — using an overwhelming military force, in the air and on the ground, to smash through the enemy's lines at high speed and then keep going. The strategy relied upon the enemy being taken by surprise and being unable to respond quickly and effectively. Remarkably, despite the decoding of secret messages concerning the invasion, repeated warnings from Soviet spies, the massing of German troops on the Polish border, and repeated reconnaissance flights over Soviet territory, the Germans managed to maintain an element of surprise. Stalin refused to believe that an attack was imminent, although he did believe that war against Germany was inevitable once Britain had been overrun, and vast numbers of troops were already assembled behind the Russian border.

OPERATION BARBAROSSA

Operation Barbarossa, the largest military operation in history, began at 3:00 on Sunday, June 22, 1941. The troop numbers on both sides are almost unimaginable, with more than three million German and Axis troops confronting more than two million Soviet troops. The rapid advance and victories of the Axis forces in the first few days appeared to fully justify Hitler's optimism. Within three days the Luftwaffe had destroyed more than three thousand Soviet planes, with minimal losses of their own. In the first week of the offensive more than half a million Soviet soldiers were killed, wounded, or captured, and the three Army Groups achieved all their immediate campaign objectives. Indeed, their advance was so rapid that in the north, although they were almost within striking distance of Leningrad, the panzer (tank) groups had to wait a week for the infantry divisions to catch up. This gave the Soviets an opportunity to strengthen the defense of the city.

A FATAL DELAY

During the course of July, German progress slowed dramatically. In the north a period of heavy rain turned the

THE RED ARMY

Hitler was certainly right in thinking that the Soviet army would be weak and disorganized. Stalin had carried out a purge of the Red Army in the late 1930s in which the majority of its generals, admirals, and commanders had been removed and tens of thousands of soldiers had been executed. The result was a command structure largely made up of young and inexperienced men unwilling to act without clear orders. Above all, Hitler's contempt for Communism led him to suppose that the Soviet structure would collapse once they suffered initial defeats.

roads into mud, and the German tanks were less able to deal with the conditions than the Soviets. The German troops had also moved ahead of their supply lines and had to wait for munitions and other supplies to reach them. Furthermore, Soviet resistance was far greater than predicted, and the Soviet armies, although they had suffered terrible losses, were being replenished by new reserves.

On July 15 the Germans captured the city of Smolensk, and by the end of the first week in August the road to Moscow was open for them. What happened next can be seen, with hindsight, as a turning point in the campaign, if not in the war as a whole.

Hitler, reasoning that depriving the Soviet army of its supplies would give Germany the advantage, made the

WAR CRIMES

Hitler called for the invasion of the Soviet Union to be a "struggle for existence." As a result he authorized crimes against Soviet prisoners and showed total disregard for the Geneva Convention, which defined the basic rights of wartime prisoners. Mass killings undertaken by German soldiers and collaborators were common and an estimated two million Soviet prisoners of war died during Operation Barbarossa. Killing squads also conducted large-scale massacres of Jews (an estimated one and a half million), communists, and other civilians, including women and children, during the German occupation of the Soviet Union.

decision to send panzer divisions from Army Group Center southward to support the advance in the Ukraine. This meant delaying the advance on Moscow. His commanders were adamant that this was a mistake, that taking Moscow—the center of communication and munitions production—was the highest priority, but they were overruled. Once Kiev had been taken, on September 19, the panzers returned northward to Army Group Center and the advance on Moscow began again on October 2. It was a delay that the Russian winter would not forgive.

WINTER TAKES HOLD

As the German forces approached Moscow, the weather steadily

Delaying the German advance on Moscow was a turning point in the campaign, if not in the war as a whole.

deteriorated. Neither the men nor their equipment were prepared for temperatures that fell to –40°F (–40°C). The supply lines were now so long, and so subject to attack by Russian forces, that it was difficult to get fuel and munitions through. Food was in short supply, and winter clothing wasn't even on the list of priorities. By early December, although German troops were within sight of the spires of the Kremlin in Moscow, some divisions had been reduced to half their strength by the terrible conditions. Machinery began to break as oil thickened and grease froze, and the Luftwaffe planes were unable to fly. The Soviet troops, on the other hand, had quilted clothing, thick boots, and fur hats, and their equipment was designed for this climate. On December 5, half a million Soviet troops launched a successful counterattack that drove the Germans back some 200 miles (320 km).

Moscow would not fall to the Nazis, and although the war on the Eastern Front would last for another three years, it would end with the Soviet flag being raised in Berlin.

FREEZING WEATHER
German troops march at the Eastern Front, 1941. With the sub-zero temperatures, snow and ice crystals have formed on their head protection and eyebrows.

JAPAN ATTACKS PEARL HARBOR

December 7, 1941

Main Culprits: Emperor Hirohito and Japanese Imperial General Headquarters

Damage Done: Killed more than 2,000 US servicemen and women, but ultimately led to the defeat of Japan

Why: Intended to stop the US from standing in the way of Japan; the attack actually drew the US into World War II

Japanese planes—fighters, dive-bombers, and aerial torpedo planes—attacked the US Pacific Fleet in Pearl Harbor, on the Hawaiian island of O'ahu, shortly before 8:00 am on December 7, 1941.

In less than an hour and a half, twenty-four hundred people were killed, nine ships were sunk, and twenty-one were seriously damaged. The following day Franklin D. Roosevelt referred to the event as "a date which will live in infamy." In the words of a Japanese admiral, "We won a great tactical victory at Pearl Harbor and thereby lost the war."

INCREASING TENSIONS

Although the time and the place of the attack took the Americans completely by surprise, the US had been expecting an act of war by the Japanese for months. Relations between the two countries had been especially tense since the Japanese invasion, in 1931, of Manchuria in northwest China. Throughout the 1930s the nationalist-dominated Japanese government had been increasing the country's military strength and looking to expand its territory, which threatened the colonial territories of the US, Britain, France, and the Netherlands. When Japan attacked China in 1937, pitching those two countries into full-scale war, the US and other Western powers supplied financial and military aid to China. In 1940 and 1941 Japan moved into north and south Indochina (now Cambodia, Laos, Vietnam, Burma, and Thailand), cutting off the supply route into China. In the meantime, Japan had signed the Tripartite Pact with Germany and Italy, whereby the three countries promised to come to one another's aid if they found themselves at war. This was clearly intended to keep America out of the war, but with Nazi aggression to its east and Japanese expansion to its west, the US was being forced to be more directly involved in the conflict.

Relations between the US and Japan had been strained for over a decade.

Already the US was aiding Britain with financial and material support and by protecting merchant ships supplying Britain across the Atlantic. Now the US imposed trade sanctions on Japan, froze Japanese assets in the US, and on August 1 banned all US fuel exports to Japan (which constituted 80 percent of that country's total supply).

NEGOTIATIONS BREAK DOWN

Discussions between the two countries took place over the next few months but no progress was made. Plans to launch an attack on Pearl Harbor had been made since the start of 1941, and on November 5 the Japanese emperor Hirohito gave his approval for the planned attack to go ahead, but in a last diplomatic effort Japan submitted two proposals to the US. These offered a partial withdrawal of the Japanese from

JAPANESE SQUADRON

More than four hundred Japanese planes were involved in the aerial attack on Pearl Harbor, bombing, strafing, and dropping torpedoes to destroy the US fleet.

China and a withdrawal from southern Indochina on condition that the US stop supplying aid to the Chinese Nationalist Government and restore oil supplies to Japan. Both of these were rejected by the US. By this point, Japan was already planning for war and had dispatched warships to Indochina. On November 26 Japan was presented with a US demand for the complete withdrawal of Japanese troops from both China and French Indochina. In fact, a fleet of six aircraft carriers carrying more than four hundred planes for the attack on Pearl Harbor was already en route across the Pacific. The fleet was not called back.

US BADLY PREPARED

There is no doubt that President Roosevelt and Secretary of War Henry L. Stimson were aware that a surprise attack by the Japanese was likely. It was not thought, however, that the target would be Pearl Harbor (Thailand and the Philippines were considered more likely), and no preparations for an attack were made. In fact, the US base was ill-prepared in several ways:

• No troops were on operational alert.
• Planes had been parked wingtip to wingtip in the center of the airfield, and could not be moved in a hurry.
• The shallow water of the harbor was thought to be safe from attack by air-launched torpedoes, so no torpedo netting had been installed. (In fact, the British had in 1940 sunk half the Italian fleet in the port of Taranto in water of a similar depth using aerial torpedoes.)

SHIPS DESTROYED

The Japanese attack sank four US naval battleships and three destroyers. On the land, 188 planes were destroyed and 155 were damaged.

• To avoid causing alarm, the mobile anti-aircraft guns had not been deployed around the island, and the shells were being stored in arms depots.
• There were few long-range reconnaissance aircraft at the base, which could have detected the approaching Japanese fleet.

> *"We won a great tactical victory at Pearl Harbor and thereby lost the war."*
>
> **—A Japanese admiral sums up the attack**

JAPANESE BOMBERS AND FIGHTER PLANES

The first wave of the air attack comprised 183 planes made up of bombers, dive bombers, and fighter planes. They proceeded to bomb and torpedo the battleships in the harbor, and to dive-bomb and fire on the onshore bases. A second wave of some 170 planes followed, and there was little that the US forces could do to respond. The scene was one of devastation, and the loss of life was terrible, but the real cost to the US was far less than the Japanese had hoped for. In many respects, the lack of preparedness on the part of the Americans proved to be a blessing. Had the fleet put to sea to meet the oncoming attack vessels, the loss of life would have been far greater, and so would the loss of vessels. As it was, many members of the ships' crews were ashore at the time and several of the ships, having sunk in shallow water rather than the open ocean, were recovered and repaired within a few weeks. It was also fortunate for the US that the three aircraft carriers of the Pacific Fleet were away at the time. As the war in the Pacific developed, aircraft carriers, rather than destroyers, proved to be the key to success, and those of the US had suffered no damage. Japan had assumed that the Pacific Fleet would be so crushed that the US would have to negotiate a settlement and leave Japan to achieve its goals in the Pacific, but the gamble hadn't paid off.

US DECLARES WAR

On the international front, events moved quickly. The day after the attack, the US received notice of Japan's declaration of war (it had been meant to arrive shortly before the attack began, but due to the

THE SLEEP OF THE SAVED

"To have the United States at our side was to me the greatest joy. Now at this very moment I knew the United States was in the war, up to the neck and in to the death. So we had won after all!… Hitler's fate was sealed. Mussolini's fate was sealed. As for the Japanese, they would be ground to powder."

—**British prime minister Winston Churchill, recalling his feelings on receiving a phone call from Roosevelt informing him of the attack. That night he "slept the sleep of the saved" knowing that the US would now enter the war, which meant one thing…victory.**

Japanese Embassy's delays in decoding and delivering the message, it arrived late). In the US, outrage at the attack rapidly overcame popular opposition to entering the war, and America immediately declared war on Japan (as did Britain, Australia, and other Allied powers). In accordance with the Tripartite Pact, Germany and Italy then declared war on America, and the US responded in kind. America was to play an important role in the Allies' victory over Nazi Germany, but an even greater one in the Pacific War. Here the defeat of the Axis powers led to the surrender of Japan, more than two million of its citizens dead, its navy destroyed, the Allies on the brink of invading the country, and the Japanese cities of Hiroshima and Nagasaki flattened by atomic explosions.

BRITAIN PARTITIONS INDIA

August 15, 1947

Main Culprits: Hindus, Muslims, and the British government

Damage Done: Conflict between Muslims and Hindus led to widespread violence and thousands of deaths—the tensions and violence continue to this day

Why: The British believed that separating the Muslims and Hindus geographically was the only way to avoid civil war in India

In 1947 British rule ended in India and the country was split into two separate states: predominantly Muslim Pakistan and predominantly Hindu India. Whether or not the British had any choice in the partition remains a matter of argument. Violence was breaking out, civil war was looming, and there appeared to be no viable alternative. However, the speed with which this major political decision was implemented, and the consequent lack of preparation for what would follow, can certainly be criticized. The effect of partition led to one of the greatest migrations of people ever seen and to terrible loss of life. The aftershocks are still being felt in the daily lives of the people of both countries.

Although some 1.3 million Indians chose to serve in the British Indian army

> **The effect of partition led to one of the greatest migrations of people ever seen and to terrible loss of life.**

during World War I, there was already a growing Indian independence movement that sought to put an end to the domination of Britain in India. (The British Raj had ruled India since 1858.) This was especially evident in Bengal and Punjab.

RELIGIOUS DIVISION

After the Amritsar Massacre of 1919, which saw the British ordering troops to fire on a crowd of Indian protestors, killing four hundred, Indian people flocked to join the Indian National Congress (INC). The INC initially enabled educated Indians to communicate with the British Raj about issues of government. Now it became a mass movement, transformed into a voice for Indian demands for independence. Although initial opposition to the Raj united Muslims and Hindus alike, their fears and ambitions soon separated. The INC, with Gandhi as its president, remained the voice of the Hindus, whereas the Muslim League, under the leadership of Muhammad Ali Jinnah, spoke for the Muslims. From the

GANDHI
An advocate of peaceful protest to attain independence, Mahatma Gandhi was strongly opposed to the partition of India. In January 1948 he was assassinated by a Hindu extremist.

Hindu perspective, it was the Muslims, in the form of the Moghul Empire, who had been the occupying invaders before the British. The Muslims feared that in an independent India they would be ruled by a Hindu majority that already dominated the government.

AN END TO BRITISH RULE

During the 1920s and '30s, various measures were introduced to include Indians in the electoral process and in governmental decision-making (except in the fields of defense and foreign affairs)

but these fell far short of satisfying the nationalists. Their call now was for dominion status for India and a complete end to British rule. When, in the 1937 provincial elections, Hindus won control in eight of the eleven provinces, Muslim fears of Hindu domination appeared justified, and the Muslim League began to demand a separate state of their own. Gandhi and the Congress Party were equally intent upon preserving Indian unity. Rivalry between the Hindus and Muslims continued to grow.

At the end of World War II, the new Labour government in Britain was anxious to solve the "Indian problem" as soon as possible, and the rivalry between the Muslims and Hindus seemed the greatest stumbling block. A plan was put forward in which political power would be transferred as much as possible to the provinces, the idea being that Muslims would have a greater say in decision-making in the few provinces that had a Muslim majority.

By this means, there would be no need for a separate Muslim state. The idea was accepted in principle and the head of the INC, Nehru, was invited to oversee a temporary government.

Although Nehru included two Muslims in his cabinet, the Muslim League was distrustful. When the INC rejected the Muslim League's call for a separate and independent Muslim state of Pakistan, the League called for a day of "direct action" to protest.

AMRITSAR MASSACRE

In 1918, the British passed legislation that allowed trials to be conducted without juries (so only a judge hears and decides on a case) and imprisonment without trial for people suspected of troublemaking. Lawyer and human rights activist Mahatma Gandhi called for non-violent protest against these laws, but in the first week of April 1919 protests in several towns in Punjab flared into violent anti-British riots. In Amritsar, several Europeans were murdered and banks were looted and burned. On April 13, following the arrest of two Indian nationalists, at least five thousand (and possibly as many as twenty thousand) peaceful protesters gathered in the city to voice their opposition, despite a ban on public meetings. Brigadier-General Rex Dyer, in the belief that India was on the brink of a full-blown rebellion, ordered a force of more than fifty Gurkhas (Nepalese fighters) and Sikh infantrymen to open fire on the packed crowd with rifles. Almost four hundred men, women, and children were killed and some fifteen hundred injured. The British establishment initially accepted that the massacre had been necessary to put down a rebellion. The authorities later distanced themselves from Dyer's actions after the full details of what had happened became known, but the damage was done. It was a turning point in the relationship between India and the British Raj.

DIRECT ACTION

On the morning of the Day of Direct Action (August 16, 1946) sporadic acts of violence broke out in the city of Calcutta, where Hindus largely dominated the economy in a state—Bengal—that had a Muslim majority. In the course of the day the violence increased dramatically, with groups of Hindus and Sikhs against Muslims, each attacking and literally hacking each other to pieces. The British were slow to bring in the military, and in the course of more than a week of rioting and looting an estimated five thousand people were killed and as many as one hundred thousand were wounded. The violence also spread to other parts of India, and a civil war was erupting. It became clear that a unified India after independence no longer looked possible.

PARTITION IN JUST TEN WEEKS

On June 4, 1947, the Viceroy of India, Lord Louis Mountbatten, announced the plan that two independent dominions—India and Pakistan—would come into existence in just ten weeks' time, on August 15. The result was the beginning of a mass migration as Muslims and Hindus crossed the borders, the mayhem heightened by the fact that the exact borders had not yet been determined. For months it had seemed probable that Punjab would be split in two, and it had been a focus of violence since March. Now brutal atrocities here and in Bengal, where many people would also find themselves on the wrong side of a border, increased to a horrifying degree.

The Dominion of Pakistan and the Union of India came into being on August 14 and 15 respectively, and full responsibility for managing one

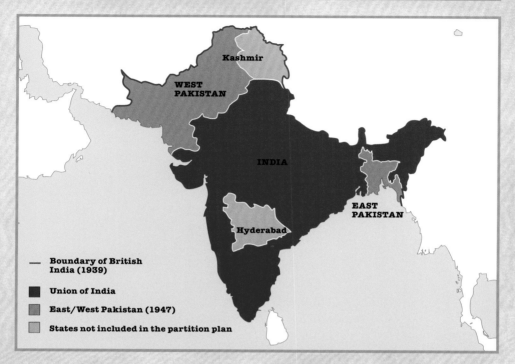

Kashmir

WEST
PAKISTAN

INDIA

EAST
PAKISTAN

Hyderabad

— Boundary of British
India (1939)

■ Union of India

■ East/West Pakistan (1947)

■ States not included in the partition plan

of the largest migrations in history fell upon the shoulders of the newly formed governments. It is estimated that approximately fifteen million people crossed the Pakistan/India borders in the months that followed, with roughly equal numbers moving in each direction. The army and the security services, in the process of being divided by religion and allocated to the new states, were unable to police the situation adequately. At least half a million Muslims, Hindus, and Sikhs were hunted down and killed by marauding groups that attacked cross-border trains and buses, as well as refugees traveling by foot, all trying to

DIVIDED

The greatest migration and the worst violence took place in the northwest, where Punjab was divided by the India/Pakistan border, and in the east, where the creation of East Pakistan split Bengal. Hyderabad became part of India in 1948, and Kashmir remains torn to this day, with control of the region being divided between Pakistan, China, and India.

make their way out of what had become, virtually overnight, enemy territory. The end of the Raj and the Partition of India may have been inevitable, but the speed at which they were accomplished came at a terrible human price.

At least half a million Muslims, Hindus, and Sikhs were hunted down and killed during the partition.

THE VIETNAM WAR

1955–1975

Main Culprits: American foreign policy officials

Damage Done: Caused untold economic, ecological, and humanitarian damage to Vietnam, and involved the US in its longest and most unpopular war

Why: To try—unsuccessfully—to prevent the spread of Communist ideology

In the course of the Vietnam War, which started in 1955, the United States was drawn into an ever greater commitment of manpower and weaponry in its support for the Republic of Vietnam (South Vietnam) against the Communist-led Democratic Republic of Vietnam (North Vietnam). At one point, more than half a million US troops were in Vietnam, actively fighting on the ground, but they were unable to defeat the guerrilla forces of North Vietnam. (Guerrilla forces are independent fighters who are not members of the government's military or police.)

As public sentiment in the United States grew increasingly opposed to US involvement in the war, the government was eventually forced to acknowledge that it could not be won. It had lasted almost twenty years and cost the lives of almost sixty thousand American servicemen but it was time to go. The last American troops were pulled out of the conflict in 1973, and the north and south regions were reunited as the Socialist Republic of Vietnam.

FRENCH INDOCHINA

By the end of the nineteenth century, France had colonial control over much of what are now Vietnam, Laos, and Cambodia, an area known at the time as French Indochina. In 1941, during World War II, the Communist revolutionary Ho Chi Minh led the Viet Minh independence fighters against the French and then, with support from China and the US, against the occupying Japanese. When Japan surrendered to the Allied Powers at the end of the Pacific War, many of the Japanese weapons ended up in the hands of the Viet Minh, who then opposed French attempts to re-establish control of the region.

The United States, led by Harry Truman, allowed the French to reassert their authority, and the French Indochina War began, but initially without active US support. However, fearing the spread of international Communism, the US began to fund the French war effort. Nonetheless, the French were unable to defeat the Viet Minh.

FRENCH INDOCHINA
A French Foreign Legion
soldier walks ahead of an
advancing tank. The French
were ultimately defeated by
the Viet Minh.

PEOPLE'S WAR

In 1955, in order to support
the independence of South
Vietnam, the US, under
President Dwight D.
Eisenhower, sent in its first
group of military advisers.
The US-backed presidency
of Ngo Dinh Diem ruthlessly
crushed any opposition.
A South Vietnamese rebel
group calling itself the Viet
Cong and using guerrilla
tactics against the forces of
Ngo Dinh Diem was quickly
suppressed and driven into
remote areas of the country.
After 1957 the North gave increasing
support to the rebels. In 1959 the North
Vietnam Communist Party authorized a
"People's War" against the South, with
support from the People's Army of
Vietnam (PAVN).

NAPALM AND AGENT ORANGE

In 1961, the year in which John F.
Kennedy's presidency began, violent
attacks against the South increased
dramatically, and although he was
opposed to deploying ground troops,
Kennedy sent in eighteen thousand
advisers and began supplying South
Vietnam with napalm incendiary jelly
(used in bombs), powerful chemical
defoliants such as Agent Orange (used to
clear forests and crops), helicopters, and
jet aircraft. These did little to lessen the

NORTH AND SOUTH

In peace negotiations, the French and the
Vietnamese agreed to temporarily divide
the north and south of the country on the
understanding that elections would take
place in 1956 prior to reunification of the
country. The Viet Minh under Ho Chi
Minh controlled the region of North
Vietnam, with their capital in Hanoi,
while the southern state of Vietnam,
with its capital in Saigon, was under
Emperor Bao Dai. His prime minister,
Ngo Dinh Diem, soon deposed the
emperor and took control himself.
With US backing, Ngo Dinh Diem then
refused to participate in elections as the
United States feared that Ho Chi Minh
would win the election and the whole
of Vietnam would then be under
Communist control.

JUNGLE WARFARE

US troops had little experience of the kind of warfare they were going to face in Vietnam. Although there were some conventional battles during the war, much of the conflict took place in dense jungle, giving the Viet Cong guerrilla fighters a decisive advantage. In an attempt to redress the balance, the US used napalm and chemical defoliants in vast quantities to try to destroy vegetation, villages, and crops, theoretically leaving the Viet Cong with no cover, no food, and no rural support.

successes of the Viet Cong, however, and the US began to lose faith in Diem's ability to defeat the Communist insurgency, which by now had Chinese backing. In 1963 Ngo Dinh Diem was murdered and his government was overthrown, to be replaced by a military coalition.

A PHONY BATTLE?

In the hope of a quick victory, the North Vietnamese PAVN increased its troop numbers to more than three hundred thousand, and by the end of 1964 it looked as though the Saigon government might collapse. However, President Lyndon B. Johnson had found an excuse to use military force without having to ask for congressional approval to declare war. On August 2, 1964, the USS *Maddox* was maneuvering off the coast of North Vietnam when it was apparently attacked by three North Vietnamese torpedo boats. In the ensuing sea battle, the Vietnamese ships were damaged, four of their crew were killed, one of the US planes was damaged, and the USS *Maddox* was hit by a single bullet. Two days later the *Maddox* and another ship reported another attack.

Before the day was over, President Johnson had broadcast the details to the American people and approved US Defense Secretary Robert McNamara's calls for retaliatory air strikes. He presented a resolution to Congress requesting the authority to conduct military operations in Southeast Asia, which Congress approved. This was a turning point in the Vietnam War—and it was founded on a fiction. In the case of the first attack, it was later revealed not only that the USS *Maddox* had been inside Vietnamese territorial waters but that the US ship had fired the first shot. As for the second attack, it hadn't taken place at all. The USS *Maddox*'s captain blamed "freak weather effects on radar and overeager sonar men" for the mistaken report. Robert McNamara had known this before Johnson gave permission for air strikes but hadn't told him.

TROOPS SENT IN

In any case, Johnson now had the authority he needed, and the US began a campaign of bombing North Vietnamese cities and industrial targets. By the end of 1965 there were 200,000 US troops in Vietnam, and this number eventually rose to more than 550,000.

Much of the conflict took place in dense jungle, giving the Viet Cong guerrilla fighters a decisive advantage.

In 1968 the Viet Cong adopted a new tactic. The Lunar New Year celebrations fell on January 30, and there was an agreed ceasefire in place. The Viet Cong, however, smuggled fighters, weapons, and explosives across South Vietnam and launched a major offensive, shooting and bombing civilians, attacking air bases and the US Embassy in Saigon. The fighting continued for more than a week, and several thousand South Vietnamese were killed. The Viet Cong lost an estimated forty-five thousand soldiers, but it was a political triumph. Scenes of the carnage had been broadcast in the US, and support for the war flagged, while the anti-war movement gained momentum.

ENGAGEMENT
Lyndon B. Johnson (center) and Robert McNamara (right) were selective in their use of the intelligence coming from the Gulf of Tonkin and brought the US into the Vietnam War.

US SOLDIERS COME HOME
In January 1969, Richard Nixon became president, and after initially increasing American involvement (including a massive bombing campaign in Cambodia), he implemented a policy of "Vietnamization," replacing US troops with Vietnamese troops and bringing the US soldiers home.

In 1973 US involvement in the war came to an end, although the government knew that without US support the Republic of Vietnam would soon be defeated. On April 30, 1975, Saigon fell to the North, and the two halves of the country were reunited as the Socialist Republic of Vietnam in 1976. The war had cost more than $100 billion, killed an estimated two million Vietnamese and fifty-eight thousand American soldiers, injured almost six times as many, deeply divided US public opinion—and achieved absolutely nothing.

FRANCE TRIES TO HOLD ON TO ALGERIA

1954–1962

Main Culprit: The French government

Damage Done: Led to the first conflict in which torture and brutal urban terrorism played a major role

Why: France didn't want to abandon more than a million French settlers in a country that would accept nothing less than independence

The French government's response to Algerian demands for greater say in government and ultimately for independence led to eight years of war and the deaths of thousands of native Algerians, European-Algerian settlers, and French military. Successive presidents failed to see they were fighting a losing battle.

France first began its invasion of the North African country of Algeria in 1830. By 1847 some fifty thousand French were settled in the country, farming land that had been confiscated. In 1848 Algeria was declared to be a part of France, and it was the only French colonial possession to be treated as a province in this way. After World War I, in which many Algerians fought for France, a movement calling for more rights for Algerians and a greater say in the running of their country began. Over the following decades several political parties were formed in Algeria with these aims on their agenda.

SÉTIF MASSACRE

The call for independence gained considerable momentum after an event that took place on May 8, 1945. In the town of Sétif, a parade by some five thousand native Algerians celebrating Victory in Europe Day turned into an anti-colonial demonstration. In clashes with the French police several protesters were shot and killed. In the riots that followed, more than a hundred French settlers were killed by Muslim Algerians. The French police and army then carried out revenge attacks, including the bombing of villages and the shelling of a coastal town by a naval gunship, in

[*"I will not agree to negotiate with the enemies of the homeland. The only negotiation is war!"*
—**French foreign minister François Mitterrand**]

Algeria to become an independent state with its own government within the French federal system, rather than being a province of France. The French government would not agree to this demand, and as attitudes on both sides hardened, the movement for Algerian independence gained strength. In the spring of 1954, the French were defeated in Vietnam, and in the aftermath the newly appointed prime minister Pierre Mendès-France negotiated French withdrawal from the region of Indochina. In Algeria, this prompted the Front de Libération Nationale (FLN) to launch armed attacks throughout the country on November 1, demanding a self-governing Algerian state. France responded by deploying troops, and French foreign minister François Mitterrand stated, "I will not agree to negotiate with the enemies of the homeland. The only negotiation is war!" Bloody All-Saints' Day, as it became known, marked the start of the Algerian War of Independence.

which several thousand Algerians were killed. The "Sétif Massacre" had a profound effect on relations between the two countries, and on the political climate in Algeria.

GROWING DEMAND FOR INDEPENDENCE

Faced with demands for radical reform to give greater equality to the Algerian people, the French government offered a range of concessions, including giving French citizenship to all Algerians. In 1946, however, the Democratic Union of the Algerian Manifesto called for

FEUDING GROUPS

The situation in Algeria was chaotic, with the Organisation de l'Armée Secrète and Front de Libération Nationale fighting each other and both using terrorist tactics against French government supporters in Algeria. There were also feuds between radical groups in Algeria. In France the battles were political, as new parties formed in support of French Algeria on one side and in opposition to the war on the other.

SAVAGE ATTACKS

The war escalated in August 1955 when the FLN launched an attack on the town of Philippeville. More than a hundred people were killed, including Muslim politicians, in acts of extreme savagery. At least a thousand (possibly several thousand) Muslim Algerians died in revenge attacks by both French troops and unofficial gangs of French settlers that followed swiftly. A year later, at the end of September 1956, the FLN began planting bombs in public spaces in the capital city of Algiers. The intention was to spread insecurity among the public and this was the first time that this tactic had ever been used. The French, in turn, resorted to torture and the swift execution of any troublemakers in order to stamp out the terrorists. This had the unintended effect of fueling a growing anti-war movement in France, and the French government now found itself caught between the conflicting wishes of its citizens at home and more than one million French settlers in Algeria.

INDEPENDENCE

Algerians take to the streets to celebrate the 1961 referendum in which voters opted for independence for Algeria.

CHARLES DE GAULLE

By 1958, French settlers and military leaders in Algeria were concerned that the socialist government in France was going to grant Algeria independence (Morocco and Tunisia had already gained their independence in 1955 and 1956 respectively). On May 13, 1958, the army seized power in Algeria.

unless power was handed over to de Gaulle the army would revolt and seize Paris. They weren't kidding, and fifteen hours before the deadline for implementing "Operation Resurrection" the government voted to hand power over to de Gaulle, which he accepted. The move was seen as a breakthrough by Algerians and French on both sides of the Mediterranean.

In June, de Gaulle visited Algeria, championing "French Algeria" and proposing a range of reforms to improve the situation for native Algerians. He also offered everyone the right to vote in a referendum on a new French constitution the following year. At the same time, the French military continued the war against the FLN and its military wing, the Armée de Libération Nationale (ALN). The FLN continued the terrorism in Algeria in an attempt to force the population to reject the referendum, and the ALN brought the terrorist war to France.

INTERNATIONAL CRITICISM

The political climate in France, meanwhile, was moving toward support for a much greater degree of independence for Algeria. The mood internationally was becoming increasingly critical of France's continued colonial domination, especially given the brutal methods being used to enforce it. In 1959 de Gaulle raised for the first time the possibility of "self-determination" for Algeria. Horrified

They demanded that Charles de Gaulle be installed as the French leader, in the belief that he would ensure the continued occupation of Algeria and its further integration with France. On May 24, French paratroopers from Algeria took the French island of Corsica, and army leaders declared that

French paratroopers from Algeria took the French island of Corsica, and army leaders declared that unless power was handed over to de Gaulle the army would revolt and seize Paris.

CEASEFIRE

As the French minister for Algerian affairs, Louis Joxe was a senior negotiator of the Évian Accords between France and the FLN, signed at Évian-les-Bains in 1962.

that a negotiated settlement and Algerian independence were now being discussed, French reservists (a military force made up of volunteer citizens) and settlers staged an uprising in Algiers early in 1960. However, the army and police, under orders not to fire on the rioters, remained loyal to the government. The ringleaders were arrested, but they were later involved in forming the French terrorist group known as the Organisation de l'Armée Secrète (OAS).

SEIZURE OF POWER

In January 1961, a referendum on independence for Algeria was held. Three-quarters of those who voted in France and Algeria opted for independence. This gave de Gaulle the backing he needed, and he entered into supposedly secret talks with the FLN. Senior figures in the French army, however, were still determined to prevent France from abandoning Algeria. In April they organized a coup (a seizure of power) that became known as the Generals' Putsch, intending to take control of Algeria first and then Paris. On the night of April 21, with the support of a thousand soldiers, they arrested key civil and military people in Algiers and took control of the country.

Within a year almost the entire French-Algerian population of over one million people had fled for France.

The French government had received intelligence reports on the uprising and was able to arrest its leaders in Paris, close all airfields around Paris, and order the army in France to hold off the takeover. President de Gaulle made a speech on the radio calling on all French people to come to the aid of their country, and commanding army conscripts not to accept orders from the rebel officers. By April 26 the coup had been crushed.

BODIES IN THE SEINE

Talks between the French government and the FLN continued, and in the course of 1961 the details of French withdrawal from Algeria were finalized. A ceasefire was to take effect on March 18, 1962, but the fighting was by no means over. The FLN embarked on a bombing campaign in France, and when some twenty thousand pro-FLN Algerians held a march in Paris in October 1961 the French police (apparently under orders from Prefect of Police Maurice Papon) carried out a massacre of some two hundred Algerians, throwing the bodies into the River Seine.

In the first half of 1962, the right-wing OAS and French Algerians made a last attempt to prevent the ceasefire and to block the creation of an independent Algeria in which the French Algerians would make up just 10 percent of the population. In March 1962, the month in which the ceasefire came into effect, the OAS exploded more than three thousand bombs in a campaign of urban terrorism designed to provoke the FLN group into breaking their part of the bargain, but they were largely unsuccessful. The French army and police were also targeted, as was de

Gaulle himself. On their way from central Paris to Orly airport on August 22, he and his wife survived one of many assassination attempts when OAS gunmen ambushed their motorcade and opened fire on the presidential car, riddling it with 140 bullets and killing two motorcycle bodyguards.

THE SUITCASE OR THE COFFIN

Following further referenda on Algerian independence in France and Algeria, where the vast majority voted in favor, de Gaulle declared Algerian independence on July 3. Although the French settlers were guaranteed protection, they were already leaving the country in droves, mindful of the Algerian nationalists' motto *La valise ou le cercueil*—"the suitcase or the coffin." Their fears proved to be well founded, as the FLN began a campaign of violence against the settlers, beginning with a massacre of Europeans in the town of Oran in which hundreds were killed. Within the year almost the entire French-Algerian population of over one million people had fled Algeria for France.

As many European colonies around the world gained their independence, the end of French colonial domination of Algeria had always been inevitable. It was the huge numbers of French settlers in Algeria and their withdrawal from the country that made the colony different from almost any other territory. The hostility between the various opposing sides led to a level of violence on an unprecedented scale. It is estimated that during the war and in its aftermath casualties may have been as high as a million Muslims and twenty-seven thousand French. The aftershocks are still being felt in French society today.

THE US FAILS TO TOPPLE CUBA AT THE BAY OF PIGS

April 1961

Main Culprit: The US government

Damage Done: The failed invasion brought Cuba and the USSR closer and revealed US involvement

Why: The US was responding to the perceived threat of Communism on its doorstep

When John F. Kennedy became president of the United States in January 1961 he inherited a plan that had been developed by the CIA (Central Intelligence Agency) and approved in its basic form by his predecessor, President Dwight Eisenhower. The plan was to bring about the overthrow of the recently installed Communist regime in Cuba and establish a government friendly to the US. Kennedy decided to go ahead with the plan, against the advice of senior government officials and mounting evidence that the plan was flawed. It resulted in the "Bay of Pigs" invasion of Cuba on April 17, a disastrous fiasco that left the US with egg on its face and strengthened ties between Cuba and the Soviet Union.

FIDEL CASTRO

In January 1959, the Cuban dictator Fulgencio Batista had been overthrown in an armed revolt led by Fidel Castro, who was now prime minister of the Communist-dominated Cuban government. In the US, the sweeping reforms taking place in Cuba, the reduction of civil rights, the imprisonment and execution of many thousands of objectors, and the closening relationship between Castro and Nikita Khrushchev, head of the Soviet Union, raised fears about the growing influence of Communism in the region. The US was also experiencing a massive influx of exiles from Cuba.

US COVER-UP

The US plan relied upon the Cuban people and some of the military supporting the invasion, and creating a popular uprising that would overthrow Castro and his government. Crucially, "deniability" had to be maintained—there could be no evidence that the US was directly involved—and with a plan on such a large scale this was a tall order. Within the White House fears were

"Deniability" had to be maintained—there could be no evidence that the US was directly involved.

expressed that there wasn't enough anti-Castro sentiment within Cuba and that the US involvement could not be kept secret. The US would then be seen as violating a host of international agreements as well as its own constitution.

Nonetheless, throughout 1960 some fourteen hundred Cuban exiles—to become known as Brigade 2506—were trained at several US military bases in Florida, Panama, and Guatemala. Elaborate preparations were made to cover up any US involvement, including the painting of six World War II B-26 attack bombers in the colors of the Cuban Air Force. A further twenty of these aircraft were prepared for the mission and four freighter ships, chartered for use in transporting the brigade, were fitted with anti-aircraft guns and landing craft.

The plan was for the invasion force to go ashore at the port of Trinidad on the south coast of central Cuba. This would mean that they could, if necessary, find shelter in nearby mountains, where counter-revolutionary forces were already active. When this location was rejected by the State Department, the CIA opted instead to stage the night landings in a swampy area some 60 miles (97 km) to the west, around the Bay of Pigs (Bahía de Cochinos). There was an airfield there and, being more remote, it was thought the Cuban forces would be less able to respond quickly to the invasion. However, the force would be a long way from any kind of shelter.

OPEN SECRET

The date for the invasion was set for April 17, 1961. Although the exact date was kept under wraps, the planned operation was an open secret, with articles even appearing in the US press,

JOHN F. KENNEDY
The new president went along with the plan to support an invasion of Cuba. It failed to achieve its objective and attracted international disapproval.

including *The New York Times*. There is evidence that Castro knew of the planned invasion as early as October 1960, that Cuba and the Soviet Union had more detailed information in the days prior to the invasion, and that the CIA knew they knew but did not inform President Kennedy.

UNITED NATIONS MISLED

At dawn on April 15, eight CIA B-26 bombers in Cuban Air Force colors took off from Nicaragua and bombed three Cuban airfields to put as many planes out of action as possible. The Cuban exile pilots reported a major success, but it was revealed the following day that they had largely missed their targets. However, Kennedy ruled against a further bombing run for fear that US involvement would be too obvious.

To keep the pretense up, another of the disguised planes, bearing the same number as one of the planes used in the bombing, its engine covers riddled with bullet holes, was flown to Miami where its Cuban pilot was granted political protection. This was to give the impression that he had defected (turned against the regime in Cuba) and that the raids on the Cuban airfields had been carried out by rebel Cuban Air Force personnel. When, at the United Nations, Cuba accused the US of orchestrating the bombing, the US Ambassador to the UN, Adlai Stevenson, was able to show photographs of the "Cuban" bomber on the runway in Miami and deny that the US had had any involvement. It was soon pointed out, however, that the nose of the plane differed from the planes used

COLD WAR TENSIONS

The 1950s had seen rising paranoia about the spread of Communism in the US. Cold War tensions and mistrust between the US and the Soviet Union had fueled this fear, which resulted in the pursuit and repression of thousands of suspected Communists during what became known as the "McCarthy era" (named after US Senator Joseph McCarthy). It was against this background that President Eisenhower had approved the CIA's plan to invade Cuba, and from March 1960 the CIA had been recruiting and training Cuban exiles in preparation for an invasion of their homeland.

Che Guevara is said to have sent a note to President Kennedy thanking him for the Bay of Pigs operation and saying, "Before the invasion, the revolution was weak. Now it's stronger than ever."

by Cuba, suggesting that the US was behind the event. Stevenson was not aware of the cover-up, but within a few hours it was obvious to all that he had been misled by the CIA and the White House.

DISASTROUS INVASION

The troops of Brigade 2506 left Nicaragua by ship on April 14 and reached the landing zone the night of April 16. A small military post was captured, but not before the Cubans there had radioed the armed forces and told them of the invasion. The landings took longer than expected; it was dark and coral reefs damaged the boats as they went ashore, and the Cuban forces responded much more quickly than expected. At dawn, six Cuban planes attacked the landing vessels and one, the *Houston*, was hit by rocket fire and forced to beach. The remaining troops on board went ashore without adequate equipment. An hour later, an airdrop of Brigade 2506 paratroopers and heavy equipment failed when the equipment fell into the surrounding swamp and the troops were unable to secure the road. Castro mobilized an estimated twenty thousand troops, and hundreds of Cuban militia reached the nearby town of Palpite by midday, forcing the invading troops to flee to the west. Over the next few days the fighting continued, with

US planes attacking Cuban supply convoys, including one carrying civilians. However, the Cuban Air Force dominated the skies.

By April 19 it was clear that the invasion force was in serious trouble and the White House authorized the sending in of six unmarked US fighter planes to defend the brigade's B-26 bombers, which arrived an hour after the fighter planes (probably due to a mistake about time zones), and two were shot down. The invasion force was overwhelmed the following day, with one hundred killed, almost twelve hundred taken prisoner, and a few dozen escaping to the coast to be picked up by waiting US ships. On the Cuban side, 176 soldiers were killed and several hundred were wounded. The prisoners were held for more than twenty months, returning to the US in late December 1962 in exchange for more than $50 million worth of medicine and baby food supplied by US manufacturers at the request of the US government.

EMBARRASSING FAILURE

The failed coup not only caused the US government severe embarrassment—the US was seen to have lied repeatedly to the UN and to have broken several international treaties, as well as elements of its own constitution—but it also increased support for the new government in Cuba. Furthermore, the Bay of Pigs strengthened ties between Cuba and the Soviet Union and may have helped to bring about the Cuban Missile Crisis, bringing the world to the brink of nuclear war.

BAHÍA DE COCHINOS
The Bay of Pigs was not a good place to land. The coast was reef-strewn and the bay was surrounded by swamps.

Havana

CUBA

Bay of Pigs

Guantánamo Bay

■ Communist-controlled Cuba

CHARLES DE GAULLE FACES DOWN THE STUDENTS

MAY 1968

Main Culprit: Charles de Gaulle and his brand of authoritarian government

Damage Done: Caused a small student protest to escalate into violent mass demonstrations and a national strike that brought the French economy to a standstill

Why: A stubborn unwillingness to listen to those calling for a re-examination of the government's policies

Charles de Gaulle came to power in France in 1958, and was inaugurated as the first president of the Fifth French Republic the following year. He brought welcome stability to a country that was tired of political infighting and indecision. He was re-elected in 1965, but his highly conservative and ultra-nationalistic style of politics was increasingly at odds with the changing times. This was an era of social change in Europe and the US, of anti-Vietnam War demonstrations, flower power, freedom of expression, pop music, and the miniskirt—which, incidentally, his equally conservative wife Yvonne tried to persuade him to ban in France.

OLD-STYLE GOVERNMENT
Against this backdrop there was growing discontent, particularly among students, with repressive aspects of the state, which controlled radio and television. They were also unhappy with the economic system of Western capitalism and with de Gaulle's old-fashioned, authoritarian style of government, especially in the fields of employment and education.

STUDENTS PROTEST
The events that were to shake French society to its core began on March 22, 1968, when some 150 students occupied a building in the University of Paris Nanterre. They were protesting against the French class system and government control of educational funding, and the university administration responded by calling in the police. The protest ended peacefully, but the conflict continued for several weeks until, on May 2, the administration closed the university and

This was an era of social change in Europe and the US, which contrasted sharply with de Gaulle's outmoded, authoritarian style of government.

threatened to expel the ringleaders. The following day, students at the Sorbonne university in Paris declared their solidarity with the Nanterre students and occupied a number of buildings. Police then invaded the university and it, too, was shut down.

This heavy-handed response exemplified state control of the education system, and on May 6 some twenty thousand students from the national students' union, supported by teachers, marched on the Sorbonne and confronted the police. They reacted with a baton charge and the situation turned violent as protesters—with some support from the local people—built barricades and hurled chunks of broken paving slabs at the police, who fired tear gas into the crowd and arrested hundreds of students. The following day the university students and teachers were joined by high-school students and workers in a rally at the Arc de Triomphe. Together, they called for the release without charge of all the arrested students, for an end to the police occupation of the Sorbonne, and for the reopening of Nanterre and the Sorbonne, none of which was granted.

FROM BAD TO WORSE

In the course of the following week, the numbers of protesters and the level of violence escalated dramatically. The Latin Quarter of Paris became a battlefield, as protesters hurled gasoline bombs and hundreds of police and demonstrators were injured. On the night of May 10, when negotiations once again failed, confrontations that lasted all night were covered live on radio, and television the following day showed footage of the events. The protesters had now occupied the Latin Quarter and forced the police to leave. The Communist Party of France and the main trade unions, unwillingly drawn into the clash, called a one-day general strike for Monday, May 13. More than a million people thronged the streets of Paris while

UNSWERVING
The political demands of the Paris students and the authoritarian General Charles de Gaulle met head on in the spring of 1968.

A NATION REAWAKENED

"In the afternoon, M. Mendès-France, the former President of the Council and, in his own right, probably the most universally respected political personality in the country, said that the Government must resign. By its comportment over the past ten years, he said, the Government had created a revolutionary situation. It could no longer resort to force without releasing tragic consequences; nor could it begin a useful dialogue with the masses who were rising against its policy... And he ended by paying tribute to the students and the young workers who had joined them to reawaken the nation."

— Nesta Roberts, Paris, May 19, 1968, writing in the *Guardian*

demonstrations sprang up in towns across the country. At this point General De Gaulle's prime minister Georges Pompidou agreed to the release of those who had been arrested and to the reopening of the Sorbonne. The protesters, however, were now in no mood for compromise, calling for a greater say in the workplace, in government, and in education. By the end of the week the Communist Party and the unions, which were seen as too willing to negotiate with the government, had lost control of the workers and more than two million were staging unofficial strikes. In the course of the next week, that number increased to a staggering ten million—two-thirds of the entire French workforce. When the trade unions negotiated a highly beneficial pay deal with the employers, the workers rejected it, as they did a subsequent offer from the Ministry of Social Affairs. They were seeking much more fundamental reforms of workers' rights.

TALKING ABOUT A REVOLUTION

By now the government was considering the use of force to put down what amounted to a rebellion and what might soon become a revolution, and the army was placed on standby. Georges Pompidou suggested that General de Gaulle dissolve the French government's National Assembly and call for a general election, but de Gaulle thought his party would lose and therefore refused. On May 29, acknowledging that the nationwide strikes and demonstrations were a challenge to his legitimacy as president, General de Gaulle packed his bags and took his family to the French military headquarters in Germany. Here he was reassured that the armed services would support him and he was persuaded to return to France the following day. By this time almost half a million people were marching through the streets of Paris celebrating his departure, but the rest of the country was more subdued.

In the course of a week, a staggering ten million French workers were staging unofficial strikes.

GENERAL STRIKE

Protests that began in the universities of Paris soon spread to workers throughout the country and to a general strike and march in Paris that attracted more than a million people.

De Gaulle's sudden disappearance had unnerved the people of France and given them pause for thought.

De Gaulle now accepted Pompidou's suggestion of dissolving the National Assembly and announced that there would be a general election the following month. He also stated that he would declare a national state of emergency unless there was a return to work.

GENERAL ELECTION

The crisis was over. As the election campaign got underway, the strikes and demonstrations subsided. To the surprise of many, de Gaulle's Union for the Defense of the Republic party won a landslide victory in the elections, as the nation recoiled from the chaos thrown up by the events of the previous month. The new government soon announced significant reforms to the education system, including the opening of more than sixty new universities and the introduction of a more democratic system of governing councils.

DE GAULLE RESIGNS

The election result was not, however, a vote for Charles de Gaulle. France after May 1968 was a different country, one that was more willing to embrace its own social changes and those taking place beyond its borders. The traditionalist, authoritarian de Gaulle was of the old school. In 1969 he lost a national referendum on political reform on which he had staked his reputation, and he resigned as president.

IDI AMIN EXPELS THE ASIAN POPULATION FROM UGANDA

1972

Main Culprit: Idi Amin, third president of the Republic of Uganda

Damage Done: Amin supervised the killing and torture of tens of thousands of Ugandans, the deportation of the entire Asian community, and the destruction of the Ugandan economy

Why: Ignorance, paranoia, megalomania, and merciless bloodthirstiness

The name of Idi Amin, the dictator of the East African country of Uganda from 1971 to 1979, is associated with corruption and inhuman brutality. During his years of rule at least one hundred thousand, and quite possibly more than a quarter of a million, Ugandans were executed for their personal or political opposition, for being members of the wrong tribe, or simply as a result of their leader's paranoia. Thousands more were tortured or imprisoned. Uganda's economy went into a dramatic decline and suffered rampant inflation, fueled by Amin's sudden decision to expel Uganda's highly successful Asian population—all fifty thousand of them. The mainstay of the country's trade and industry, many Asians also occupied key positions in the civil service. His action not only crippled Uganda's economy but also caused untold hardship for those who were forced to flee the country.

HEAVYWEIGHT SOLDIER AND BOXER

Born in northern Uganda in about 1925, Idi Amin began his military career with the British army, as a cook in the King's African Rifles. He rose through the ranks, fought for the British in Kenya during the Mau Mau revolt, and held the title of Ugandan heavyweight boxing champion throughout the 1950s. In 1961 he became a commissioned officer (only the second black Ugandan to do so) despite being almost completely uneducated and illiterate. In 1962 he led a force to northern Uganda to stop the theft of cattle by tribesmen from the Turkana region of Kenya where, it later came to light, his troops had tortured, murdered, and even buried alive the cattle rustlers. However, with Uganda about to be given its independence from Britain, and Amin being one of the

> During Amin's rule, at least one hundred thousand and quite possibly more than a quarter of a million Ugandans were executed.

country's few black officers, no action was taken against the overzealous leader of the "Turkana Massacre."

TAKING POWER

The new prime minister of Uganda, Milton Obote, clearly thought that Idi Amin displayed admirable qualities, for he made him Commander of the Ugandan Army and Air Force two years later, promoting him to Major General in 1968. However, relations between the two deteriorated and Amin was demoted in 1970. On hearing that Obote planned to arrest him on charges of stealing military funds, Amin decided to launch a military takeover of the government, which was successful.

TRUE COLORS

Promising elections and equality for all Ugandans, regardless of ethnic or tribal background, his self-proclaimed presidency was welcomed by the majority, but he soon showed his true colors. Obote

supporters within the security services were rounded up, tortured, and executed. The army was purged of members of the Acholi and Lango ethnic groups, possibly as many as six thousand of them, and their horribly mutilated bodies were dumped in forests and waterways. Anyone who spoke out against the atrocities became an immediate target, and that included the Anglican archbishop, Janani Luwum (whose body was found in a poorly simulated car crash), and Ben Kiwanuka, chief justice and leader of the Democratic Party.

TOLD TO LEAVE

Asians, who had been brought to Africa by the British Empire and almost all of them from India and Pakistan, made up

POWER MAD

With deluded self-importance and a vicious sadistic streak, Idi Amin plunged his country into a decade of bloodshed, oppression, and economic chaos.

the largest non-Ugandan ethnic group in the country. They faced considerable hostility under Obote's rule because of their economic success. Asians were involved in banking, clothing, farming, ranching, import/export, and some thriving industries, which gave rise to a great deal of envy, and Obote had made the most of this to demonize the Asian community. To Amin they were a convenient scapegoat and a potential source of wealth, and in 1972 he announced that God had spoken to him and instructed him to expel all Asians from the country. Amin accused them of purposely ruining the country's economy—which was far from the truth—and of sending all their money out of the country, which was partly true. The Asian population had been made to feel so insecure in Uganda that many had indeed chosen to send some of their hard-earned wealth overseas. On August 4 they were told they had to leave the country within ninety days, taking with them only what they could carry, or face the consequences. No compensation was offered for the businesses and homes they were being forced to abandon, and even as they were leaving on buses to get to the airport, valuables were taken from them. Many left with absolutely nothing and were forced to start from scratch in their new lives, about half of them in

The civil service degenerated into chaos and annual inflation reached 1,000 percent.

Britain (as they had UK passports), many in Canada and India, and the rest scattered around the globe.

MIDDLE CLASS ELIMINATED

The majority of the businesses and land, houses, cars, and personal possessions that they left behind were divided between Amin and his supporters, especially members of the army whom he needed to keep on his side. It has been estimated that more than five thousand business enterprises, including ranches and agricultural estates, were distributed in this way. At a stroke, Amin had virtually eliminated the Ugandan middle class, and their once-productive businesses were now in the hands of individuals and organizations that had neither the expertise nor the experience to run them properly. Production, distribution, and imports of goods were completely disrupted. When Amin decided in the following year to take over British-owned businesses (again, without any compensation, causing Britain to cut all ties with the country), the economic situation deteriorated rapidly. The civil service degenerated into chaos, annual inflation reached 1,000 percent, and even Uganda's principle export, coffee, went into decline because no money was reaching the growers.

AMIN FLEES TO LIBYA

In October 1978, turning his attention away from the country's economic hardships, Amin invaded Tanzania, with help from Libyan forces. His aim was to annex a portion of that country for Uganda. Under the leadership of President Julius Nyerere, Tanzania responded with a force that included several thousand Ugandan exiles.

LORD OF ALL THE BEASTS

"Excellency, President for Life, Field Marshal Al Hadji Doctor Idi Amin Dada, VC, DSO, MC, Lord of All the Beasts of the Earth and Fishes of the Seas and Conqueror of the British Empire in Africa in General and Uganda in Particular."

— Title bestowed upon himself by Idi Amin. He had never received the DSO or MC, but gave himself a Victoria Cross and a Doctorate in Law. He also claimed to be king of Scotland.

They successfully repelled Amin's troops, who were more focused on looting the towns and villages through which they passed than they were on fighting. The Tanzanian army advanced into Uganda, joined with the Ugandan National Liberation Army, and in April 1979 the capital Kampala was taken. Amin fled to Libya, where he stayed for ten years, and then to Saudi Arabia, where he died in 2003.

ASIAN REFUGEES MAKE GOOD

As for the dispossessed Asian refugees, some have returned to Uganda since Amin's downfall, but most have remained in their newfound homes and flourished. In the UK, for example, Asian families from East Africa made up the majority of small corner store owners, and a disproportionate number run their own multi-million-dollar businesses. For many countries, Uganda's loss has proved to be their gain.

PRESIDENT NIXON AND THE WATERGATE AFFAIR

July 1972–August 1974

Main Culprit: Republican US President Richard Nixon

Damage Done: Was forced to resign to avoid being charged with misconduct; shook America's trust in its political system (but not before time)

Why: He wanted to destroy the Democrats' chances in the forthcoming election, and was willing to allow the use of illegal methods to do it, as well as participate in the cover-up

It is amazing how often people in positions of power make risky decisions that they know could end in their downfall—and get caught. President Richard Nixon's use of unethical undercover operations to undermine the Democrats' election campaign and his involvement in a cover-up ultimately led to the greatest, and most public, fall from political grace in the history of America.

DEMOCRAT HQ BREAK-IN

The "–gate" ending that has been applied to the titles of so many scandals—from Irangate to Monicagate—has its origins in the Watergate Hotel and office building in Washington, D.C., where the Democratic Party had its headquarters in 1972. In the early hours of the morning of July 17, a security guard in the sixth-floor offices noticed that latches on several doors had been taped so that they would close without locking, and he called the police. Five men were caught photographing and stealing documents, and placing wiretaps (listening devices) on phone lines. They were arrested, charged in September, and convicted the following January, but their discovery was the start of a trail that was ultimately to lead to the president.

The break-in was part of an election campaign plan to bug, spy on, and generally sabotage the Democratic Party. The plan was put together by the Republicans' "Committee for the Re-election of the President" (CRP), which included former Attorney General John Mitchell and Presidential Counsel John Dean. The break-in operation had been coordinated by G. Gordon Liddy,

The break-in was part of an election campaign to bug, spy on, and generally sabotage the Democratic Party.

a former FBI agent, aided by E. Howard Hunt, a former CIA agent. They were both also involved in a secret security operation known as the White House Plumbers, the purpose of which was to prevent leaks of sensitive information from the president's administration to the media, and they had been using unofficial methods to achieve their goals. The FBI quickly discovered Hunt's name in the address books of two of the burglars, so to prevent the truth coming out, President Nixon ordered his chief-of-staff to get the CIA to block the FBI's investigation on the grounds of national security.

FLEETING POPULARITY

According to the journalist Hunter S. Thompson, Nixon was "a man with no soul, no inner convictions, with the integrity of a hyena and the style of a poison toad."

SMELLING A RAT

Two reporters with *The Washington Post* — Carl Bernstein and Bob Woodward — had already smelled a rat. With the help of an informant in the FBI (revealed more than thirty years later to be Mark Felt, the FBI's associate director), whom they referred to only as "Deep Throat," they soon began uncovering connections between the break-in and the Nixon administration. These included the fact that one of the burglars was a Republican Party security adviser (strenuously denied by John Mitchell), that a check in the account of another burglar had originally been given to Nixon's campaign fund, and that when he was attorney general, Mitchell had managed a fund that paid for secret information-gathering operations against the Democrats. By October, the FBI had established the connection between

Watergate and a large-scale undercover operation in support of Nixon's re-election, but that didn't prevent him from being re-elected the following month in a landslide victory.

UNDERCOVER JOB

By the spring of 1973, the word on everyone's lips was "cover-up," and at the highest levels. One of the burglars informed the judge who had overseen his trial that he had committed perjury (told an untruth while under oath), and that he and the others had been under pressure to do so. Another of the burglars told US attorneys that John Dean and John Mitchell had been involved. Nixon's advisers, meanwhile, were telling the attorney general that no one in the White House had had any prior knowledge of the break-in.

In April, US attorneys informed the president that his two most important advisers—John Ehrlichman and

MAN AT THE TOP

"In any organization, the man at the top must bear the responsibility. That responsibility, therefore, belongs here, in this office. I accept it. And I pledge to you tonight, from this office, that I will do everything in my power to ensure that the guilty are brought to justice and that such abuses are purged from our political processes in the years to come, long after I have left this office."

—Nixon's first Watergate Speech, April 30, 1973

There was no doubt that Nixon had been lying throughout the whole affair.

H. R. Haldeman—were involved in the cover-up, and Nixon then asked them for their resignations, going on TV to tell the nation what a difficult decision it had been. He also announced the departure of John Dean, whom he had fired.

NIXON TAPES

In the meantime, the Senate had approved the meeting of a special committee to investigate the Watergate affair, and it sat for the first time on May 17, 1973. The hearings were aired live on TV, shared between three networks. In June, a White House assistant revealed that President Nixon had had an automatic recording system installed in the Oval Office and other key areas, and that all conversations had been taped. The "Nixon tapes" were immediately requested at court, but the president refused to hand them over and ordered the special prosecutor to drop the request—which he refused to do. Nixon then used strong-arm tactics to have the special prosecutor dismissed, a highly unpopular move that increased the public's negative perception of the president. Suspicions were heightened when Nixon's lawyers disclosed that there was an eighteen-and-a-half-minute gap in the tapes, and his secretary's explanation that she had accidentally erased this section was widely disbelieved.

By March of the following year, seven of Nixon's advisers had been accused of obstructing the Watergate investigation, and the noose was drawing tighter.

ADDRESSING THE NATION
President Nixon after his televised address in April 1974. He sits beside transcripts of his secret tapes, which he was ordered to hand over at the end of July.

procedure to formally accuse (impeach) the president on the grounds of obstruction of justice, abuse of power, and contempt of Congress.

SMOKING GUN
A tape made shortly after the break-in was released by the White House on August 5, and it was the clincher. It soon became known as the "smoking gun," because it contained conversations with the president in which Haldeman discussed the Watergate burglaries and outlined the cover-up plan, and Nixon gave his approval. There was now no doubt that he had been lying throughout the whole affair, and it was clear that the impeachment of the president would have more than enough support to succeed. On August 8, seated in the Oval Office, he announced his resignation to the American people.

Soon after taking over as president, former Vice President Gerald R. Ford kindly pardoned Nixon of all charges in connection with the Watergate affair.

Nixon narrowly missed being accused with them, but he still maintained that he had known nothing about the break-in or the cover-up. In July 1974 the Supreme Court ordered Nixon to hand over the tapes to the special prosecutor, which he finally did at the end of the month. The contents did not reveal any specific offense, but they demonstrate the president's contempt for democratic government. It was clear, too, that he had approved of payments being made to the accused in the Watergate investigations, after the event if not before. In July, the House Judiciary Committee began the

ARGENTINA INVADES THE FALKLAND ISLANDS

April 2, 1982

Main Culprits: General Leopoldo Galtieri and the ruling military junta

Damage Done: Hundreds killed and injured

Why: To divert the attention of the Argentine people from social and economic problems at home and strengthen the position of the military government

A satellite image reveals two large and ragged barren islands fringed by a few smaller barren islands, one of which is named Barren Island. From the ground the picture is only slightly different. So what could possibly have prompted the Argentine government to contest Britain's rule of the remote and windswept Falkland Islands in the South Atlantic? There were actually several reasons, but one thing is certain: it was a bad decision.

ISLAS MALVINAS

After their discovery in the sixteenth century, the Falkland Islands (or Islas Malvinas to give their Spanish name) were claimed by the Spanish, the French, and the British, all of whom built settlements there in the course of the eighteenth century. When Argentina gained its independence from Spain in 1816 it claimed the Islas Malvinas as its own. In 1833, however, a disagreement with America over fishing and hunting rights led to US warships shelling the Argentine colony on the Falkland Islands, Puerto Soledad. Britain subsequently reclaimed the islands and in 1844 established a colony there, the immigrants coming largely from Scotland and Wales. Sheep farming became the staple of the economy, a harbor was built at Stanley, and the islands proved to have strategic importance during both the World Wars.

SEEDS OF WAR

Throughout this time, the issue of the Malvinas continued to rankle in Argentina, and when the United Nations was formed in 1945, Argentina took its grievance to the United Nations.

Galtieri thought it unlikely that Britain would commit
a military response to events happening on an insignificant
group of rocks some 8,000 miles from home.

Their claim to the islands was based on its geographical closeness to their country and the inherited rule from the Spanish, but it had little success. Nonetheless, the issue became a popular and important one to the Argentine people. Britain, meanwhile, was able to point to more than a hundred years of continuous and peaceful settlement by some two thousand loyal and strongly pro-British Falkland Islanders.

In the early 1980s, the Argentine ruling military was facing growing dissent from a populace suffering economic hardships and reduced civil rights. The Argentine president General Leopoldo Galtieri saw the Malvinas as a means to divert attention from the shortcomings of the government and rally the people behind him. He thought it unlikely that Britain would commit a military response to events on an insignificant group of rocks some 8,000 miles (13,000 km) from home. As a result, in the spring of 1982, Galtieri

SHEEP AND THE ISLANDS
Despite their inhospitable appearance, the Falkland Islands became an important piece in the political games of both Britain and Argentina.

decided to invade the Falklands and impose Argentine rule.

SOUTH GEORGIA

In March 1982, a group of some forty workers employed by an Argentine scrap metal merchant arrived on the island of South Georgia, situated in the southern Atlantic Ocean 800 miles (1,300 km) from the Falkland Islands. This was done with the knowledge of the British authorities. However, when the Argentines planted their national flag on the island, the British responded by dispatching their naval ship, HMS *Endurance*, from the Falkland town of Stanley with half the garrison's forces — twenty-two Royal Marines and one Lieutenant. Argentina, however, sent a warship and landed a hundred troops to "defend" its nationals, and the British forces had little choice but to move back and observe.

GALTIERI INVADES

On April 2, using South Georgia as justification, four thousand Argentine troops landed on East Falkland Island and Stanley was occupied. On hearing this news, the marines on South Georgia surrendered to the Argentines.

At this point, Galtieri perhaps thought the islands were his for the taking, but he had failed to take into account both the character of the British prime minister Margaret Thatcher and her own need for popularity in the light of a forthcoming general election.

THATCHER'S RESPONSE

Britain moved quickly to gain support from international bodies, including the United Nations, which passed a resolution calling for an end to hostilities. At the same time, Britain, under the leadership of Margaret Thatcher, launched its military response: "Operation Corporate." A British naval taskforce, consisting of twenty warships, eight amphibious ships, and a supply fleet of forty vessels, was soon on its way. The task force was made up of some fifteen thousand personnel, including a landing force of seven thousand marines and soldiers.

On April 12 Britain declared a 200-mile (320-km) Total Exclusion Zone

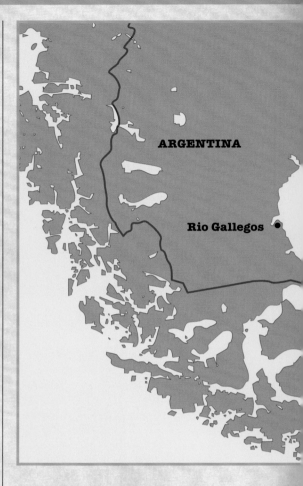

The sinking of the Argentine cruiser *General Belgrano* led to a loss of more than three hundred lives.

around the Falklands Islands, to block the movement of troops and supplies from Argentina. This was also enforced by three nuclear-powered attack submarines that had already reached the area. The US had, in the meantime, put forward peace proposals but these were rejected by Argentina, and by the end of April the US was giving both diplomatic and military support to Britain.

On April 25 British marines, under cover of naval gunfire, retook South Georgia from the occupying Argentine garrison, and by the end of April several

TOTAL EXCLUSION ZONE

The Falkland Islands

British aircraft carrier ships and warships had reached the Falkland Islands. With winter approaching, British military operations began on May 1 with bombing raids on the runway at Stanley to prevent Argentine planes from using it.

SINKING OF THE *BELGRANO*

The following day, the British nuclear submarine *Conqueror* fired three torpedoes at the Argentine Navy cruiser *General Belgrano*, sinking the ship with the loss of more than three hundred lives. The event

EXCLUSION ZONE
The British declaration of a no-go area around the Falklands succeeded in preventing the Argentine navy from operating in the area.

proved to be a contentious one, with critics pointing out that the ship was outside the Exclusion Zone and was possibly headed toward the South American coast rather than toward the islands. The British navy maintained that the ship posed a potential threat, and senior figures in the Argentine military

CONSCRIPTS VERSUS CAREER SOLDIERS

The British troops, made up of experienced career soldiers who had trained under conditions similar to those found on the islands, had a real advantage. The Argentine troops were young and poorly trained conscripts led by an elitist officer class that did all it could to avoid the hardships of the battlefield. In the absence of adequate leadership, the inexperienced Argentine soldiers were all too ready to fall back when British troops advanced on them.

agreed that the sinking was legal in the context of the hostilities. In any case, the Argentine navy retired to coastal waters for the rest of the conflict and efforts were focused on airborne attacks launched from the Argentine mainland.

HMS *SHEFFIELD* AND SURRENDER

Two days later, on May 4, Britain's HMS *Sheffield* was struck by a missile fired from an Argentine fighter, causing a major fire, killing twenty crew members and seriously injuring twenty-four others. The Argentine Air Force continued to inflict considerable damage on the British vessels that now surrounded the islands, but also suffered significant losses. On May 21 British commandoes landed on the island by helicopter and amphibious craft. Over three weeks the troops advanced across the difficult terrain, taking Argentine positions while aircraft from both sides fought overhead and

SURVIVORS
When HMS *Sheffield* was struck by an Exocet missile on May 4, 1982, the resulting fires caused serious injuries to many of the crew. The ship sank six days later.

British ships and Harriers shelled and bombed strategic targets. The British suffered a major setback on May 25 when an Exocet missile sank the vessel carrying most of the task force's troop-

British landing craft, killing fifty soldiers and injuring many more. Nonetheless, by early morning on June 14 the Argentines had lost all the high ground and the commandoes were on the outskirts of Stanley, where some eight thousand Argentine troops were effectively trapped. At 9:30 that evening, after several hours of negotiations, the Argentine forces formally surrendered.

END RESULT

The outcome had been by no means a foregone conclusion. The logistical difficulties of conducting a British military operation so far from home were considerable. The Argentine Air Force, who were widely praised for their bravery and professionalism, also had problems operating at the limit of their fuel range and lost more than half of their combat aircraft in the conflict. These, then, are some of the factors that made invading the Falklands a bad idea. Even if the territory could have been held by the Argentines, the level of casualties was unacceptably high, with Argentine losses put at 635 killed and 1,068 wounded, and British losses of 255 killed (including three Falkland Islanders) and 777 wounded.

For the Argentine ruling military junta, the invasion was also a bad decision because the defeat ultimately led to its downfall. For the Argentine people, the silver lining was a gradual return to democratic rule, and in 1983 Margaret Thatcher reaped the reward of a second term in office.

carrying Chinook helicopters. Twelve seamen were killed and soldiers were forced to make a 60-mile (100-km) march across East Falkland Island. On June 4 Argentine bombs struck two

The defeat ultimately led to the downfall of the Argentine military junta and a gradual return to democratic rule, while in the UK Margaret Thatcher reaped the reward of a second term as prime minister.

IRAQ INVADES KUWAIT

August 2, 1990

Main Culprit: President Saddam Hussein

Damage Done: Cost the lives of thousands of Kuwaiti civilians and Iraqi military, and devastated the oil fields of both countries

Why: Saddam Hussein mistakenly thought he could annex Kuwait without incurring a military response

When the Iran-Iraq War ended in August of 1988—a fruitless and costly war started in 1980 by Iraq under the leadership of President Saddam Hussein—Iraq found itself in a very serious economic situation. The war had brought economic growth within the country to a standstill, and oil production in the Basra oil fields had been seriously disrupted. The cost of the war had been astronomic and Iraq had borrowed heavily. It now had an international debt of more than $130 billion, $14 billion of which it owed to its neighbor Kuwait. Their financial support for Iraq had resulted in Iranian reprisals and repeated attacks on Kuwaiti oil tankers in the Persian Gulf. Now that the war was over, however, tensions between Iraq and Kuwait were mounting, for several reasons.

OIL FIELDS
Unable to pay back the loans, Iraq requested Kuwait (among others) to cancel its debt, which Kuwait refused to do. Kuwait also refused Iraq's request to reduce its oil production. Iraq was desperate to get as high a price as possible for the small amount of oil that it was producing. Kuwait's much bigger output was keeping oil prices down and was costing Iraq billions of dollars a year. High-level talks continued at OPEC (an association of oil-producing countries in the region) while Iraq steadily built up the numbers of its troops along the border with Kuwait. When Iraq accused Kuwait, whose border cut through the Rumaila oil field, of using slant drilling techniques to extract oil from Iraqi territory, this was seen by outside observers as part of an Iraqi plan to further its territorial ambitions and gain control of the oil supplies. On July 25, 1990, OPEC announced that Kuwait had agreed to limit its oil production, but by this time Iraq had around one hundred thousand of its troops positioned along the border.

IRAQ INVADES
At a meeting between Iraq and Kuwait, held in Saudi Arabia on August 1, negotiations quickly degenerated into disagreement. On the following day, Iraq invaded Kuwait. Despite worsening

> *"The war will end in dignity, glory, and triumph."*
> —Saddam Hussein in a radio broadcast, January 19, 1991

diplomatic relations over the preceding months and the large numbers of troops massed on the border, the invasion took the Kuwaiti military by surprise. As Iraqi armored divisions and mechanized infantry troops headed for Kuwait City, helicopter gunships and transport helicopters carrying commandoes began an assault on the city, as well as taking airbases and airports. Iraqi planes quickly gained supremacy in the air, and one fifth of the Kuwait Air Force's planes were lost before the remainder flew to bases across the border in Saudi Arabia. The deposed emir of Kuwait and the royal family, along with senior government officials and many of the retreating military, also sought refuge there. Within forty-eight hours Iraq had control of the entire country, and Saddam soon installed a "Provisional Government of Free Kuwait," annexing the country as Iraq's nineteenth province.

SADDAM HUSSEIN

The oppressive ruler of Iraq invaded Kuwait as a means of gaining oil-rich territory for his country and avoiding the repayment of financial debts owed to Kuwait.

OPERATION DESERT SHIELD

Condemnation of the invasion by the international community—including countries formerly friendly toward Iraq—was instant. The United Nations Security Council passed Resolution 660, calling for the unconditional withdrawal of all troops from Kuwait. At the same time, the Arab League called for a solution to the crisis without the intervention of non-Arab nations. The banning of arms and economic sanctions (commercial penalties) followed, and the UN authorized a naval blockade to achieve these. On August 7, in response to a request by King Fahd, the US sent troops to Saudi Arabia, a country with justifiable fears about Iraqi aggression. It shared a long border with Iraq, its oil fields were within easy reach of the Iraqi forces, and, like Kuwait, it was owed many billions of dollars by Iraq after the Iran-Iraq War. This was the start of Operation Desert Shield, ultimately leading to the stationing of more than half a million US troops in Saudi Arabia.

UN GIVES DEADLINE

On August 12, Saddam Hussein sought a compromise solution, linking Iraq's withdrawal from Kuwait to the withdrawal of Israel from the occupied Palestinian territories, and calling for all US troops in Saudi Arabia to be replaced by Arab forces. The US, anxious that Iraq should in no way be rewarded for its actions, was opposed to any such linkage and remained adamant that the Iraqi withdrawal be unconditional. Various other compromise proposals by Saddam met with a similar response over the next few months, and on November 29 the UN gave Iraq a deadline of January 15, 1991, after which force would be used to remove Iraqi troops from Kuwait.

OPERATION DESERT STORM

By the time that date was reached, thirty-four countries had joined the US in a coalition, prompted not only by outrage at Iraq's initial act of aggression but also by the perceived threat to Saudi Arabia and other Middle East countries. There were also reports of human rights violations within Kuwait (some of which later turned out to be false), and by Iraq's use of chemical and biological weapons. Some of the participants were undoubtedly swayed by financial incentives or by threats to withdraw aid. Operation Desert Storm began on January 16, 1991, with an air campaign that lasted thirty-eight days and targeted

Iraq suffered at least twenty thousand military casualties and thousands of Kuwaiti civilians had lost their lives.

GREEN LIGHT?

On July 25, 1990, at a meeting requested by Saddam Hussein at the presidential palace in Baghdad, the US ambassador to Iraq, April Glaspie, asked the president for an explanation for the military build-up on the Kuwait border. Saddam replied that unless Iraq's dispute with Kuwait could be settled through negotiations then he would be unwilling to give up his goal of controlling the whole of the Shatt al-Arab waterway "to defend our claims on Kuwait to keep the whole of Iraq in the shape we wish it to be. What is the United States' opinion on this?" According to one version of the transcript of this conversation, US Ambassador Glaspie replied, "We have no opinion on your Arab-Arab conflicts, such as your dispute with Kuwait. Secretary of State [James Baker] has directed me to emphasize the instruction, first given to Iraq in the 1960s, that the Kuwait issue is not associated with America." Opinions are divided over whether or not these words gave Iraq the "green light" to invade Kuwait. (Ambassador Glaspie later said that she did not think that Iraq intended to annex the whole of Kuwait, possibly implying that the US did think Iraq might attempt to push its border south to encompass the Rumaila oil field.) In any case, Saddam apparently smiled at this response.

the Iraqi Air Force, anti-aircraft defenses, missile launchers, and the Iraqi navy. The attacks—conducted in both Kuwait and Iraq—utterly disrupted Iraq's military and destroyed morale. The ground campaign was launched on February 23, and within one hundred hours Kuwait City was in the hands of coalition and Kuwaiti forces as the Iraqis retreated northward, setting fire to hundreds of Kuwaiti oil wells, and thousands of Iraqi troops surrendered. Coalition forces followed the retreating army into Iraq before declaring a ceasefire on February 28. In April, Iraq agreed to UN terms for a permanent ceasefire, which included the destruction of all stockpiled weapons.

PUBLIC ENEMY NUMBER ONE

The occupation of Kuwait had lasted seven months, Iraq had suffered at least twenty thousand military casualties and huge financial costs, thousands of Kuwaiti civilians had lost their lives, the oil fields of both countries had been

MILITARY RESPONSE

A coalition of nations sent in troops to free Kuwait from Iraqi occupation. Operation Desert Storm lasted less than six weeks.

devastated, and Saddam Hussein had made himself public enemy number one. The international community continued to view Saddam in this light especially when there was mounting evidence that he was developing weapons of mass destruction. Removing Hussein from office became official US foreign policy in 1998, and after the September 11 attacks on the US in 2001, President Bush announced his "War on Terror." A US-led invasion of Iraq was launched on March 20, 2003, and by early April the coalition force had occupied much of Iraq. Saddam fled and was later captured in December 2003. He was imprisoned and eventually found guilty of crimes against humanity in 2006 and hanged on December 30 that year.

MARGARET THATCHER INTRODUCES THE POLL TAX

1989–1990

Main Culprit: Margaret Thatcher

Damage Done: Lost her the leadership of the Conservative Party

Why: She had become overconfident and failed to see that the policy was seen as deeply unfair by the general public

When King Richard II of England introduced a head, or "poll," tax in 1377 it was, to say the least, unpopular. When he tripled the tax fourteen years later and insisted that some poor people pay the same amount as the wealthy, it ignited the smoldering discontent that the peasants felt for the landowners and the governing classes. The outcome was the Peasants' Revolt. In June 1381, armed peasants from the counties of Kent and Essex met in London, where they stormed the Tower of London and captured the Lord Chancellor, Simon Sudbury, and the Lord High Treasurer, Robert Hales. The two men, seen as the prime movers in the poll tax, were later beheaded at Tower Hill. Margaret Thatcher, British prime minister from 1979 to 1990, might not have championed the "community charge" had she studied history at Oxford instead of chemistry.

CONSERVATIVE THINKING

Prior to the general election of 1987, local government services in the United Kingdom were funded by a property tax called rates, an annual sum payable by every house owner on the basis of an assessed rental value for the property. It may not have been perfect, but it had been in place for almost four hundred years and it worked.

To Margaret Thatcher, however, the rates tax was not in line with Conservative thinking. It meant that the wealthy paid more, the poorest paid nothing, and the middle class, who could be seen as the core of her popular support, were paying for the services being provided to those at the bottom of the social scale. It had to be changed. Indeed, the rates system of tax had been in her sights since 1974, five years before she became prime minister. It had also been part of the Conservative Party manifesto (a public declaration of party policies and aims) since then.

> To Margaret Thatcher, the rates system of tax was not in line with Conservative thinking. It had to be changed.

COMMUNITY CHARGE

In 1986, a government Green Paper proposed that the rates should be replaced by a community charge, a flat-rate tax paid by every adult regardless of their income. In other words, a poll tax. Margaret Thatcher was fully in support of this and the proposed change became part of the Conservative manifesto prior to the 1987 general election. It clearly did appeal to a majority of voters, as the Conservatives won the election and came to power for a third four-year term.

The community charge was introduced in Scotland in 1989, and in England and Wales in 1990. It didn't take those same voters long to realize that the poll tax, even with reductions for students, the elderly, and the very poor, was outrageously unfair, as the opposition Labour Party quickly pointed out. While the wealthy in large and expensive homes would find themselves paying less, large families in small homes would pay more—sometimes far more, as it turned out.

BATTLE OF TRAFALGAR

Even before the tax was officially introduced, opposition to it was being voiced in Scotland and then throughout the UK, and anti–poll tax unions were formed to make those voices heard. In November 1989, the All Britain Anti–Poll Tax Federation was set up to coordinate the protest, and in the spring of 1990 a march was organized for Saturday, March 31, a few days before the introduction of the community charge in England and Wales. The march, from Kennington on the South Bank of the Thames in London, was to end with a rally in Trafalgar Square.

THE IRON LADY
Although she was renowned, and sometimes admired, for her strong will, Thatcher's refusal to give way on the community charge was politically foolish.

Trafalgar Square can hold about sixty thousand people. Police estimates put the size of the crowd that marched at around two hundred thousand. The result was chaos, as demonstrators crowded into the square and the length of Whitehall, which runs past Downing Street and the prime minister's residence. As police and mounted riot police attempted to control the crowd, violence broke out, and throughout the evening and the course of the night London saw its worst rioting in more than a hundred years. Over a hundred people (including police) were injured, some of them seriously, and there were several hundred arrests.

A LADY NOT FOR TURNING

Although, throughout her occupancy of 10 Downing Street, Margaret Thatcher attracted more than her fair share of criticism, even hatred, no one has ever doubted that she was a woman of principle. Far from caving in to pressure from the public, and even from her colleagues, to drop the tax, she made keeping it a matter of personal pride. She effectively nailed the community charge firmly to her own masthead as well as that of the Conservative Party and ignored the question of whether, at a certain point, principle should perhaps give way to common sense or fairness.

TRAFALGAR

In March 1990, a protest rally in central London turned nasty as police tried to control unexpectedly large numbers of people. Rioting continued through the night, vehicles were burned, and stores were looted.

As chance would have it, while the riots were in progress, the prime minister was attending a Conservative Party conference at which the community charge was the central topic. The evident unpopularity of the tax raised the first ripples of doubt about Margaret Thatcher's leadership.

TIDAL WAVE OF "CRIMINALS"

In the following months, anti–poll tax unions urged people not to pay the community charge. Many, up until then, law-abiding citizens—up to 30 percent of them in some districts—followed the

[
"I fight on. I fight to win."

—Margaret Thatcher just before she was forced to resign, 1990
]

calls and refused to pay. Councils, police, and the courts were wholly unprepared and unable to deal with such a tidal wave of "criminals."

This was just one of the unforeseen hiccups in implementing the tax. Whereas the rates had been levied on homeowners, the poll tax applied to all adults. Tracking down the portion of society that were living in rented accommodation, many of whom moved around a lot, proved to be a mammoth task and greatly increased the cost of collecting the tax.

FORCED TO RESIGN

As non-payment of the tax increased and polls showed that a vast majority of the British people (98 percent in one poll) were opposed to the community charge, the Conservatives' popularity plummeted in the opinion polls. Much of the discontent was directed at Margaret Thatcher and she began to look like a problem for the Conservative Party. In November of 1990, Michael Heseltine challenged her in a leadership election and received 40 percent of Parliament's vote, which didn't give Thatcher enough of a margin for an outright win. Rather than risk probable defeat in a second ballot, Margaret Thatcher resigned as prime minister and party leader.

The subsequent leadership election was won by John Major. Michael

Heseltine was appointed as environment secretary and given responsibility for replacing the community charge. The following March, the introduction of the council tax—a tax based on the market value of a householder's property—was announced, and it came into force in 1993. It is not unlike the rates system.

RESIGNATION

Margaret Thatcher faces the press on the steps of Downing Street. She was finally forced to resign after failing to win a big enough majority in a leadership election.

A vast majority of the British people were opposed to the poll tax and the Conservatives' popularity plummeted.

THE UN FAILS TO PREVENT GENOCIDE IN RWANDA

1994

Main Culprit: The countries of the United Nations Security Council

Damage Done: The brutal rape and slaughter of three-quarters of the Rwandan Tutsi population

Why: A failure to recognize the dreadful nature of what was happening, and a lack of political will to intervene

In 1994, despite abundant evidence that the Hutu people were carrying out an organized wholesale massacre of the Tutsi people, the United Nations Security Council refused to take the necessary steps to prevent it. The carnage that followed left a stain on the reputation and credibility of the United Nations.

HUTU-DOMINATED STATE

When the territory of Rwanda fell under German colonial control at the end of the 1800s, the two largest ethnic groups in the country were the Hutus and the Tutsis. The Hutus, who were mostly farmers, were by far the bigger group. The Tutsis were cattle herders and of higher status, but there was some fluidity in the different groups and a Hutu that became a cattle owner effectively became a Tutsi. The Germans, and later the Belgians, nonetheless established their

own system of rules. They gave greater political power to the Tutsis, whom they felt to be more "European-like" as they were lighter skinned and taller than the Hutus. The Belgians insisted that everyone must have an identity card stating whether they were Hutu or Tutsi, based on how many cattle they owned. In addition, Tutsis were generally more willing to convert to Catholicism, and were therefore given greater opportunities for education. The overall effect was to make the ethnic divisions in the society more rigid.

Throughout the 1950s, Hutu resentment against the ruling Tutsi minority grew. Assaults on Hutu political leaders in 1959 led to the Hutus killing tens of thousands of Tutsis. Some 150,000 Tutsis were exiled to the neighboring countries of Burundi, Tanzania, and Uganda, and a policy of deliberate discrimination against the Tutsis in Rwanda was put in place. Over the next thirty years, Tutsis were increasingly excluded from professional employment and positions of influence, until Rwanda became a one-party, Hutu-dominated society.

The only thing necessary for the triumph of evil is for good men to do nothing.

HUTU/TUTSI CONFLICT

Similar Hutu/Tutsi conflicts had raged in neighboring Burundi in the 1970s, and there were three years of war in the 1990s in Rwanda during which both sides committed numerous human rights violations. Eventually a peace agreement was signed in August 1993. The agreement called for the establishment of a transitional government in Rwanda, for the reunification of the army, and for a United Nations peacekeeping force to oversee the process.

Many Hutus, however, were opposed to the agreement, and as ethnic tensions rose, the Hutu-led government used print media and state radio stations to spread anti-Tutsi propaganda and incite racial hatred. They referred to

COLONIAL DIVISIONS

Rwanda's tribal problems date back to the early period of colonization. Count Gustav Adolf Von Götzen, one of the first Germans to set foot on Rwandan soil, was governor of German East Africa in the early 1900s.

the Tutsis as "cockroaches," claiming that they intended to enslave the Hutus, and blamed them for the country's economic problems.

KILLING GROUPS

Aware that the situation was likely to become violent, in October 1993 the UN Security Council established the United Nations Assistance Mission for Rwanda (UNAMIR) under the leadership of Canadian general Roméo Dallaire. It took contributing nations five months to supply the twenty-five hundred troops needed. In December 1993, General Dallaire was warned that the powerful Hutu elite had formulated a plan to hold onto power by eliminating the Tutsis. The Rwandan Armed Forces and seventeen hundred militia in organized civilian "killing groups" had been armed with rifles and grenades, and more than half a million machetes (a broad, heavy knife) had been imported. The UN, however, told Dallaire that he could not interfere in the internal affairs of the country unless an act of genocide was being perpetrated. (Genocide is defined as the deliberate killing of a large group of people, especially those of a particular ethnic group.) Meanwhile the anti-Tutsi media statements, as well as propaganda inciting the rape of Tutsi women, increased over the next few months.

HUTU PRESIDENTS MURDERED

On April 6, 1994, an event took place that lit the fuse. The Rwandan president and the president of Burundi, both Hutus, were killed as their plane, hit by missiles, crash-landed at the airport in Kigali, the capital of Rwanda. The task of leadership now fell to the prime minister, Agathe Uwilingiyimana, but her

authority was disputed by the army and especially by Colonel Bagosora, who was the prime mover behind setting up and arming the "killing groups." General Dallaire sent ten Belgian peacekeepers to guard Uwilingiyimana's home. During the night of April 7, however, soldiers and the presidential guard disarmed the Belgians and then shot Uwilingiyimana and her husband. The Belgian soldiers were murdered later that day.

WHOLESALE SLAUGHTER

Then the killing began in earnest, an organized countrywide effort to eliminate as many Tutsis as possible from Rwanda. As mass violence broke out on an unprecedented scale, the UN directed Dallaire and UNAMIR to help in the evacuation of foreign nationals. Shortly afterward, the United Nations ordered the withdrawal of all but 270 of the peacekeepers, despite Dallaire's reports on what was happening and his requests for an additional fifty-five hundred peacekeepers to prevent the slaughter. The US actually called for all UNAMIR troops to be withdrawn and refused to

When a peacekeeping force was removed from a school in which two thousand Tutsis, including many children, were seeking shelter, the Hutus waiting outside rushed in and murdered every one of the refugees.

use its technology to block the radio stations broadcasting racial hatred.

In the course of the next hundred days, an estimated eight hundred thousand people—mainly Tutsis, but also moderate Hutus who tried to help them—were shot or literally hacked to pieces by the army, the killing groups, and by Hutu civilians forced at gunpoint to murder their neighbors. Tutsi women and girls, as many as five hundred thousand of them, were brutally and systematically raped.

TOO LITTLE TOO LATE

General Roméo Dallaire and his utterly inadequate force of peacekeepers did their best to create safe areas in which they could protect would-be victims of what was now quite clearly an act of genocide. They succeeded in saving tens of thousands of Tutsis, but Dallaire's reports and pleas for additional support were largely ignored by the UN. The member countries were unwilling to become caught up in something that they refused to accept was genocide. Such an acknowledgment would have required them to respond with money and manpower. Finally, after five weeks of horrifying violence, the UN did vote to send in the requested 5,500 extra peacekeepers, but by the time they had been mobilized it was too late.

As the genocidal war against the Tutsis raged, a civil war was taking place between the Rwandan Armed Forces and the Rwandan Patriotic Front. By mid-July the RPF had succeeded in taking control of the country and only then did the genocide come to an end. It was replaced by the mass fleeing of some two million Hutus into Zaire and other neighboring countries, creating overcrowded and disease-ridden refugee camps.

NO ONE CAME

"Twelve years ago in a small African country a group of citizens met and decided the only way they could maintain power was to simply eliminate 1.2 million people by mutilation killing. A hundred days into the genocide, they had slaughtered 800,000 and over 3 million had been displaced and refugeed of which not only the Tutsis but the moderate Hutus who supported them also suffered. And no one came."

—**Excerpts from a speech given by General Roméo Dallaire at the national commemoration of Holocaust Memorial Day in Cardiff, Wales, on January 26, 2006**

UN TO BLAME

The UN commissioned its own inquiry into the events of 1994, and its results were made public in December 1999. The report concluded that responsibility for the failure to halt the 1994 genocide in Rwanda lay with the UN system, members of the UN Security Council— the US and UK in particular—and other UN member states. It also stated that the UN mission had not been planned, deployed, or instructed in a way that would have enabled it to stop the genocide. UNAMIR, it said, was the victim of a lack of political will in the Security Council and by other members. In the report's words, "This international responsibility is one which warrants a clear apology by the organization and by the member states concerned to the Rwandese people."

MASSACRE AT SREBRENICA

July 1995

Main Culprits: Bosnian Serb soldiers, paramilitary, and police

Damage Done: Mass murder of thousands of Bosnian Muslim men and boys, forced deportation of women and children, and widespread rape

Why: The horrific and unjustifiable crimes committed by the Serbian troops made no sense on military grounds, and can only be viewed as acts of ethnic hatred

In 1991, the Republic of Bosnia and Herzegovina was part of the Socialist Federal Republic of Yugoslavia, which had been formed at the end of World War II. Its population was made up principally of 43 percent Muslim Bosnians (later known as Bosniaks), 31 percent Orthodox Christian Serbs, and 17 percent Croats, who are mainly Catholic. These three groups were represented by three parties in the democratically elected coalition government.

THE BREAK-UP OF YUGOSLAVIA

In the fall of 1991, the parliament of Bosnia and Herzegovina passed a resolution as a first step toward declaring its independence from Yugoslavia. It faced opposition from all the Serbian delegates, who then formed their own "Assembly of the Serb People in Bosnia and Herzegovina." The following January the Serb assembly proclaimed the Republic of the Serb People of Bosnia and Herzegovina, creating four separate administrative districts in areas of Bosnia and Herzegovina where Serbs were in the majority. In these Serbian regions, an overwhelming majority voted to remain within the Yugoslavian Federation, but in a referendum held by the Bosnian parliament, the rest of the country voted equally forcefully for independence, which was declared in March 1992. The Serbs then announced their separation from Bosnia and Herzegovina and the creation of the Serb Republic (Republika Srpska), a separate state within the territory of Bosnia and Herzegovina.

[*"The tragedy of Srebrenica will forever haunt the history of the UN."*
—Kofi Annan, General Secretary of the UN, 2000]

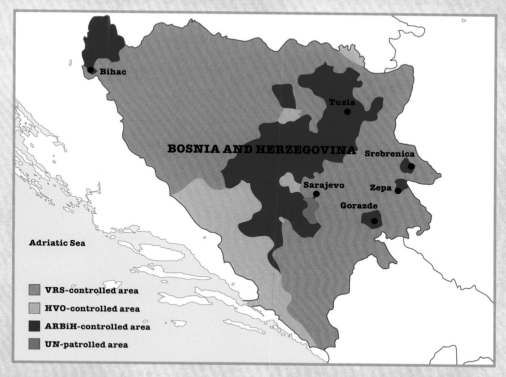

Bihac

Tuzla

BOSNIA AND HERZEGOVINA

Srebrenica

Sarajevo

Zepa

Gorazde

Adriatic Sea

- VRS-controlled area
- HVO-controlled area
- ARBiH-controlled area
- UN-patrolled area

AREAS OF CONTROL

With a few areas under Croatian control (HVO), the majority of the country was held by the Bosnian Serbs (VRS). Although the central portion was controlled by the Army of the Republic of Bosnia and Herzegovina (ARBiH), the Muslim Bosnians in the east were surrounded.

VICIOUS WAR

The army of the former Socialist Federal Republic of Yugoslavia, together with all its weaponry and vehicles, became the Army of the Serb Republic or Vojska Republike Srpske (VRS). The eighty-thousand-strong VRS force soon began a war against the (principally Bosniak) Army of the Republic of Bosnia and Herzegovina (ARBiH) for territorial control, and not just for those areas proclaimed as the Serb Republic.

Lasting for three years, it was a vicious war in which terrible war crimes were committed, mainly by the VRS, against the civilian population. The massacre at Srebrenica was the worst of these, made all the more noteworthy by the international community's failure to prevent it.

ETHNIC CLEANSING

As the Bosnian Serb forces took control of ever larger areas of Bosnia and Herzegovina, they attempted to "ethnically cleanse" those areas by removing or killing the Bosnian Muslims. In the extreme east of the country, close to the border with Serbia, the predominantly Muslim town of Srebrenica and the surrounding region, made up of some three hundred small villages, found itself isolated and under attack from Serb forces. For a period of twelve months from the spring of 1992 the town and villages were systematically shelled and bombed. As villages were destroyed, many of their inhabitants made their way to Srebrenica, and by the spring of 1993 the town was surrounded, hugely overcrowded and effectively under siege, without adequate electricity, medical supplies, food, or water. The commander of the United Nations Protection Force (UNPROFOR) visited the town and declared that the UN would protect it, and several thousand residents were evacuated to the main government-held region of central Bosnia. The government had mixed feelings about the evacuations because they could be seen as helping the Serbs to achieve the ethnic cleansing they desired.

UN "SAFETY ZONE"

The Serbian troops then issued an ultimatum saying that they would attack the town unless all the Bosniaks surrendered and agreed to be evacuated. The Bosniaks refused. Within days, an area of less than 1 square mile (2.6 square km) incorporating Srebrenica was declared by the UN Security Council a "safe area which should be free from any armed attack or any other hostile act." Six hundred Dutch soldiers were brought in to protect the people there. It was also declared a demilitarized zone, which made little difference to the

RATKO MLADIC
Accused of committing war crimes, the Bosnian Serb leader was arrested in northern Serbia in May 2011 and was sent to The International Court of Justice at The Hague.

poorly equipped soldiers of the Bosnian Muslim troops within the town, and no difference at all to the fifteen hundred or so Serbian troops surrounding the town, who refused to remove their heavy armaments. The situation remained at a stalemate for the next year, but the Serbian troops kept up their pressure on the town and allowed access to fewer and fewer relief convoys. Conditions for the

The president of the Serb Republic, Radovan Karadžic, issued the directive to "create an unbearable situation of total insecurity with no hope of further survival or life for the inhabitants of Srebrenica."

trapped Bosniaks and UN peacekeepers steadily deteriorated, and in June 1995 people started dying of starvation.

THE FALL OF SREBRENICA

In March 1995, the president of the Serb Republic, Radovan Karadžic, had issued a directive to the VRS to "create an unbearable situation of total insecurity with no hope of further survival or life for the inhabitants of Srebrenica." In early July, the Serb troops under the leadership of General Ratko Mladic began advancing into the "safe zone" from the south. The remaining four hundred men of the UN Protection Force did little to prevent them. Their commanding officer urgently requested help from NATO, which ran air strikes against VRS gun positions and the advancing tanks until the Serbs threatened to kill the UN hostages that they were holding and to shell the UN compound at Potocari, a village outside the town.

MASS SLAUGHTER

In the meantime, the Bosniaks in Srebrenica fled to Potocari, a few miles away, and by the evening of July 11 there were more than twenty thousand refugees in the compound and in the surrounding fields and outbuildings. The Bosnian Serb troops followed, and in the following days they carried out tens (some reports say hundreds) of killings, taking away young men—and even children—and then shooting them or slitting their throats. Women and young girls were tortured and raped; mothers were forced to watch their children being killed. The details of what happened to countless individuals are horrific. The Dutch UNPROFOR soldiers could only look on, helpless.

As the evacuation got underway, women, children, and the elderly were herded onto buses to take them to the Bosniak-controlled central region of the country, but some of those buses went in other directions, and their passengers were almost certainly massacred. The men and boys were held separately, and by night the Serb army carried out mass executions behind industrial buildings in the village, the bodies being bulldozed into communal graves dug with heavy equipment. Members of UNPROFOR who tried to investigate were prevented by Serb soldiers. Thousands of men, captured within Potocari or on the roads leading away from Srebrenica, were

WAR CRIMES

"During several days of carnage after the fall of Srebrenica, more than 8,000 Muslim men and boys, who had sought safety in this area under the protection of the United Nations Protection Force (UNPROFOR), were summarily executed by Bosnian Serb forces commanded by General Mladic and by paramilitary units, including Serbian irregular police units which had entered Bosnian territory from Serbia...nearly 25,000 women, children and elderly people were forcibly deported, making this event the biggest war crime to take place in Europe since the end of the Second World War."

—Excerpts from the European Parliament Resolution on Srebrenica, January 15, 2009

Butchers of Bosnia

Radovan Karadžic was arrested in
2008 and held by the International
Criminal Tribunal for the former
Yugoslavia (ICTY), which has
ruled that the Srebrenica massacre
was indeed an act of genocide.
On March 24, 2016, he was found
guilty of genocide in Srebrenica,
war crimes, and crimes against
humanity, and sentenced to forty
years' imprisonment. Ratko Mladic
was arrested in Serbia in 2011 and
deported to the International Court
of Justice at The Hague. Accused
of committing war crimes, crimes
against humanity, and genocide, his
trial formally began on May 16, 2012.

marched or bused to collection points
to the northwest, outside the so-called
safety zone. Some were killed
individually or in small groups, but
the vast majority were gathered in
warehouses and a football field and,
beginning on July 13, they were taken
to isolated fields in the area and
systematically lined up and shot in
well-organized mass executions. (In one
instance, more than a thousand men in
a farm warehouse were killed when Serb
soldiers threw in hand grenades and
opened up with gunfire.) Heavy earth-
moving equipment was used to bury the
thousands of bodies in gigantic mass

graves, and in some cases the corpses
were thrown into rivers.

MARCH TO TUZLA

On the night of July 11, while most of
the Bosniaks were retreating to Potocari,
the poorly armed soldiers of the Bosniak
28th Division, together with several
thousand civilian men and a few women,
started the 35-mile (60-km) march
northwest toward Tuzla, in Bosniak
government-held territory. They saw
this as their only chance of survival.
When the VRS realized what had
happened, orders were issued to prevent
the refugees from reaching safety.
Some were captured soon after setting
off, and were later executed with the
other male prisoners from Potocari.
Others made it into the countryside,
but over the next three days the column
of some twelve thousand people was
bombed, shelled, and ambushed as they
made their way, without food or water
at the height of the summer, through
mountainous terrain. At one point more
than two hundred were captured and
then mown down by machine-gun fire.

As they approached Tuzla, the
remains of the column broke through the
VRS troops that were blocking the way,
with help from the Bosniak 2nd Division
that attacked the Serb army from the
Bosnian side. After negotiations, a
corridor was opened for them to make
their way through to Tuzla, but it is
estimated that more than eight thousand
people died on the march. Certainly less

**In one instance, more than a thousand men in a farm warehouse were killed
when Serb soldiers threw in hand grenades and opened up with gunfire.**

than half of those who had left
Srebrenica completed the journey.
Emaciated and delirious with hunger,
many of them barefoot and wounded, the
survivors were seething with anger at the
UN for its failure to protect them and at
their own army for refusing to send
reinforcements to help the 28th Division.

END OF WAR
The war was finally brought to a close
after a UN bombing campaign to crush
the Army of the Serb Republic in the
first three weeks of September 1995.
The Dayton Peace Agreement was
signed by all parties in November 1995.
That same month, Radovan Karadžic
and Ratko Mladic were charged for their
roles in the atrocities. It was established
that more than eight thousand Bosnian

IN MEMORIAM
On July 11 every year in Potocari, Bosnia
and Herzegovina, a memorial ceremony is
held at the monument for victims of the
July 1995 Srebrenica massacre.

Muslims who had sought, and been
guaranteed, refuge in the "safe area"
of Srebrenica were massacred.
  Since the end of the Bosnian War,
there has been an international effort to
locate the mass graves in the area, and to
identify the thousands of bodies they
contain using DNA analysis. So far more
than sixty-five hundred have been
identified and given proper burials.
To this day there are Serbs who deny that
the massacre ever happened, and former
soldiers of the army of the Serb Republic
who express pride in what they achieved.

REPEALING THE GLASS-STEAGALL ACT

November 1999

Main Culprits: The financial industry and the US government

Damage Done: Shattered the US economy and forced millions of Americans to lose their homes and their jobs

Why: Created a culture of corporate greed, personal profit, and public risk

In November 1999, the Glass-Steagall Act, which placed limitations on the banking industry in the US, was dropped. In its place, the Gramm-Leach-Bliley Act brought in a new era of less rigorous regulation, and new possibilities for huge profits. The repeal of Glass-Steagall was a major contributing factor in the sub-prime mortgage collapse and the subsequent financial crisis that sent shock waves around the world.

CONFLICT OF INTERESTS

After the Wall Street Crash of 1929 and the Great Depression that followed it, part of the blame was laid at the doors of the commercial banks for having invested heavily in the stock market (where industry shares and bonds are bought and sold). This placed their depositors' savings at risk but also led the banks to make loans to companies

Homeowners kept borrowing and the banks kept lending and selling. Then it all went wrong.

in which they had invested and then encourage clients to buy those stocks. To prevent a repeat performance, the Glass-Steagall Act (GSA) was passed in 1933 to separate banking from investment activities, the combination of which was seen as creating a conflict of interests. Banks were required to choose between the two. The GSA also led to the creation of bank deposit insurance, which guarantees bank customers that their deposits will be protected and reimbursed should the bank be forced to close.

GREATER FREEDOM

From the 1960s on, the banks were lobbying to have the restrictions of the GSA loosened so they could broaden the range of their financial activities. In 1986 the US banking authority, the Federal Reserve, "reinterpreted" the GSA to allow banks to take 5 percent of their total revenue from investment banking, and later to deal in municipal bonds (which are issued by local government to raise money for day-to-day costs and construction projects) and mortgage-

BILL CLINTON
US President Bill Clinton signed the
Gramm-Leach-Bliley Act which led to the
housing bubble over the next decade,
which burst in 2008 in the financial crisis.

backed securities (mortgage loans that
are sold on). Further weakening of the
GSA followed, especially under the
Federal Reserve chairman Alan
Greenspan, who allowed banks to deal
in a wider range of investments. At the
same time, the major banks had invested
millions of dollars to persuade the
government of the need to give them
greater freedom.

MEGA-BANKS

Throughout the 1990s, the weakening of
the regulations led to the steady grouping
of banks into a smaller number of much
larger institutions. In 1998 the chairmen
of Travelers Insurance Group (Sandy
Weill) and Citicorp (John Reed)
announced plans to merge (combine

two companies into one big company).
The merger was technically in violation
of the GSA and would require the newly
formed Citigroup, Inc. to stop its
involvement in the insurance business
within two years. However, having
spoken to Alan Greenspan, Treasury
Secretary Robert Rubin, and President
Clinton, Sandy Weill was confident that
the GSA would be repealed before
that became necessary. He was right.
(Incidentally, Robin Rubin left the
Treasury in 1999 and joined the board
of Citigroup.)

In November 1999, after spending
twenty years and $300 million lobbying
for the repeal of the GSA, the financial
companies got their payback plus
interest. It was accomplished with the
passing of the Gramm-Leach-Bliley
Act, otherwise known as the Financial
Services Modernization Act.

SUB-PRIME BOOM

The newly liberated mega-banks now
had the go-ahead to deal in a whole range
of different financial "instruments" and
to create innovative new ones. One of the
new areas into which they moved was
home mortgages (property loans).
New kinds of mortgages were developed,
such as mortgages with an adjustable
rate of interest (the money on top of a
loan that the borrower pays), interest-
only mortgages (borrowers only pay the
interest on a debt, meaning the loan itself
is not paid off), and even negative-
amortization mortgages (the homeowner
pays less than the necessary amount each
month and the debt keeps increasing).
Wall Street, the home of the New York
Stock Exchange, began to bundle these
mortgages together and sell them
as mortgage-backed securities.

The government-sponsored Federal National Mortgage Association (Fannie Mae) and Federal Home Loan Mortgage Corp (Freddie Mac) had been selling these to pension funds, insurance companies, and foreign governments for years, but now Wall Street was able to get a piece of the action. The revenue was used to provide further mortgages to bundle and sell and so on and so on.

HIGH-RISK LENDING

As the lucrative cycle continued, both the private banks and Fannie and Freddie gave mortgages to borrowers with lower and lower credit ratings (credit ratings score how reliable people are in repaying debt). This created a boom in sub-prime (meaning "high-risk") mortgage lending. Interest rates were low, house prices were rising at record rates, and even a mortgage higher than the value of a property wasn't that big a risk for the lender, as the property would be worth that in a few months' time anyway. Homeowners kept borrowing (increasing their level of debt significantly), the banks kept lending and selling, and the hedge funds (a group of investors that make high-risk investments) and insurance companies kept buying. And then, in mid-2006, it all went sour.

FANNIE AND FREDDIE

Fannie Mae (with its headquarters, seen here, in Washington, D.C.) and Freddie Mac had combined losses of almost $15 billion and required a massive bailout by the US government.

> **The major banks had invested millions of dollars to persuade the government to give them greater freedom.**

FINANCIAL FREEFALL

House prices started to fall, interest rates began to rise, adjustable-rate mortgages were reset at higher rates, and homeowners who had been sold mortgages that they couldn't afford were unable to make repayments. Some who found themselves with negative equity (the amount they borrowed was more than the value of their property) simply handed back the keys to the house. Others found the banks taking back possession of their properties. The mortgage-backed securities, held by just about every financial institution, lost their value dramatically, causing some institutions to close, as investors withdrew their money.

Of the five largest investment banks, one went bankrupt, two were taken over, and two received massive bailouts from the government. Fannie Mae and Freddie Mac went into receivership (meaning the companies were bankrupt and others were handling their financial affairs). The total debt of these seven institutions amounted to $9 trillion—the equivalent of two-thirds of the US GDP (the total value of goods or services produced in a year). The credit squeeze that followed, meaning that people couldn't borrow as much money as before, stifled economic growth. It affected not just the US, where the auto industry suffered a major crash, but across the globe.

The repeal of the Glass-Steagall Act was by no means the only factor that brought about the financial crisis, but it was certainly a major one. The deregulation of the financial sector demonstrated the unhealthy relationship that exists between big business and political power—a state of affairs that has become known as corporatocracy. It wasn't a surprise to most people.

NEW ACT

The Financial Services Modernization Act cleared the way for the creation of huge banking companies that offered a broad range of financial services, with less external regulation and supervision. In the words of President Bill Clinton, it:

"… makes the most important legislative changes to the structure of the US financial system since the 1930s. Financial services firms will be authorized to conduct a wide range of financial activities, allowing them freedom to innovate in the new economy. The Act repeals provisions of the GSA that, since the Great Depression, have restricted affiliations between banks and securities firms. It also amends the Bank Holding Company Act to remove restrictions on affiliations between banks and insurance companies. It grants banks significant new authority to conduct most newly authorized activities through financial subsidiaries."

AL-QAEDA ATTACKS THE US

September 11, 2001

Main Culprits: Al-Qaeda Islamic terrorists

Damage Done: Killed 2,753 people, provoked a tide of anti-Islamic feeling, and began an era of fear and suspicion

Why: In retribution for America's economic, political, and military involvement in the Middle East

No one who has seen the televised footage of the collapse of the Twin Towers—and who hasn't?—can fail to have been struck by a sense of horror at the enormity of the tragedy. Even those who were behind the world's most deadly act of terrorism must have been staggered by the sheer scale of the devastation. It was an event that reshaped the political landscape and caused fear, suspicion, and insecurity on a global scale. Yet, did it further the aims of Al-Qaeda or was it just a pointless act of venomous hatred?

TWIN TOWERS

When they were completed in December 1970 and July 1971, towers 1 and 2 of the World Trade Center were the tallest buildings in the world, dominating New York City's Lower Manhattan skyline. Each standing 110 stories high, the "Twin Towers" were largely made up of offices, many of them leased by companies involved in the financial sector. Some fifty thousand people came to work in the towers every day, and more than one hundred thousand members of the public passed through the doors each day to visit the public spaces. These included the rooftop observatories and the famous Windows On The World restaurant on the 106th and 107th floors of the North Tower. As emblems of America's economic influence in the world they were instantly recognizable icons.

AMERICAN AIRLINES FLIGHT 11

At 8:46 am on the clear, bright morning of Tuesday, September 11, 2001, Boeing 767 American Airlines Flight 11 from Boston to Los Angeles carrying ninety-two people crashed through the north face of the North Tower between the 94th and 98th floors, severing the

A giant fireball roared through the elevator shafts and started a huge fire that engulfed the upper floors of the North Tower in thick, toxic smoke.

stairwells. The fuel in the jet's wings
exploded into a giant fireball that roared
through the elevator shafts up and down
the building and started a huge fire that
engulfed the upper floors in thick, toxic
smoke. People in the floors below the
impact zone immediately began to
evacuate the building, but those above it
were trapped. Within minutes, news of
the plane crash and fire were being
broadcast on radio and TV; the

SECOND STRIKE

As smoke poured from the North Tower,
and photographers and film crews trained
their cameras on the disaster, the South
Tower was hit by a second plane, to the
horror of millions who were watching.

assumption being that this was a terrible
accident. Emergency vehicles were soon
rushing through the streets of Manhattan
toward the World Trade Center, some
arriving within minutes of the collision.

AMERICAN AIRLINES FLIGHT 175

At 9:03 am, seventeen minutes after the North Tower was hit, a second Boeing 767, United Airlines Flight 175, also flying from Boston to Los Angeles, crashed into the south face of the South Tower. The plane, traveling at almost 600 mph (950 kph) and carrying sixty-five people, was banking hard when it struck the building, slicing into floors 77 through 85. As in the North Tower, the floors of the South Tower burst into flame. Television film crews were by now covering the incident in the North Tower,

PRESIDENT BUSH
George Bush addresses the rescue workers on the site of Ground Zero two days after the attack.

and the approach and impact of the second plane were broadcast live to a horrified audience. There was now no doubt that this was a coordinated terrorist attack.

CHOKING SMOKE

All 157 people in the two planes died instantly as the planes hit the buildings, as did people working on the floors that were struck directly. In the North Tower, the few floors above the impact zone were rapidly affected by the fire from below. Soon after the impact, people in these upper floors found themselves unable to breathe and sought fresh air at the windows, but as the fire, heat, and smoke

VITRIOLIC HATRED

"How do I respond when I see that in some Islamic countries there is vitriolic hatred for America? I'll tell you how I respond: I'm amazed. I'm amazed that there is such misunderstanding of what our country is about, that people would hate us. I am, I am—like most Americans, I just can't believe it. Because I know how good we are, and we've got to do a better job of making our case. We've got to do a better job of explaining to the people in the Middle East, for example, that we don't fight a war against Islam or Muslims. We don't hold any religion accountable. We're fighting evil. And these murderers have hijacked a great religion in order to justify their evil deeds. And we cannot let it stand."

—**President George W. Bush responds to the attacks at a press conference on October 11, 2001**

became overwhelming, some chose to jump from the building, plunging more than 1,000 feet (300 m) to the ground below. At least a hundred, and probably two hundred, died in this way.

In the South Tower, one stairwell remained open after the impact, but rather than face the choking smoke that filled it, people on the upper floors made their way upward, hoping to be rescued from the roof of the building. However, the only doors providing access to the roof were locked, and in any case no helicopter could have landed on the roof, which was engulfed in thick smoke. Only four people chose to descend through the smoke and debris and succeeded in making their way to safety. No one on the floors above the impact zone in the North Tower would survive.

TOTAL DEVASTATION

A rescue worker signals to a colleague amid the burning rubble of Ground Zero, where 343 firefighters and twenty-three police officers lost their lives on September 11.

GROUND ZERO

Just before 10:00 am, less than an hour after being struck, the South Tower collapsed down on itself, its steel structure weakened by the impact of the plane and by the raging fire. Half an hour later, the North Tower crumpled. Although the lower floors in both buildings had largely been evacuated, many rescue workers had entered the towers in an attempt to save those trapped. Only twenty people who were in the buildings at the time survived the collapse of the towers. The total death toll was 2,753 individuals, including 343 New York Fire Department firefighters and twenty-three officers of the New York Police Department. More than 1,300 vehicles were crushed beneath the collapsed buildings, including ninety-one fire and emergency vehicles. The fires at Ground Zero, as the site of the collapsed towers became known, burned for the next ninety-nine days, and the cleanup of the site was to take eight months.

TERROR SPREADS

In addition to the two passenger planes that were flown into the Twin Towers on September 11, 2001, two others had been hijacked at about the same time. All four were scheduled to fly to California, and the hijackers had chosen these long-distance flights because they would be carrying the maximum amount of fuel.

American Airlines Flight 77, a Boeing 757 bound for Los Angeles, took off from Dulles, North Virginia, at 8:20 am carrying six crew and fifty-eight passengers,

The fires at Ground Zero burned for the next ninety-nine days.

including five hijackers. Half an hour into the flight the hijackers took control, forced the passengers to the back of the cabin, and turned the plane back toward Virginia. Passengers had time to call their families on cell phones and tell them what was happening. At 9:37 am the plane crashed into the side of the Pentagon, the headquarters of the US Department of Defense, killing 125 people in the building as well as everyone on the plane.

United Airlines Flight 93, a Boeing 757 bound for San Francisco, was the last of the four to take off. Carrying seven crew and thirty-seven passengers, including four hijackers, it was scheduled to leave Newark International Airport at 8:00 am but was delayed on the tarmac and did not take off until 8:42 am, just minutes before American Airlines Flight 11 struck the WTC South Tower. Three-quarters of an hour into the flight the hijackers took control. The terrorist pilot announced to the passengers that there was a bomb on board and that the flight would be returning to Newark. Over the next half hour, using cell phones, the passengers learned what had happened in New York and realized that the bomb story was a hoax and that this was a suicide mission. At 10:00 am they bravely stormed the cockpit and the hijackers were forced to abandon their target—probably the United States Capitol, the seat of the US Congress, or the president's residence, the White House, in Washington, D.C.

> **It became clear that the horrific events of September 11 were the result of a planned attack by nineteen hijackers.**

The plane crashed instead in a field in Pennsylvania, killing everyone on board.

LETTER TO AMERICA

As it became clear that the horrific events of the morning were the result of a planned attack by nineteen hijackers (some of whom had received flying lessons in the US), suspicion immediately fell on the extremist Islamic terrorist group Al-Qaeda and the militant group's leader, Osama bin Laden. He denied having been involved. Not until three thousand civilians, he said, was justified because the US is a democracy and the actions of its government are therefore approved by its people.

As evidence against Al-Qaeda and Bin Laden mounted, the US demanded that the fundamental Islamic group, the Taliban, hand over Bin Laden, which they refused to do. In response, as part of its War on Terror, the US invaded Afghanistan. The war against Iraq was also, in part, provoked by the attack on the World Trade Center. The US devoted considerable resources to tracking down Osama bin Laden, and a CIA-led military attack on his compound in Pakistan in May 2011 resulted in his death.

SINCE 9/11

In the US and many other countries new legislation was introduced to stamp out terrorism by increasing governments' powers of gathering and sharing intelligence on suspected terrorist activity, along with the arrest and detention, and monitoring and surveillance of suspects. Some of this legislation has been criticized as eroding civil rights and personal privacy, and there is no doubt that cross-border travel, especially into the US, has been made far more difficult and far more intrusive, with everyone being treated as a potential terrorist.

Since that terrible day in September 2001, there have been more terrorist attacks, heightening fear across the globe. One of the most significant developments has been the emergence of ISIS (Islamic State of Iraq and Syria). This militant group grew out of Al-Qaeda in Iraq in the 2000s, going on to take over a large swathe of Syria and Iraq from 2011 onward, where they have imposed a brutal fundamentalist regime.

MILITARY ACTION
In response to known connections between the Taliban and Al-Qaeda, and the Taliban's refusal to hand over Osama bin Laden, the US launched Operation Enduring Freedom in Afghanistan in October 2001.

years later did he admit responsibility, writing an open letter to the US and citing America's support for Israel and US military and political involvement in the Middle East as the reasons for the attack. The murder of almost three

THE DEEPWATER HORIZON BLOWOUT

April 20, 2010

Main Culprits: BP, Transocean, Halliburton

Damage Done: Killed eleven men, injured seventeen, and released almost five million barrels of oil into the Gulf of Mexico

Why: A corporate culture that places profitability above safety

There are some disasters that result from one single and supremely bad decision, and we have seen many examples of those, but others are the consequence of a series of small acts of poor judgment that have a cumulative effect and a terrible outcome.

The explosion that took place on the Deepwater Horizon oil rig in the Gulf of Mexico and the subsequent oil spill— the largest in US history—are examples of this.

DEEPWATER DRILLING

The drilling of the Macondo well by BP (formerly British Petroleum), in an area of the Gulf known as Mississippi Canyon Block 252, was always going to be a challenge. To begin with, the seabed was 5,000 feet (1,500 m) below the surface of the ocean. Furthermore, it was expected that the rig would have to drill more than 20,000 feet (6,000 m) below sea level to reach the hydrocarbon-bearing rock (the compound hydrocarbon is the chief component of petroleum and natural gas).

The 33,000-ton (30,000-tonne) Deepwater Horizon was a gigantic, semi-submersible, "dynamically positioned," mobile offshore drilling unit (MODU) that used GPS technology and thrusters to remain positioned exactly over the well no matter what the sea or weather conditions. Owned and operated by Transocean, it took over from another rig (which had been damaged in Hurricane Katrina) in January 2010. Its first task was to put in place a blowout preventer, or BOP, on the seabed. This is a gigantic valve that is seated on top of the well and contains several methods of closing off the well in the event of an emergency. The BOP also provides a means of monitoring what is happening in the drill bore. Above the BOP, a large tube called a well-riser extends the well up through the ocean to the rig and carries power and control lines to the BOP.

MOUNTING PRESSURE

By early April of 2010, the rig had drilled to a depth of more than 18,000 feet (5,500 m) and had reached hydrocarbon-bearing rock. Drilling at these depths is a delicate balancing act. Such deep reserves of hydrocarbons, trapped in rock beneath an impermeable layer, are under enormous pressure. The well has

MEGA-RIG
The Deepwater Horizon caught fire after a blowout and explosion in 2010. The rig sank two days later and caused the largest US oil spill ever.

to be kept at a sufficiently high pressure to prevent the gases and liquids from flowing upward through the well bore and causing an uncontrolled discharge, or blowout. This is done by pumping in a complex and expensive mixture, known casually as mud, that circulates down through the drill, cooling and lubricating the drill bit. It then circulates back up to the rig carrying with it the debris from the drilling operation. Further protection is given by a tubular metal casing as the well is extended down through the rock. Cement is pumped into the space between the casing and the walls of the bore, and this keeps the hydrocarbons out of the well. It also protects the surrounding rock from the pressure of the drilling mud, which can cause the

Drilling down to such deep levels is always a delicate balancing act.

rock to fracture. In this event the mud is forced into the rock and less mud returns to the rig than is being pumped down, a situation known as "lost circulation."

On April 9, "lost circulation" is exactly what happened. It is not an uncommon occurrence, and the drilling crew responded by pumping down a special liquid to seal the fracture, but it prompted BP to stop drilling and to complete the well at that depth. The next step was to install the last section of casing (the "production casing" that would allow the oil and gas to be extracted when a production rig was brought in to replace the Deepwater Horizon). They then needed to pump down a cement foam into the space

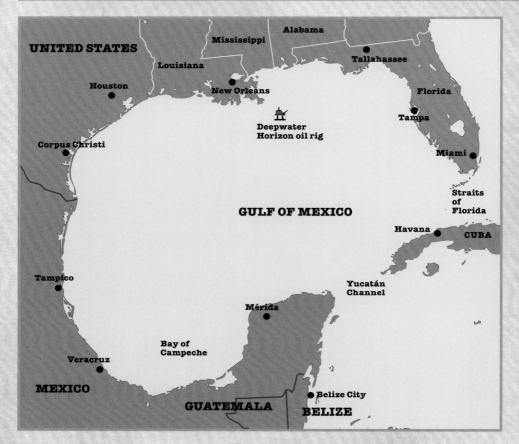

between the casing and the surrounding rock to seal off the hydrocarbon reserves from the well. This is when the problems and the sequence of bad decisions began.

SHORT CUTS

Installing the production casing was a long job, with sections being assembled and then slowly lowered to the bottom of the well. As they were assembled, centralizers had to be fitted to the casing at intervals to keep it in the center of the bore. Without these, the cement can end up "channeling" as it comes up around the casing. There were only six centralizers on the rig, which were not

MACONDO PROSPECT

The Deepwater Horizon was drilling in the United States' sector of the Gulf of Mexico, about 40 miles (65 km) off the coast of Louisiana, when the explosion occurred.

enough. A further fifteen centralizers were ordered, but when they arrived they were found to be of the wrong type. Rather than waiting for the correct ones to be sent, the decision was to go with just the six that were on hand, despite the potential risk of channeling. Sections continued to be added and lowered, and finally the top end of the 180-foot (55-m) length of casing was fitted with a pair of valves held open by a perforated tube that allowed the drilling mud to flow up through the casing as it was lowered. By April 19 it was in position at the well bottom.

Before the cement foam could be pumped down the casing, the tube holding the valves open had to be pushed down, allowing them to close and converting them to one-way valves so they would prevent the cement from rising up the well. This was to be achieved by pumping mud down through the casing to push the perforated tube down. Despite pumping at high pressure, however, the crew could not establish a flow of mud. After several attempts, the pressure suddenly dropped and the mud began to flow, but at a lower rate and a lower pressure than predicted. But rather than investigating what was causing this, the team put the low pressure reading down to a faulty gauge and concluded that the valves had successfully been converted.

CRITICAL DECISIONS
Next came the cementing, the most critical part of the process in terms of preventing a blowout. Given the fragile nature of the rock structure, BP was anxious to keep pressure at the bottom of the well to a minimum. This led to several questionable instructions being given to Halliburton, the company conducting the cementing. The first of these was not to follow the normal procedure of pumping mud through the system until material from the bottom reaches the top of the well. This practice ensures that the space between the casing and the rock is cleaned through and also allows technicians to check mud from the bottom for signs that

The cement foam used to pump through the system was found to be unstable (and therefore unsafe) but this was not brought to the attention of BP.

hydrocarbons are leaking into the well. BP elected to pump down only about an eighth of the mud needed to complete the "bottom up" procedure. They also decided to pump down less cement than would have been ideal and to pump at a lower rate than normal.

To compound the risk, laboratory tests conducted by Halliburton had already indicated that the particular cement/nitrogen foam that was to be used might be unstable (therefore unsafe to use), but this had not been brought to the attention of BP. The pumping of the cement was completed in the early hours of April 20, and technicians checked to see how much fluid flowed up from the casing when a valve was opened. The flow was slightly more than predicted but it then stopped and they concluded that the valves were holding. The procedure was declared a success and BP sent home a team of technicians who were waiting to run tests to check the strength of the cement seal. Confidence was running high.

WARNING SIGNS
The crew of the Deepwater Horizon then set about completing the procedures to seal the well and remove the riser, and began by running two standard tests. The first was a "positive pressure test" that involved raising the pressure in the well and seeing whether the pressure held. It did, indicating that there was no

COMPLACENCY

"Our investigation shows that a series of specific and preventable human and engineering failures were the immediate causes of the disaster, but, in fact, this disaster was almost the inevitable result of years of industry and government complacency and lack of attention to safety… As drilling pushes into ever deeper and riskier waters where more of America's oil lies, only systemic reforms of both government and industry will prevent a similar, future disaster."

— The National Commission co-chair William K. Reilly sums up the cause of the Deepwater Horizon oil spill

leak from the well into the surrounding rock. They then ran a "negative pressure test," reducing the pressure in the well to zero and seeing whether it remained at zero. This is designed to check both the casing and the cement seal at the bottom of the well. If the pressure rises then hydrocarbons are leaking into the drill pipe, and only the pressure of the mud in the well bore and the riser are keeping it out. In this case, the crew were unable to even get the pressure down to zero in the first place and each time the drill pipe was closed, the pressure jumped higher. The team then conducted the test on another pipe, got a satisfactory result, and declared the test successful, but failed to explain why the pressure in the drill pipe was so high. The only explanation was that there was a leak at the bottom of the well, and this was ignored.

SERIES OF EXPLOSIONS

In the course of the evening the crew pumped seawater down the drill pipe and steadily forced up the mud in the well bore and the riser. The pressure in the drill pipe gradually fell as the water replaced the heavier mud above it. However, just after 9:00 pm the pressure in the drill pipe began to rise and continued to do so for the next fifteen minutes. This is clear from the data logged by the monitoring systems, but no one on the rig appears to have noticed what was happening. All the signs indicated that there had been a "kick," a leak of oil and/or gas into the well. A recorded drop in pressure at 9:39 pm shows that a bubble of gas was rocketing up the casing, expanding as it rose, and a couple of minutes later workers on the rig saw drilling mud shooting out onto the rig floor. Valves in the BOP were quickly installed but it was too late. They failed to contain the pressure, and in any case the gas was already above the BOP and coming up the riser. It blasted out of the top of the well and ignited, causing a massive explosion. Several of the rig's crew probably died in that first fireball.

The Deepwater Horizon burned for the next thirty-six hours before finally sinking, ripping away the riser and starting an oil spill that released an estimated five million barrels of oil into the Gulf of Mexico.

One of the supervisors ran to the main control panel and activated the emergency disconnect system (EDS), which should have sheared off the drill pipe, sealed the well, and uncoupled the rig from the BOP. None of this happened, probably because the explosion had damaged the cables from the rig to the BOP. An automatic cut-off system also failed to work, possibly due to poor maintenance.

Of the 126-person crew, eleven died that night and sixteen were seriously injured. The Deepwater Horizon burned for the next thirty-six hours before finally sinking, ripping away the riser and starting an oil spill that released an estimated five million barrels of oil into the Gulf of Mexico and took three months to cap. The cost to BP ran into tens of billions of dollars. However, the cost to the environment and to the livelihoods of the people of the US Gulf Coast is incalculable.

UNACCEPTABLE RISK?

And the blame? In its "Report to the President," the National Commission on the BP Deepwater Horizon Oil Spill and Offshore Drilling spotlights poor management and a culture of risk taking in the oil industry, as well as a lack of adequate regulation. Perhaps we should all shoulder some of the blame for humankind's unconscious "decision" to rely on an energy source whose extraction and use poses an unacceptable risk to the planet.

TROUBLED WATERS
The progress of the oil slick from the Deepwater Horizon was tracked using satellite imagery. The total amount of oil that leaked from the well contaminated more than 650 miles (1,000 km) of coastline.

BUILDING REACTORS IN JAPAN'S EARTHQUAKE ZONE

March 11, 2011

Main Culprit: Tokyo Electric Power Company

Damage Done: Leaked significant amounts of radioactive material into the atmosphere and the ocean

Why: The Fukushima Daiichi nuclear power plant was built on the coast in an earthquake zone where it was known a major tsunami was possible

So when is hope a criminal offense? When it leads to the playing down of a potentially lethal risk. The earthquake and tsunami that struck the east coast of Japan in 2011 damaged the Fukushima Daiichi nuclear reactors and their systems so badly that several explosions occurred and they released large quantities of radioactive material. Why? Well, given that a seismic event of that magnitude was a realistic possibility, the decision to build a nuclear power plant of that design in that location was clearly a bad one. Unfortunately, Fukushima is not alone.

TSUNAMI WARNING

In 2008, concerns were raised in Japan and by the International Atomic Energy Agency (IAEA) about the ability of Japan's nuclear installations to withstand a significant tsunami caused by an offshore earthquake of magnitude 7 or greater. In the same year, the Tokyo Electric Power Company (TEPCO), the owner and operator of the Fukushima Daiichi nuclear power plant, carried out a study that showed that the plant could be flooded by a tsunami greater than 28 feet (8.4 m) high. As a result, they proposed that steps should be taken to improve protection at the site in case of such an event. Company officials regarded the probability of such a large earthquake or tsunami as insignificant and no action was taken. The report landed on the desk of the Japanese Nuclear and Industrial Safety Agency (NISA) on March 7, 2011.

On March 11, 2011, at 2:46 pm, a magnitude 9 earthquake occurred 80 miles (128 km) off the east coast of Honshu Island and 230 miles (370 km) northeast of Tokyo. The shock waves

The first tsunami to hit the power plant was 46 feet high, more than twice the height the plant had been designed to withstand.

from the Great East Japan Earthquake caused no fewer than eleven nuclear reactors at four sites on Japan's northeast coast to shut down automatically.

The Fukushima Daiichi power plant has six nuclear reactors. Units 4, 5, and 6 had been shut down for routine maintenance, and the fuel rods in Unit 4 had been removed and placed in the spent fuel pool. Units 1, 2, and 3, which were in operation at the time, shut down automatically, inserting the control rods into the core to slow the nuclear reaction. The earthquake cut off the external electrical power supply to the facility, but the backup diesel generators (two for each of five reactors and three for Unit 6) started up and power was restored to all six units. So far, so good.

About fifty minutes after the earthquake struck, the first of a series of tsunamis hit the coast. It was 46 feet (14 m) high,

BEFORE THE BLAST

When hydrogen gas that had accumulated in Unit 1 (nearest) exploded on March 12, 2011, the top half of the building was blown off. Unit 3 building exploded two days later, followed by Unit 2 on the 15th.

more than twice the height of wave that the plant had been designed to withstand, and it crashed over the nuclear power plant, flooding the facility and knocking out the diesel generators in all but Unit 6. Operators managed to connect the Unit 6 generator to run Unit 5 as well, and both were now safe, but the other four were in a state known as "station blackout."

HEADING FOR MELTDOWN

Although Units 1, 2, and 3 had been shut down, each of the reactor cores contained extremely hot fuel rods and still needed to be cooled, as did the fuel rods in the spent fuel pool in Unit 4. As various safety features could not be operated without an electricity supply, the temperatures in the reactor cores began to rise and the water level in each of them fell as the water evaporated. Despite their courage and diligence, there was little that operatives could do to remedy the situation. Within hours of the tsunami, the water level in Unit 1 fell below the top of the fuel rods, allowing them to heat up rapidly and

FAILING TO PLAN FOR THE WORST

The US Nuclear Regulatory Commission (NRC), in its earthquake engineering criteria for nuclear plants, uses the concept of the Safe Shutdown Earthquake (SSE). This states that a nuclear reactor must be designed so that, in the event of an earthquake, it doesn't lose reactor coolant, it can be shut down safely and kept that way, and it doesn't leak radioactive material into the surrounding area. Sounds reasonable enough, but the seismic events that struck in March 2011 were so far beyond the SSE that the Fukushima reactors failed on all three counts. Clearly the SSE was set too low. The NRC regulations also state, "Seismically (earthquake) induced floods and water waves...must be taken into account in the design of the nuclear power plant so as to prevent undue risk to the health and safety of the public."

damaging the core. The following day, March 12, the pressure in the reactor vessel rose and, without electricity, could not be let out through vents remotely. Workers entered the reactor to vent it manually, taking an enormous risk, but an hour later there was an explosion that tore the top off the building, caused by hydrogen escaping into the reactor.

At 7:00 in the evening, the decision was made to start injecting seawater into the reactor to cool it, using fire department pumping trucks. Although it was not realized at the time, the core of the Unit 1 reactor had already completely melted and slumped to the bottom of the reactor vessel.

The following day, March 13, the water levels in Units 2 and 3 were causing concern, falling to the level of the top of the fuel rods. The pressure in Unit 2 was high, and it was thought that in Unit 3 there might be a partial meltdown. At 11:00 am the next morning, the Unit 3 reactor building exploded violently, killing six workers. The explosion was heard 25 miles (40 km) away. Within hours, a large proportion of the fuel had fallen to the bottom of the reactor vessel. Meanwhile, the water level in Unit 2 had fallen farther, damaging the core, and on March 15 it, too, suffered an explosion, followed shortly by a fire in Unit 4 where it was thought the water in the spent fuel pool may be boiling.

On March 16, radiation levels at the plant rose to a dangerous level and the majority of the workers were evacuated temporarily. A range of measures was taken to try to keep the reactor cores and the spent fuel pools cool by spraying water into the reactors from fire trucks and dropping water from helicopters, which succeeded in refilling the Unit 4 pool.

EXCLUSION ZONE
A house sits on the scarred landscape inside the exclusion zone close to the Fukushima Power Plant. The area is closed to residents due to radiation contamination.

RADIATION LEAK

Over the next two days, high radiation levels were detected almost 20 miles (32 km) northwest of Fukushima, and the following week high levels of radioactivity were found in Tokyo's drinking water. At the plant it was discovered that water in the reactor buildings was contaminated with radioactive material, and that this contaminated water was leaking into the ocean.

The work to make the plant safe continued throughout 2011, but it was not until December 16 that TEPCO and the Japanese government were able to announce that the reactors had achieved a state of cold shutdown. In January 2012, hundreds of tons of highly radioactive water were still being discovered beneath the plant. So what had gone so horribly wrong?

NOT WORTH THE RISK

The disaster has fueled the anti-nuclear debate in Japan, and in other countries around the world, and has stimulated research into other forms of renewable energy, including plans to build a wind farm off the coast of Japan. Japanese prime minister Naoto Kan ordered one of the country's oldest reactors to be closed down, and the building of new reactors has been put on hold. He has been quoted as saying, "Japan should reduce and eventually eliminate its dependence on nuclear energy," and "If there is a risk of accidents that could make half the land mass of our country uninhabitable, then we cannot afford to take that risk."

Over the next two days, high radiation levels were detected 20 miles northwest of Fukushima, and the following week high levels of radioactivity were found in Tokyo's drinking water.

FURTHER READING

In general, the most useful single book for any earnest student of history is a good historical atlas. *The Times Atlas of World History* is probably the best. For general reference and fact checking without expense or inconvenience, the internet is a remarkable source, and Wikipedia (www.wikipedia.org) in particular is a great starting point, although its nature as an open-source encyclopedia to which almost anyone can contribute means you should pay close attention to the references and footnotes if you want to make the most of it. You will also find some excellent links and information at www.bbc.co.uk/history.

For the history of ancient civilizations, there is a wealth of information at the internet Classics Archive (http://classics.mit.edu/), which contains English translations of "441 works of classical literature by 59 different authors." It is an absolute treasure trove for the works of Greek and Roman historians.

BOOKS

Ackroyd, Peter. *Tudors*. Pan, 2013.

Aussaresses, General Paul. *The Battle of the Casbah: Terrorism and Counter-Terrorism in Algeria, 1955–1957.* Enigma Books, 2003.

Baritz, Loren. *Backfire: A History of How American Culture Led Us into Vietnam and Made Us Fight the Way We Did.* The Johns Hopkins University Press, 1998.

Beard, Mary. *SPQR: A History of Ancient Rome.* Profile Books, 2016.

Bin, Alberto, Richard Hill, and Archer Jones. *Desert Storm: A Forgotten War.* Praeger Publishers, 1998.

Bradbury, Jim. *The Battle of Hastings.* Sutton Publishing, 2006.

Brinkley, Alan. *The Unfinished Nation: A Concise History of the American People.* McGraw-Hill Companies, Inc., 1997.

Burg, Steven L., and Paul S. Shoup. *The War in Bosnia-Herzegovina: Ethnic Conflict and International Intervention.* M. E. Sharpe, 1999.

Chang, Jung. *Wild Swans: Three Daughters of China.* Harper Perennial, 1992.

Conquest, Robert. *The Harvest of Sorrow: Soviet Collectivization and the Terror-Famine.* University of Alberta Press, 1986.

Diamond, Jared. *Guns, Germs, and Steel.* Penguin Books, 1999.

Dicklitch, Susan. *Encyclopedia of Human Rights, Volume 1.* Editor in Chief, David P. Forsythe. Oxford University Press, 2009.

Evans, Eric J. *Thatcher and Thatcherism.* Routledge, 2004.

Evans, Martin, and John Phillips. *Algeria: Anger of the Dispossessed.* Yale University Press, 2008.

Gillon, Steven M.
*Pearl Harbor: FDR Leads
the Nation Into War.*
Basic Books, 2011.

Gregg, Pauline.
King Charles I.
Phoenix Press, 2001.

Hardin, Stephen.
*The Alamo 1836: Santa
Anna's Texas Campaign.*
Osprey Publishing, 2001.

Hart-Davis, Adam.
*History: From the Dawn of
Civilization to the Present
Day.* Dorling Kindersley
Publishing, 2015.

Hemming, John.
Conquest of the Inca.
Pan, 2004.

Herr, Michael. *Dispatches.*
Vintage, 1991.

Hopkirk, Peter. *The
Great Game: The Struggle
for Empire in Central
Asia.* Kodansha
International, 1992.

James, Lawrence.
*Raj: The Making and
Unmaking of British India.*
Little, Brown and
Company, 1997.

Kornbluh, Peter (Editor).
*Bay of Pigs Declassified:
The Secret CIA Report
on the Invasion of Cuba.*

The New Press, 1998.
**Kuntz, Phil, and Kenneth
Starr**. *The Starr Report:
The Starr Evidence: The
Complete Testimony from
President Clinton and
Monica Lewinsky.*1998.

Melvern, Linda.
*Conspiracy to Murder:
The Rwanda Genocide and the
International Community.*
Verso, 2004.

Mosse, W. E. *Alexander II
and the Modernization of
Russia.* English
Universities Press, 1958.

Norwich, John Julius. *A
Short History of Byzantium.*
Penguin Books, 1998.

Prunier, Gérard.
*The Rwanda Crisis: History
of a Genocide.* Columbia
University Press, 1995.

Read, Donald. *Peterloo:
The Massacre and its
Background.* Manchester
University Press, 1958.

Rees, Laurence.
*War of the Century:
When Hitler Fought Stalin.*
The New Press, 2000.

Robertson, William.
*A General History of
North and South America.*
Mayhew, Isaac, and
Co., 1834.

Sachs, Jeffrey.
The End of Poverty.
Penguin Books, 2005.

Singer, Daniel.
*Prelude to Revolution:
France in May 1968.*
South End Press, 2002.

Smith, Gordon.
*Battle Atlas of the Falklands
War 1982 by Land, Sea and
Air.* Naval-History, 2009.

Standage, Tom.
*An Edible History
of Humanity.*
Bloomsbury US, 2009.

Stiglitz, Joseph E.
*Freefall: America, Free
Markets and the Sinking
of the World Economy.*
W. W. Norton, 2010.

Sussman, Barry.
*The Great Coverup: Nixon
and the Scandal of Watergate.*
Seven Locks, 1992.

Taylor, A. J. P.
*The Habsburg Monarchy,
1809–1918: A History of
the Austrian Empire and
Austria-Hungary.*
Hamish Hamilton, 1948.

Wright, Lawrence.
*The Looming Tower: Al-
Qaeda's Road to 9/11.*
Penguin Books, 2007.

INDEX

A

Aaron the Israelite 13, 14, 15
Afghanistan
  British invasion of 104–7
  US invasion of 207
Agent Orange 149
Agincourt, Battle of 56–9
agriculture
  collectivization 130–1
  early 8–10, 11
Akbar Khan 105, 106, 107
Alamo 100–3
Alaska 88
Alexander the Great 20–5, 26
Alexander II, Tsar 112–15
Alexander III, Tsar 115
Alexandria 23, 46
Algerian War of Independence 152–7
Al-Qaeda 202–7
Amin, Idi 166–9
Amritsar massacre 144, 146
Anglican Communion 77
animal domestication 8
Annan, Kofi 192
Arab League 181
Argentinian invasion of the Falkland
  Islands 174–9
Arianism 46
Aristotle 21
Arkwright, Richard 94
Asculum, Battle of 28
Asian expulsion from Uganda 166–9
assassinations
  Agathe Uwilingiyimana 189–90
  Duke of Buckingham 83
  Julius Caesar 30–5
  Philip II of Macedon 21
  Tsar Alexander II 112–15
Atahualpa 70–3
Auckland, Lord 104
Austria 116–19

B

Bagosora, Colonel 190
banking industry 198–201
Bao Dai, Emperor 149
Batak 11
Batista, Fulgencio 158
Bayeux Tapestry 54
Bay of Pigs invasion 158–61
Bernstein, Carl 171
Bessus (Artaxerxes V) 23

Bible history 12–15
bin Laden, Osama 206–7
blitzkrieg 136
Blücher, Field Marshall von 91, 93
Boleyn, Anne 75, 76–7
Boleyn, Mary 75
Bosnian War 192–7
Bowie, Jim 101–2, 103
BP 208–13
Britain
  Agincourt 56–9
  British Raj 144, 146
  Church of England 77, 78
  Commonwealth 85
  Crimean War 108–11
  defeat of Spanish Armada 78–81
  English Civil War 82–5
  Falkland Islands 174–9
  invasion of Afghanistan 104–7
  Norman Conquest 52–5
  Peasants' Revolt 184
  Peterloo Massacre 94–9
  poll tax 184–7
  Roman occupation 31
  Tudor dynasty 74–7
  see also World War I;
  World War II
Brutus 34, 35
Buckingham, George Villiers,
  Duke of 83
Burnes, Sir Alexander 104, 105, 106
Burundi 188, 189
Bush, George W. 183, 204
Byzantine Empire 47

C

Caesar, Julius 30–5
Caesarion 32
Caligula 36–9
Calvinism 68, 69
Canute, king of England 53
Cardigan, Earl of 109, 110, 111
Carlile, Richard 99
cast iron 60–1
Castro, Fidel 158, 159
Catherine of Aragon 74–5, 76
Chaeronea, Battle of 21
Charge of the Light Brigade 108–11
Charles I, king of England 82–5
Charles II, king of England 85
Charles V, Holy Roman emperor 76

China
  isolationism 63
  Japanese invasion of Manchuria
  140
  scientific and technological
  prowess 60–3
Christianity 40–51
  Counter-Reformation 68
  East–West schism 47, 48–51
  monophysitism 44–7
  Nestorian Church 46, 47
  Oriental Orthodox Church 47,
  50–1
  Protestant Reformation 65–9, 74, 76
  Roman Catholicism 48–51, 64–9,
  74, 77, 78, 82
Church of England 77, 78
Churchill, Winston 143
CIA (Central Intelligence Agency)
  158, 159, 160, 171, 207
city-states, Greek 18, 19
Claudius, Emperor 39
Clement VII, Pope 75, 76
Cleopatra 32, 35
Clinton, Bill 199, 201
Cold War 160
collectivization 130–1
Columbus, Christopher 61, 62
Communism 115, 126, 127, 132–3,
  135, 148, 149, 158, 160
community charge *see* poll tax
Congress of Vienna 91
Constantine I, Emperor (Constantine
  the Great) 40, 45
Constantinople 40, 48, 50, 51
Corn Laws 96
Corsica 155
Council of Nicaea 45, 49
council tax 187
Counter-Reformation 68
Cranmer, Thomas 76
Crassus 31
Crimean War 108–11, 112
Crockett, Davy 102
Cromwell, Oliver 85
Cromwell, Thomas 76
Crusades 50, 65
Cuba
  Bay of Pigs invasion 158–61
  Cuban Missile Crisis 161
Cyril, Bishop of Alexandria 46

D

Dallaire, General Roméo 189, 190, 191
Darius I, emperor of Persia 16, 18
Darius III, emperor of Persia 22, 23
Dark Ages 60
Dayton Peace Agreement 197
Dean, John 170, 172
Deepwater Horizon blowout 208–13
diet, hunter-gatherer 11
Diet of Worms 67–8
diseases 11, 72
divine right of kings 83, 84
Dost Mohammad 104, 107
Drake, Sir Francis 78–9
Dyer, Brigadier-General Rex 146

E

earthquakes 214–15
Ebert, Friedrich 128
Edward the Confessor, king of
    England 53
Edward VI, king of England 77
Egypt, ancient
    agriculture 9
    Alexander the Great in 23
    Israelite Exodus 12–15
    Ptolemaic dynasty 32
    Roman annexation of 35
Ehrlichman, John 172
Eisenhower, Dwight D. 149, 158, 160
Elba 90, 93
elephants, war 24, 28
Eleusinian Mysteries 41
Elizabeth I, queen of England 77, 78,
    80
Elphinstone, General William 105–6
ethnic cleansing 193, 194
    see also genocide
Exodus 12–15

F

Falkland Islands 174–9
Fannie Mae and Freddie Mac 200, 201
FBI (Federal Bureau of Investigation)
    171
Felt, Mark 171
feudal system 70, 112–13
financial deregulation 198–201
FLN (Front de Libération Nationale)
    153, 154, 155, 156, 157
Flodden Field, Battle of 74
Forbidden City, Beijing 61
Ford, Gerald R. 173
Four Great Inventions 60
"Fourteen Points" 126
France
    1968 student protests 162–5
    Agincourt 56–9
    French Algeria 152–7
    French Communist Party 163, 164

French Indochina 148
Louisiana Territories 86–9
    see also World War I
Franz Ferdinand, Archduke 119
Franz-Josef, emperor of Austro-
    Hungary 116, 118
Fukushima nuclear reactor disaster
    214–17

G

Galtieri, General Leopoldo 175, 176
Gama, Vasco da 62
Gandhi, Mahatma 144, 145, 146
Gaugamela, Battle of 23
Gaul 31, 39
Gaulle, Charles de
    and the Algerian War of
        Independence 155, 156, 157
    and the student protests (1968)
        162, 163, 164, 165
General Belgrano, sinking of 177–8
Geneva Convention 138
genocide
    Rwanda 188–91
    Srebrenica massacre 192–7
    Ukraine 130, 132–3
George IV, king of Great Britain and
    Ireland 99
Germany
    Nazism 126, 129, 135
    Weimar Republic 128, 129
    see also World War I;
        World War II
gladiatorial games 30, 36, 37
Glaspie, April 182
Glass-Steagall Act, repeal of 198–201
global financial crisis 198, 201
Götzen, Count Gustav Adolf von 189
Gramm-Leach-Bliley Act 198, 199
Granicus, Battle of 22, 24
Gravelines, Battle of 81
Great Canal of China 62
Great Depression 198
"Great Game" 104
Great Wall of China 62
Greece
    Macedonian Empire 20–1, 27
    Persian invasion of 16–19
Greenspan, Alan 199
guerrilla warfare 148, 149, 150
Guevara, Ernesto Che 160
Gulf of Tonkin incident 150
Gulf War 180–3
gunpowder 60

H

Habyarimana, Juvénal 190
Hague Convention 121
Haiti 88
Haldeman, H.R. 172, 173

Hannibal 26
Hapsburg dynasty 116–19
Harald Hardrada, king of Norway 53,
    54
Hargreaves, James 94
Harold II, king of England 52, 53,
    54–5
Hastings, Battle of 52–5
Hellenistic period 25
Henry V, king of England 56, 57, 58–9
Henry VIII, king of England 74–7
Heraclea, Battle of 27–8
Heseltine, Michael 187
Hirohito, emperor of Japan 141
Hiroshima 143
Hitler, Adolf 129, 134, 135, 136, 137–8
Ho Chi Minh 148, 149
Hobbes, Thomas 11
Holocaust 134
Houston, Sam 102, 103
Huayna Capac 70
Huguenots 82, 83
Hundred Years War 56
Hunt, E. Howard 171
Hunt, Henry 96, 97, 99
hunter-gatherer society 8, 9, 10–11
Hus, Jan 64
Hussein, Saddam 180, 181, 182, 183
Hydaspes, Battle of 24

I

Incas 70–3
India 104, 105
    Amritsar massacre 144
    British Raj 144, 146
    Indian National Congress (INC)
        144
    Moghul Empire 145
    partition of 144–7
indulgences, sale of 65–7
Industrial Revolution 63, 94, 96
Ionian Revolt 16
Ipsus, Battle of 26
Iran–Iraq War 180
Iraq
    2003 invasion of 183
    invasion of Kuwait 180–3
Islam 47, 207
Israelites 12–15
Issus, Battle of 22

J

Jacob 12, 14
Japan
    Fukushima nuclear reactor
        disaster 214–17
    Pearl Harbor 140–3
Jefferson, Thomas 87, 88, 89
jihadism 207
Jinnah, Muhammad Ali 144

Johnson, Lyndon B. 150, 151
Judaism 42
Julian, Emperor (Julian the Apostate) 40–3
Julius II, Pope 74, 75, 76

K

Kalahari Bushmen 11
Karadžic, Radovan 194, 195, 196, 197
Kashmir 147
Kay, John 94
Kennedy, John F. 149, 158, 159–60
Kenya
    Mau Mau revolt 166
    Turkana Massacre 166–7
Khrushchev, Nikita 158
Kiwanuka, Ben 167
Knap of Howar 10
kulaks 131
Kuwait, Iraqi invasion of 180–3

L

Laud, Archbishop William 84
Lebensraum 134
Lenin, Vladimir 130
Leo X, Pope 66, 67
Leonidas 18
Liddy, G. Gordon 170–1
Livingston, Robert 87, 88
Lollards 64
longbows 58, 59
Loris-Melikov, Count 115
Louisiana Territories 86–9
Lucan, Lord 109, 110, 111
Lusitania, sinking of the 120–5
Luther, Martin 64–9, 76
Luwum, Archbishop Janani 167

M

McCarthy, Joseph 160
Macedonian Empire 20–1, 27
Macnaghten, Sir William Hay 104, 105, 106
McNamara, Robert 150, 151
Magellan, Ferdinand 62
magnetic compass 60
Major, John 187
Manchester 94–9
Manchuria, Japanese invasion of 140
Marathon, Battle of 16–17, 19
Mardonius 16, 19
Mark Antony 34, 35
Mary, queen of England 74, 75, 77, 78
Mau Mau revolt 166
Mayan culture 72
Mayerling Incident 116–19
Mendès-France, Pierre 153, 164
Menshikov, Prince Alexander Sergeyevich 109
Mexico 100–3

Ming dynasty 60–3
Mitchell, John 170, 171, 172
Mitterrand, François 153
Mladic, Ratko 194, 195, 196, 197
Moghul Empire 145
Molotov-Ribbentrop Pact 135, 136
Mongols 63
monophysitism 44–7
monotheism 49
Monroe, James 87
More, Sir Thomas 76, 77
Morocco 154
Moses 12–13, 14–15
Mountbatten, Lord Louis 146
Muggeridge, Malcolm 133
Muslim League 144, 145

N

Nagasaki 143
Napoleon Bonaparte
    exile 90, 93
    Hundred Days 90–3
    Louisiana Purchase 86–9
    Waterloo 92–3
Napoleonic Wars 90, 94
Naseby, Battle of 85
Native Americans 89
NATO 195
Nazism 126, 129, 135
Nehru, Jawaharlal 145
Neolithic farming 10
Neoplatonism 41
Nestorian Church 46, 47
New Model Army 85
Ngo Dinh Diem 149, 150
Nicene Creed 45, 49
Nicholas I, Tsar 112
9/11 202–7
95 Theses 67, 68
Nixon, Richard 151
    Watergate 170–3
Nolan, Captain Lewis 110
Norman invasion of Britain 52–5
nuclear reactors 214–17
nuclear weapons 143
Nyerere, Julius 169

O

OAS (Organisation de l'Armée Secrète) 154, 156, 157
Obote, Milton 167, 168
Octavian (Emperor Augustus) 35, 36
oil fields, Iraqi 180
oil spills 208–13
OPEC 180
Operation Barbarossa 134–9
Operation Desert Shield 181
Operation Desert Storm 182–3
Oriental Orthodox Church 47, 48–51

P

paganism 40, 41–2, 43
Pakistan 144, 145, 146–7
papacy 48, 49, 50, 64, 65–7
paper making 60
Paris Peace Conference 126
Passover 14
Peace of Westphalia 68–9
Pearl Harbor 140–3
Peasants' Revolt 184
Peninsular War 90
The People's Will 114, 115
Persepolis 23
Persian Empire
    invasion of Greece 16–19
    war with Alexander the Great 21–3
Peru 70–3
Peterloo Massacre 94–9
Petrine Doctrine 50
Pheidippides 19
Philip II, king of Macedon 20–1
Philip II, king of Spain 78–81
Philippi, Battle of 35
Pinckney's Treaty 86
piracy 78, 124
Pirahã 11
Pizarro, Francisco 70, 71–3
Plagues of Egypt 13–15
Plantagenet dynasty 56
Plato 41
poll tax 184–7
Pompey 31–2
Pompidou, Georges 164, 165
Pont, Pierre du 87
Porus, Hindu king 24
prehistoric life 8–10
Presbyterianism 84, 85
Preston, Battle of 85
printing 60
Protestant Reformation 65–9, 74, 76
Protestantism 68–9, 77, 78, 82, 84
Ptolemaic dynasty 32
Puritans 82
Pym, John 84
Pyrrhus of Epirus 26–9

R

Raglan, Earl of 109, 110, 111
Red Sea 15
Reed, John 199
religion
    Christianity see Christianity
    Islam 47, 207
    Judaism 42
    paganism 40, 41–2, 43
    wars of religion 68–9
religious persecution 43, 77
Renaissance 60

republicanism
    English Commonwealth 82, 85
    Roman Republic 27–9, 30–5
Richard II, king of England 184
Roman Catholicism 48–51, 64–9, 74, 77, 78, 82
Roman Empire 35, 36–43
Roman Republic 27–9, 30–5
Roosevelt, Franklin D. 140, 142
Roosevelt, Theodore 124
Rubin, Robert 199
Rudolf, Crown Prince of Austria 116–19
Russell, William 109–10
Russia
    assassination of Tsar Alexander II 112–15
    Communism 126, 127
    Crimean War 108–11
    Russian Revolution 115
    see also Soviet Union
Rwandan genocide 188–91

S
Safe Shutdown Earthquake (SSE) 216
St. Helena 93
Santa Anna, Antonio López de 100–3
Saudi Arabia 181, 182
Senate, Roman 29, 30, 33, 36, 37
September 11, 2001, terrorist attacks 202–7
Serb Republic 192, 193, 195
serfs 112–13
Sétif Massacre 152–3
settlements, early 10
Sevastopol 108, 112
Seymour, Jane 77
Shakespeare, William 34, 58
ship tax 84
Shuja Shah Durrani 104, 105, 107
Sidonia Medina, Duke of 79, 80, 81
Sixtus V, Pope 78
slavery 12, 21, 23, 87–8, 100
    serfs 112–13
Soviet Union
    Bay of Pigs invasion 158–61
    Cold War 160
    Communism 132–3
    Five-Year Plans 130–3
    German invasion of 134–9
    see also Russia; World War II
Spain
    Armada 78–81
    conquistadores 70–3
Spartans 17, 18, 19
Srebrenica massacre 192–7
Stalin, Joseph 130–3, 134–5, 137
steam power 94
Stevenson, Adlai 160

Stimson, Henry L. 142
Strafford, Earl of 84
sub-prime mortgage collapse 198, 199–201
submarine warfare 123–5
Sulla 30
Sweyn Forkbeard 53

T
Taliban 207
Tanzania 188
    Ugandan invasion of 169
Tarentum 27
Tennyson, Alfred, Lord 110
terrorism
    Algeria 154, 155
    September 11, 2001, terrorist attacks 202–7
    tsarist Russia 113–15
    see also assassinations
Texas Revolution 100–3
Thatcher, Margaret 176, 179, 184, 185, 186, 187
Thebes 21
Thermopylae, Battle of 18–19
Thirty Years' War 68, 69
Thompson, Hunter S. 171
Tiberius, Emperor 36, 37
trade unions 95, 163, 164
Travis, Lieutenant Colonel William B. 101–2
Treaty of Nonsuch 78
Treaty of Versailles 126–9
Trinity, doctrine of the 44–5, 48
Truman, Harry 148
tsunamis 214
Tunisia 154
Turkana Massacre 166–7
tyranny 34, 35
Tyre 23

U
Uganda 188
    Asian population expelled 166–9
Ukraine, famine in 130–3
United Nations
    and Falkland Islands invasion 176
    formation 174
    and the Gulf War 181, 182
    and the Rwandan genocide 188, 189, 190, 191
    and Srebrenica 194, 195, 197
United States of America
    Bay of Pigs invasion 158–61
    Cold War 160
    Deepwater Horizon blowout 208–13
    Glass-Steagall Act, repeal of 198–201
    Gulf War 181–2

    Louisiana Purchase 86–9
    McCarthy era 160
    Pearl Harbor 140–3
    September 11, 2001 terrorist attacks 202–7
    Vietnam War 148–51
    Watergate 170–3
    see also World War I; World War II
USS Maddox incident 150

V
Vetsera, Baroness Marie von 116–17, 118
Viet Cong 149, 150, 151
Viet Minh 148, 149
Vietnam War 148–51
Vikings 52, 53

W
Wall Street Crash 198
war crimes 195, 196
War on Terror 183, 207
Watergate 170–3
Waterloo, Battle of 92–3
Weimar Republic 128, 129
Wellington, Duke of 91, 92, 93
White House Plumbers 171
Wilhelm II, Kaiser 125, 128
William of Normandy 52, 53–5
William, Prince of Orange 92
Wilson, Woodrow 125, 126
Wolsey, Cardinal Thomas 76
Woodward, Bob 171
World Trade Center 202–5
World War I
    outbreak 119
    sinking of the Lusitania 120–5
    Treaty of Versailles 126–9
World War II
    outbreak of 129
    Pacific War 148
    Pearl Harbor 140–3
    Soviet Union, invasion of 134–9
Wroe, James 99
Wycliffe, John 64
Wu, King 33
Wyclif, John 83

XYZ
Xerxes, emperor of Persia 18
Yongle emperor 61
Yugoslavia, former 192
Zheng He 61, 62, 63
Zhukovsky, Vasily 113

PICTURE CREDITS

Key: t=top, b=bottom, l=left, r=right, c=center

All images public domain unless otherwise indicated:

Alamy: 114b Interfoto.

Dreamstime: 45tr Martin Mullen, 186t David Fowler, 209t Sculpies.

German Federal Archives: p136t Böhmer.

Getty Images: 27tl Dea/A. Dagli Orti/De Agostini Collection, 37t 27tl Dea/A. Dagli Orti/De Agostini Collection, 47t Library of Congress, 71tl Hulton Archive/ Handout, 85tr UniversalImagesGroup, 111t Time Life Pictures, 124–125t Rex Hardy Jr, Hoover War Library, 127b Hulton Archive/Stringer, 135t Georgi Zelma/Hulton Archive, 153tl Hank Walker, 154–155 Keystone-France, 156r STF, 165t Carlo Bavagnoli, 167b Hulton Archive, 168t George W. Hales, 178–179t Hulton Archive, 181bl Hulton Archive, 187br AFP, 194tr Pascal Guyot, 217t Christopher Furlong.

Mary Evans Picture Library: 17tl The Mullan Collection, 24b Photo Researchers, 38–39b, 50br, 54–55, 92–93, 97tl, 129br, 139b picture alliance/ZB, 204tr Everett Collection.

Shutterstock.com: 64tr aphotostory, 175t Fredy Thuerig.

Wikimedia Commons: 10t Drewcorser, 20r Andrew Dunn, 32bl Andreas Wahra, 65tl Hassan Saeed, 197t Adam Jones, 200b AgnosticPreachersKid, 203t Robert J. Fisch, 215t Kawamoto Takuo.